STAR WARS®

REBEL JAIL

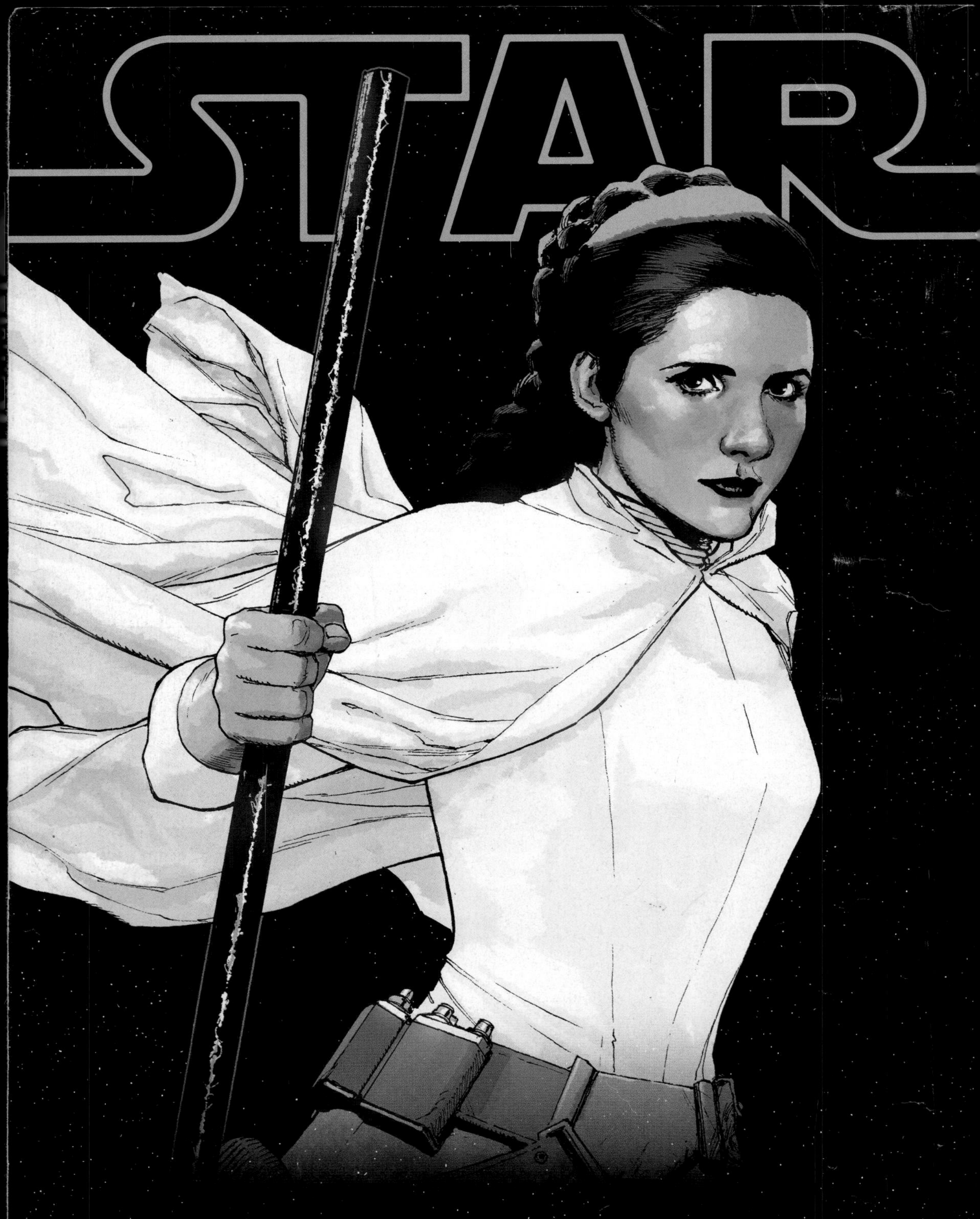
STAR

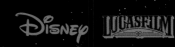

Collection Editor **JENNIFER GRÜNWALD**
Associate Editor **SARAH BRUNSTAD**
Associate Managing Editor **ALEX STARBUCK**
Editor, Special Projects **MARK D. BEAZLEY**
VP, Production & Special Projects **JEFF YOUNGQUIST**
SVP Print, Sales & Marketing **DAVID GABRIEL**
Book Designer **ADAM DEL RE**

STAR WARS VOL. 3: REBEL JAIL. Contains material originally published in magazine form as STAR WARS #15-19 and ANNUAL #1. First printing 2016. ISBN# 978-0-7851-9983-0. Published by MARVEL WORLDWIDE, INC., a subsidiary of MARVEL ENTERTAINMENT, LLC. OFFICE OF PUBLICATION: 135 West 50th Street, New York, NY 10020. STAR WARS and related text and illustrations are trademarks and/or copyrights, in the United States and other countries, of Lucasfilm Ltd. and/or its affiliates. © & TM Lucasfilm Ltd. No similarity between any of the names, characters, persons, and/or institutions in this magazine with those of any living or dead person or institution is intended, and any such similarity which may exist is purely coincidental. Marvel and its logos are TM Marvel Characters, Inc. **Printed in the U.S.A.** ALAN FINE, President, Marvel Entertainment; DAN BUCKLEY, President, TV, Publishing & Brand Management; JOE QUESADA, Chief Creative Officer; TOM BREVOORT, SVP of Publishing; DAVID BOGART, SVP of Business Affairs & Operations, Publishing & Partnership; C.B. CEBULSKI, VP of Brand Management & Development, Asia; DAVID GABRIEL, SVP of Sales & Marketing, Publishing; JEFF YOUNGQUIST, VP of Production & Special Projects; DAN CARR, Executive Director of Publishing Technology; ALEX MORALES, Director of Publishing Operations; SUSAN CRESPI, Production Manager; STAN LEE, Chairman Emeritus. For information regarding advertising in Marvel Comics or on Marvel.com, please contact Vit DeBellis, Integrated Sales Manager, at vdebellis@marvel.com. For Marvel subscription inquiries, please call 888-511-5480. **Manufactured between 6/10/2016 and 7/18/2016 by R.R. DONNELLEY, INC., SALEM, VA, USA.**

10 9 8 7 6 5 4 3 2 1

WARS

REBEL JAIL

ANNUAL #1
Writer   **KIERON GILLEN**
Artist   **ANGEL UNZUETA**
Color Artist **PAUL MOUNTS**
Letterer   **VC's JOE CARAMAGNA**
Cover Art   **JOHN CASSADAY & PAUL MOUNTS**

ISSUES #16-19
Writer   **JASON AARON**
Penciler   **LEINIL YU**
Inker   **GERRY ALANGUILAN**
Color Artist **SUNNY GHO** WITH **JAVA TARTAGLIA** (#19)
Letterer   **CHRIS ELIOPOULOS**
Cover Art   **TERRY DODSON & RACHEL DODSON** (#16-17) AND
             LEINIL YU & SUNNY GHO (#18-19)

ISSUE #15
Writer   **JASON AARON**
Artist/Cover **MIKE MAYHEW**
Letterer   **CHRIS ELIOPOULOS**

Assistant Editor **HEATHER ANTOS**
Editor   **JORDAN D. WHITE**
Executive Editor **C.B. CEBULSKI**

Editor in Chief   **AXEL ALONSO**
Chief Creative Officer **JOE QUESADA**
Publisher   **DAN BUCKLEY**

For Lucasfilm:
Senior Editor   **FRANK PARISI**
Creative Director   **MICHAEL SIGLAIN**
Lucasfilm Story Group **RAYNE ROBERTS, PABLO HIDALGO,
                       LELAND CHEE, MATT MARTIN**

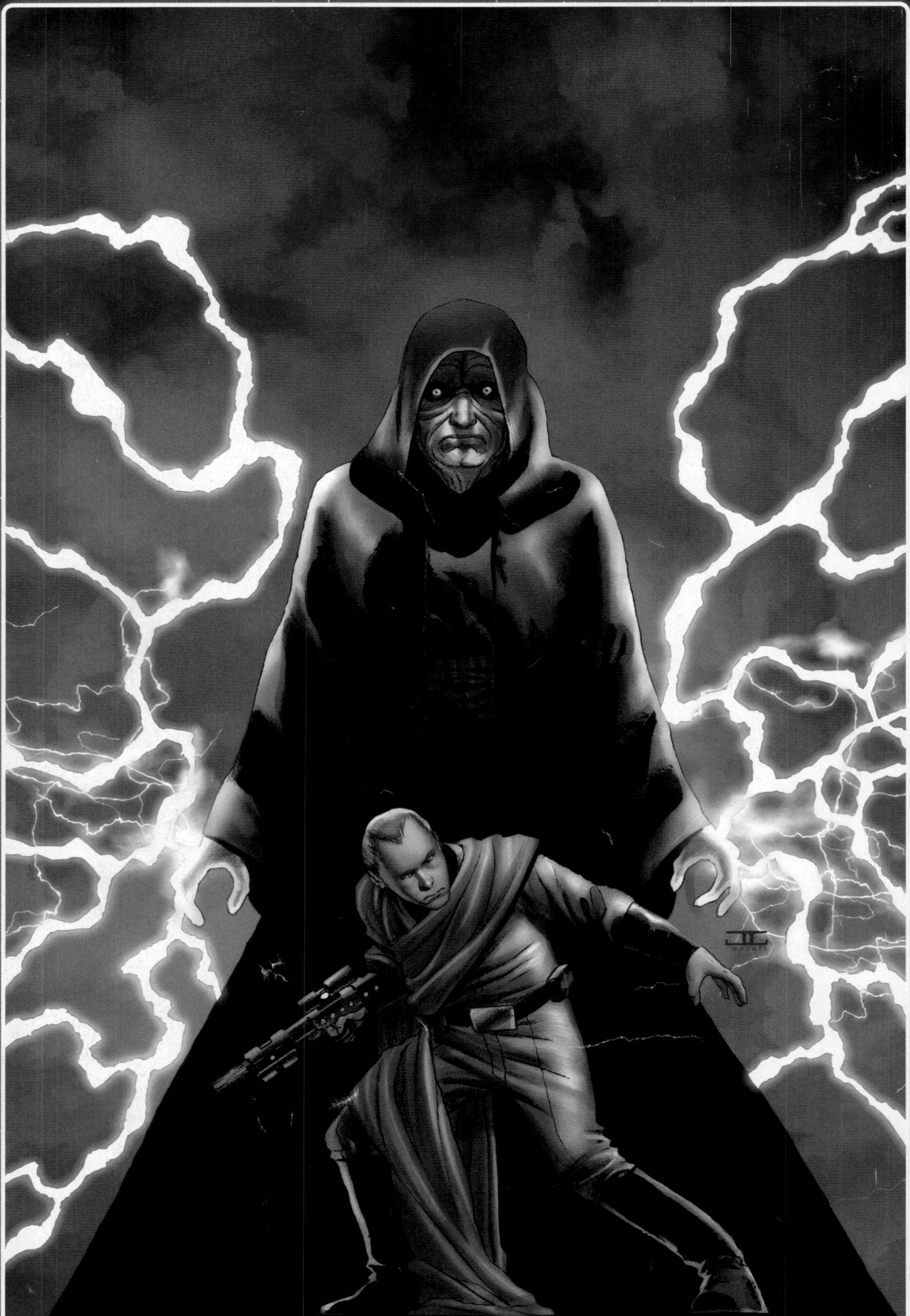

ANNUAL 1

STAR WARS

It is an era of renewed hope for the Rebellion.

The evil Galactic Empire's greatest weapon, the Death Star, has been destroyed by the young rebel pilot, Luke Skywalker. But Imperial forces still stand strong.

Rebel spy Eneb Ray has infiltrated Coruscant, working under an Imperial guise and the name Tharius Demo. He quickly learns that some missions prove to be much more complicated than others....

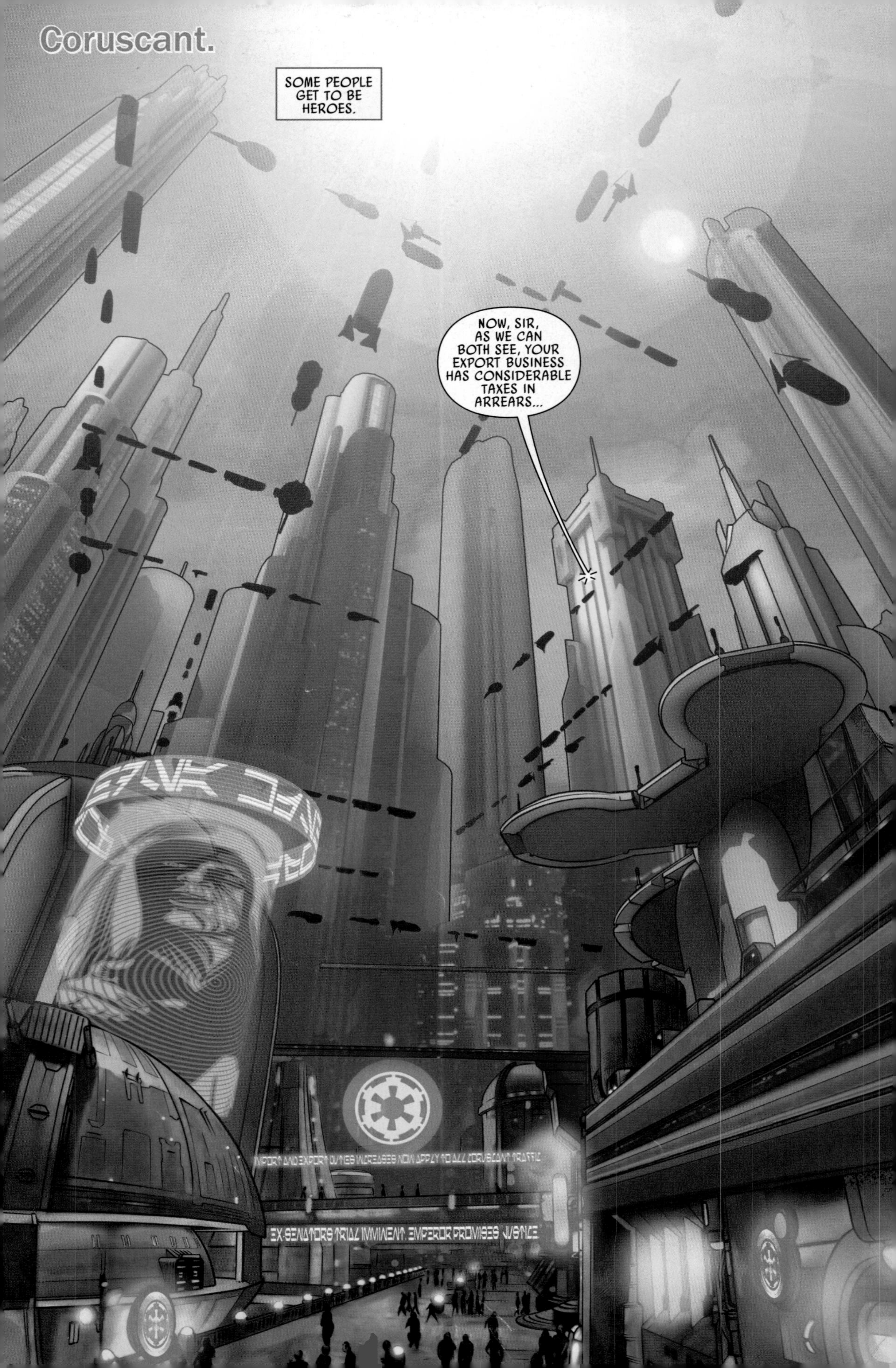
Coruscant.
SOME PEOPLE GET TO BE HEROES.
NOW, SIR, AS WE CAN BOTH SEE, YOUR EXPORT BUSINESS HAS CONSIDERABLE TAXES IN ARREARS...
IMPORT AND EXPORT DUTIES INCREASES NOW APPLY TO ALL CORUSCANT TRAFFIC
EX-SENATORS TRIAL IMMINENT. EMPEROR PROMISES "JUSTICE."

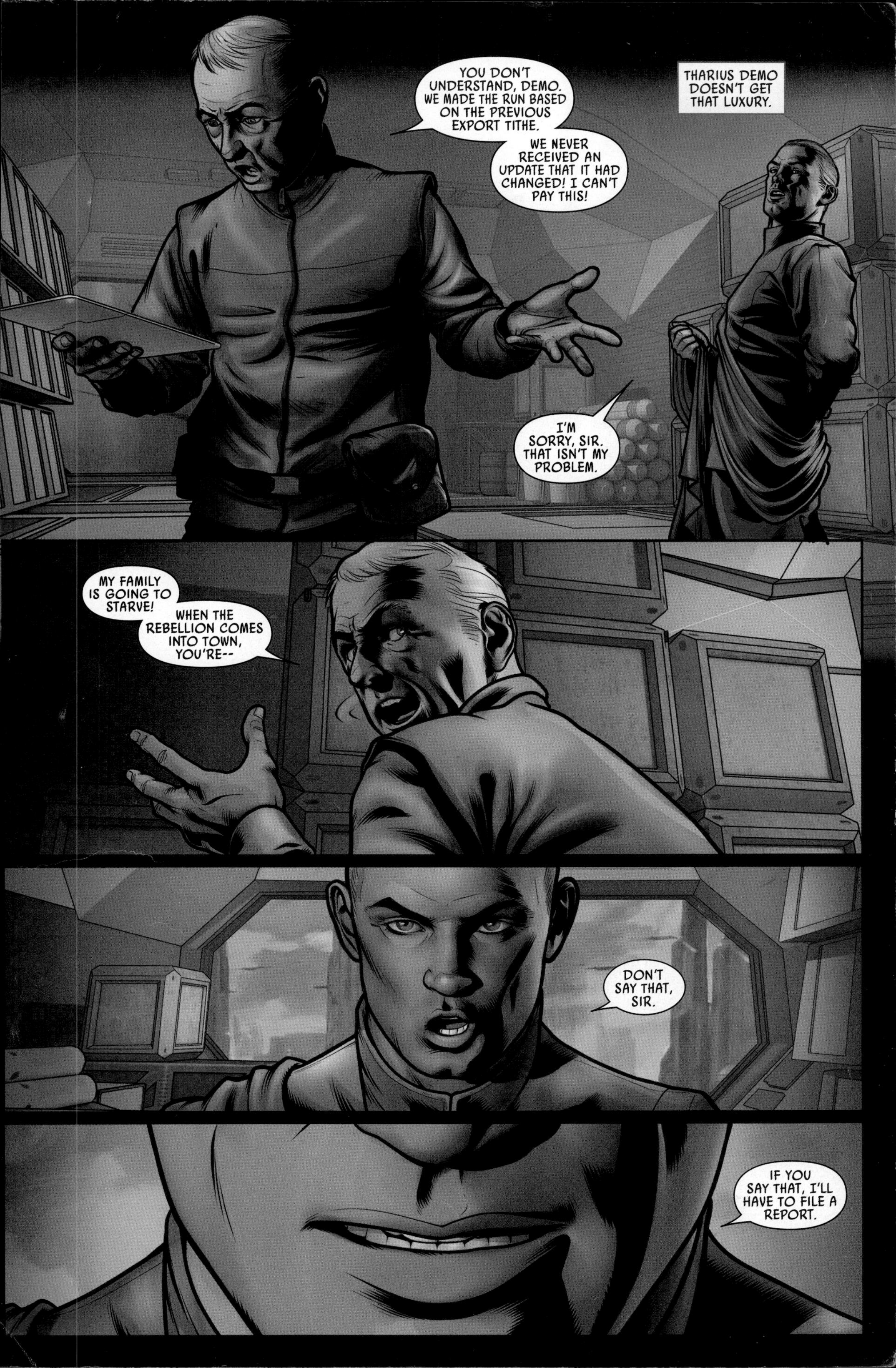
THARIUS DEMO DOESN'T GET THAT LUXURY.
YOU DON'T UNDERSTAND, DEMO. WE MADE THE RUN BASED ON THE PREVIOUS EXPORT TITHE.
WE NEVER RECEIVED AN UPDATE THAT IT HAD CHANGED! I CAN'T PAY THIS!
I'M SORRY, SIR. THAT ISN'T MY PROBLEM.
MY FAMILY IS GOING TO STARVE!
WHEN THE REBELLION COMES INTO TOWN, YOU'RE--
DON'T SAY THAT, SIR.
IF YOU SAY THAT, I'LL HAVE TO FILE A REPORT.

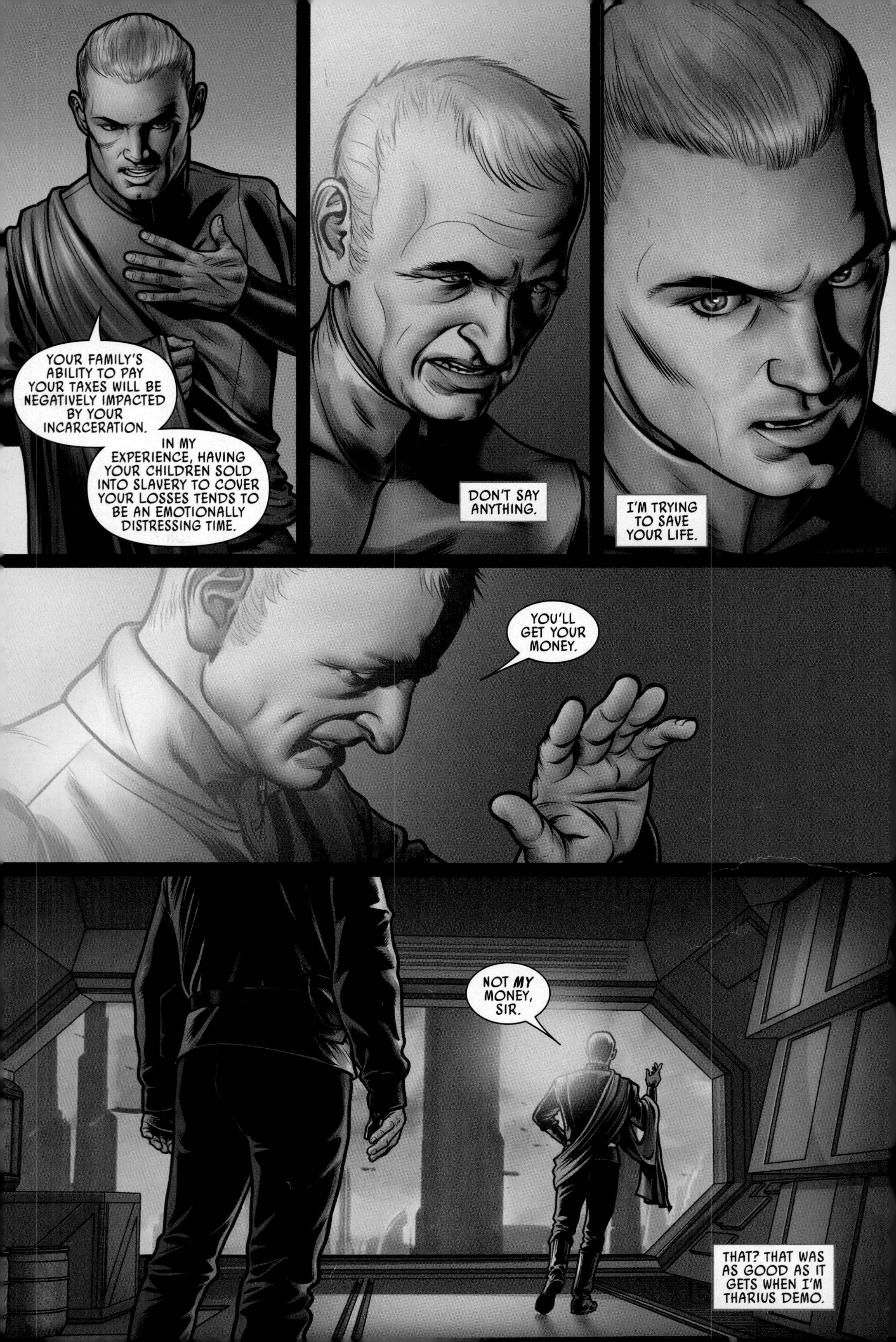

YOUR FAMILY'S ABILITY TO PAY YOUR TAXES WILL BE NEGATIVELY IMPACTED BY YOUR INCARCERATION.
IN MY EXPERIENCE, HAVING YOUR CHILDREN SOLD INTO SLAVERY TO COVER YOUR LOSSES TENDS TO BE AN EMOTIONALLY DISTRESSING TIME.
DON'T SAY ANYTHING.
I'M TRYING TO SAVE YOUR LIFE.
YOU'LL GET YOUR MONEY.
NOT MY MONEY, SIR.
THAT? THAT WAS AS GOOD AS IT GETS WHEN I'M THARIUS DEMO.

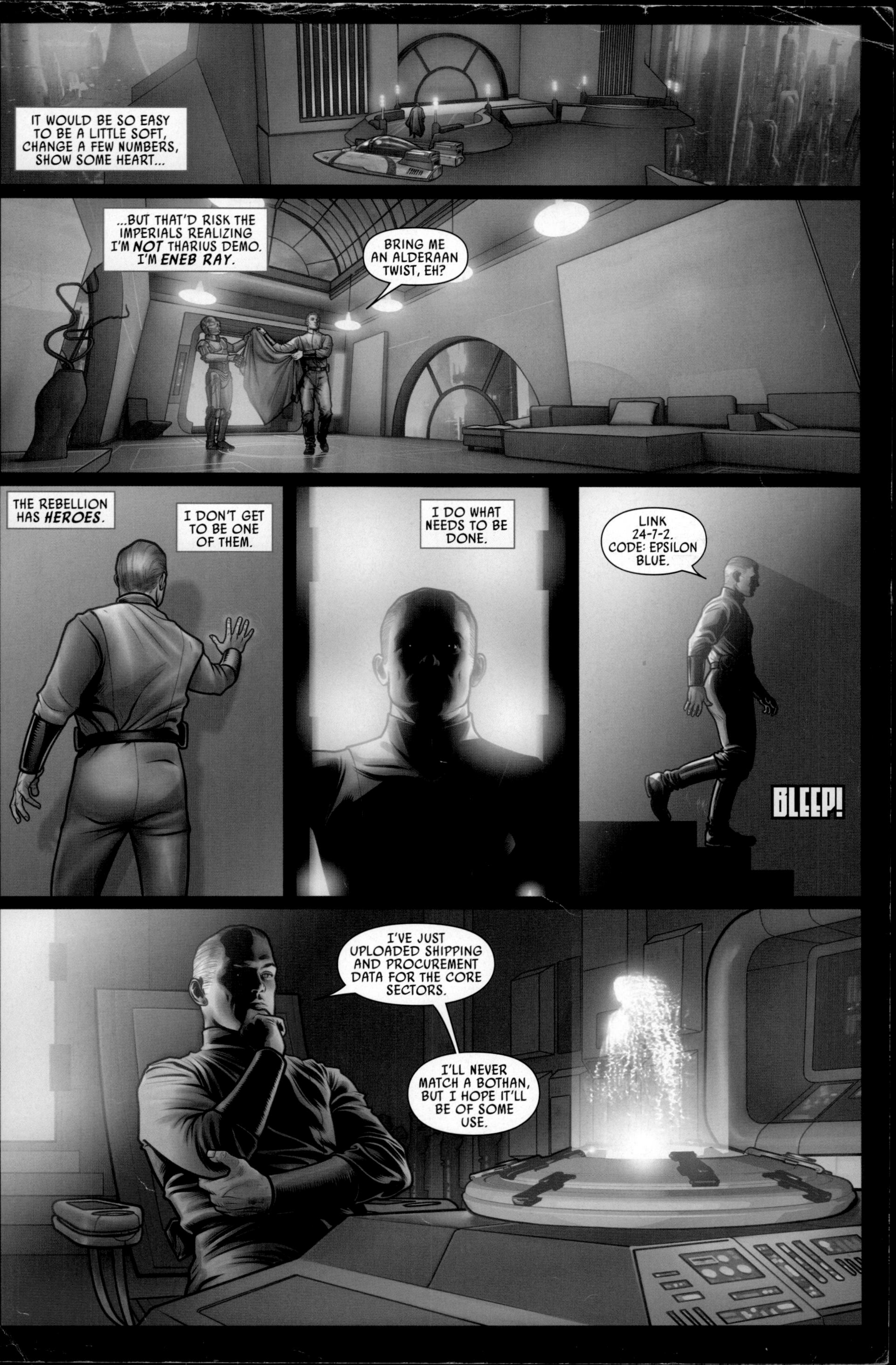
IT WOULD BE SO EASY TO BE A LITTLE SOFT, CHANGE A FEW NUMBERS, SHOW SOME HEART...
...BUT THAT'D RISK THE IMPERIALS REALIZING I'M NOT THARIUS DEMO. I'M ENEB RAY.
BRING ME AN ALDERAAN TWIST, EH?
THE REBELLION HAS HEROES.
I DON'T GET TO BE ONE OF THEM.
I DO WHAT NEEDS TO BE DONE.
LINK 24-7-2. CODE: EPSILON BLUE.
BLEEP!
I'VE JUST UPLOADED SHIPPING AND PROCUREMENT DATA FOR THE CORE SECTORS.
I'LL NEVER MATCH A BOTHAN, BUT I HOPE IT'LL BE OF SOME USE.

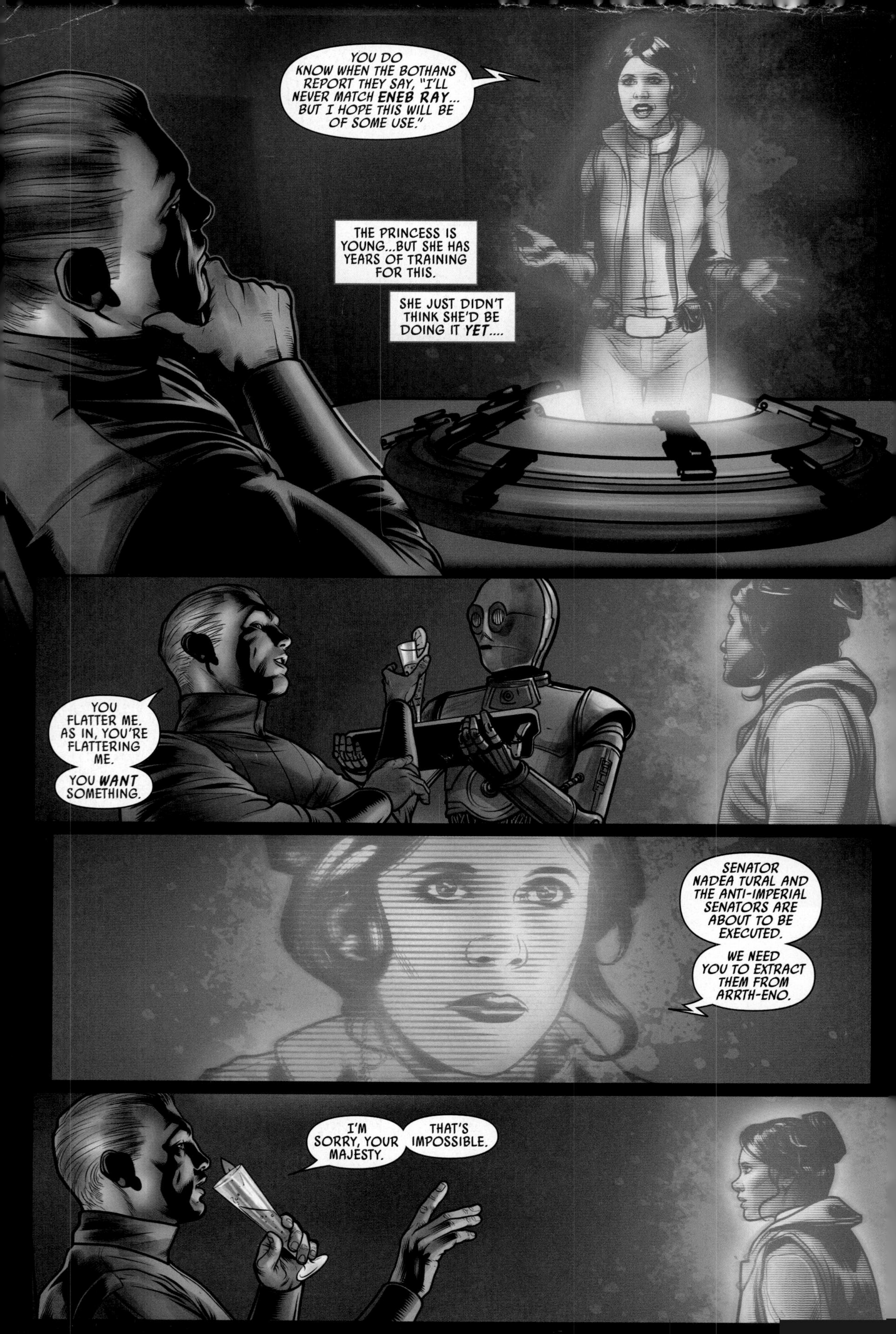
YOU DO KNOW WHEN THE BOTHANS REPORT THEY SAY, "I'LL NEVER MATCH ENEB RAY... BUT I HOPE THIS WILL BE OF SOME USE."
THE PRINCESS IS YOUNG...BUT SHE HAS YEARS OF TRAINING FOR THIS.
SHE JUST DIDN'T THINK SHE'D BE DOING IT YET....
YOU FLATTER ME. AS IN, YOU'RE FLATTERING ME.
YOU WANT SOMETHING.
SENATOR NADEA TURAL AND THE ANTI-IMPERIAL SENATORS ARE ABOUT TO BE EXECUTED.
WE NEED YOU TO EXTRACT THEM FROM ARRTH-ENO.
I'M SORRY, YOUR MAJESTY.
THAT'S IMPOSSIBLE.

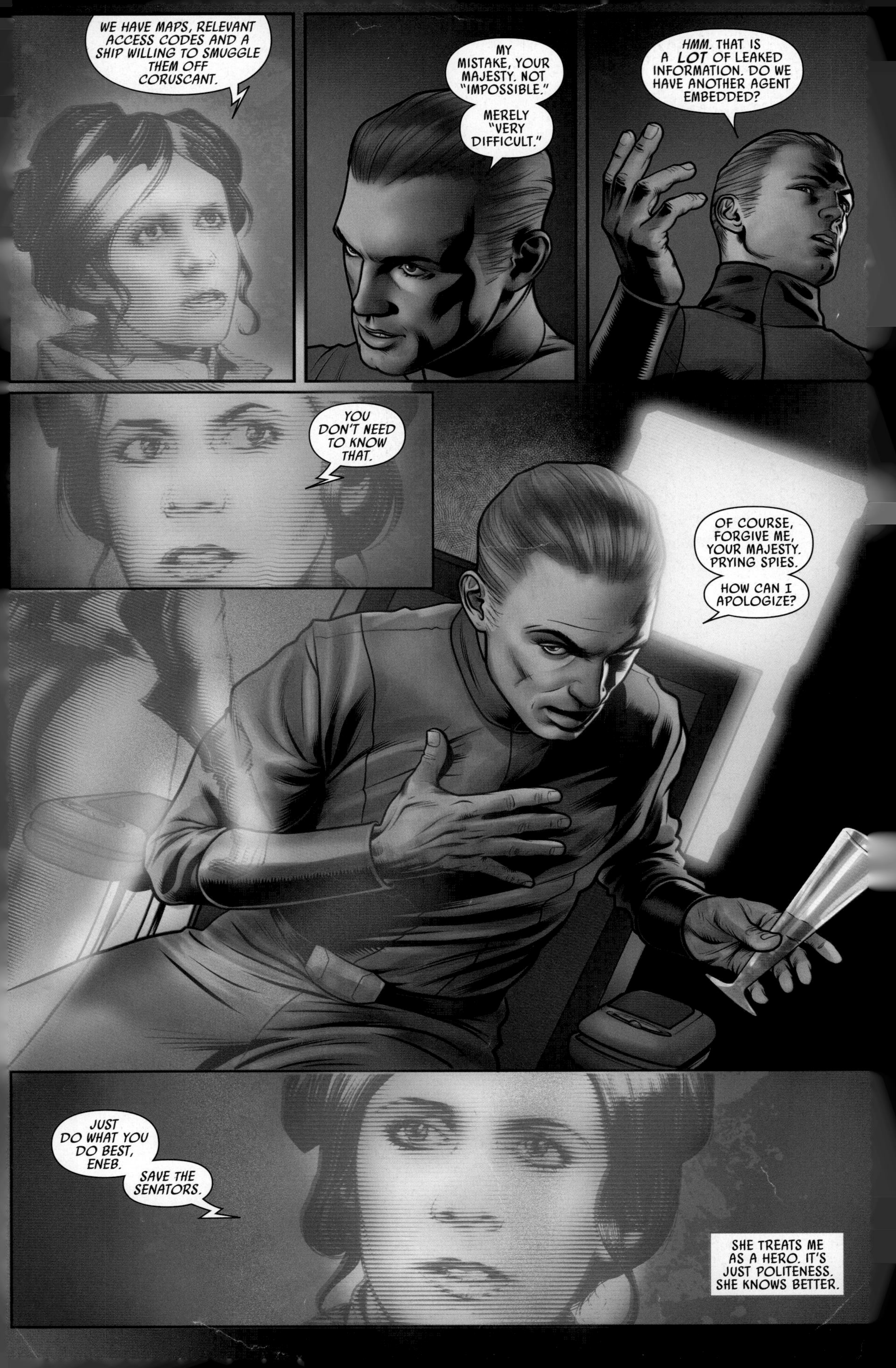
WE HAVE MAPS, RELEVANT ACCESS CODES AND A SHIP WILLING TO SMUGGLE THEM OFF CORUSCANT.
MY MISTAKE, YOUR MAJESTY. NOT "IMPOSSIBLE."
MERELY "VERY DIFFICULT."
HMM. THAT IS A LOT OF LEAKED INFORMATION. DO WE HAVE ANOTHER AGENT EMBEDDED?
YOU DON'T NEED TO KNOW THAT.
OF COURSE, FORGIVE ME, YOUR MAJESTY. PRYING SPIES.
HOW CAN I APOLOGIZE?
JUST DO WHAT YOU DO BEST, ENEB.
SAVE THE SENATORS.
SHE TREATS ME AS A HERO. IT'S JUST POLITENESS. SHE KNOWS BETTER.

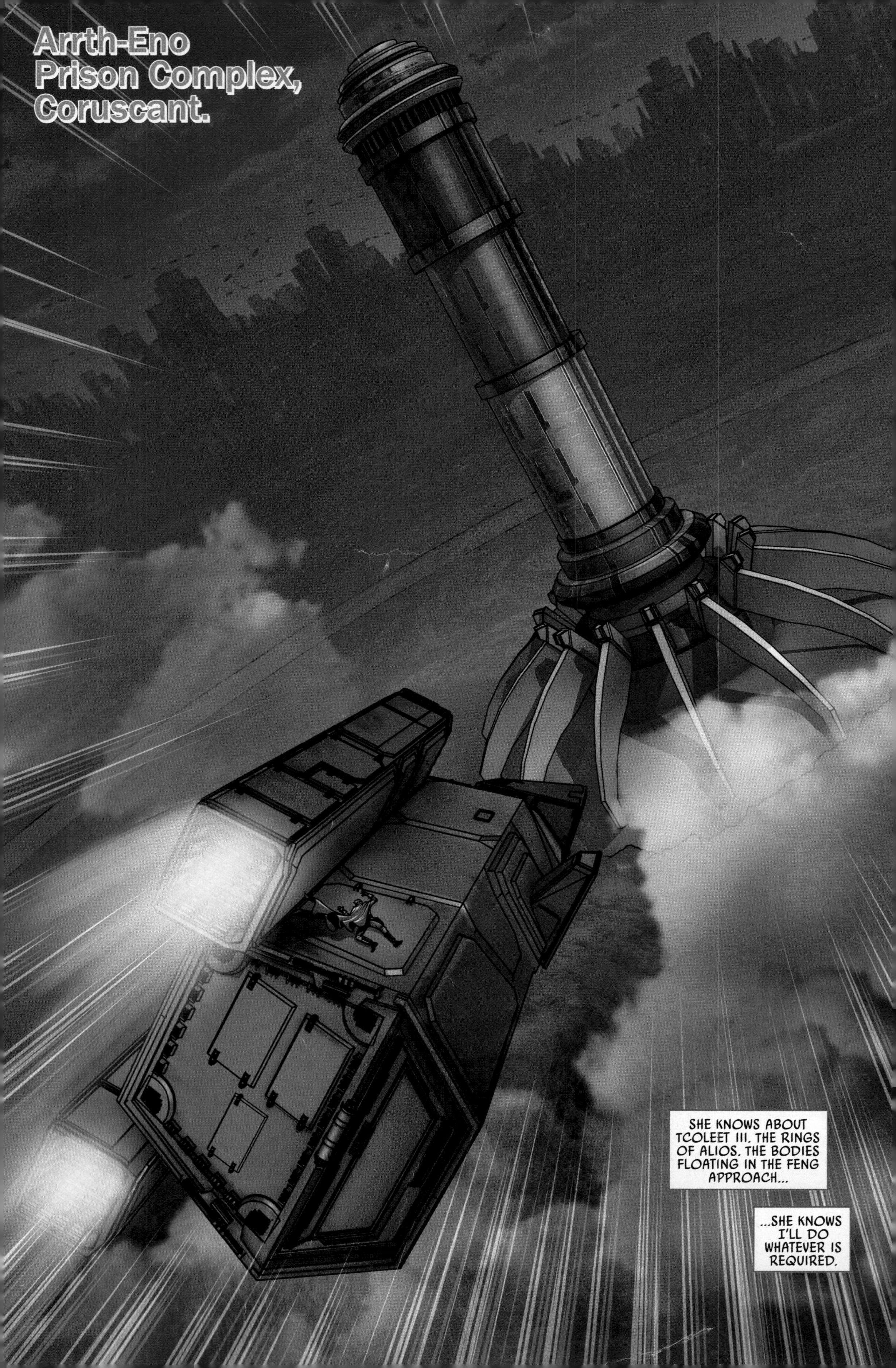
Arrth-Eno Prison Complex, Coruscant.
SHE KNOWS ABOUT TCOLEET III. THE RINGS OF ALIOS. THE BODIES FLOATING IN THE FENG APPROACH...
...SHE KNOWS I'LL DO WHATEVER IS REQUIRED.

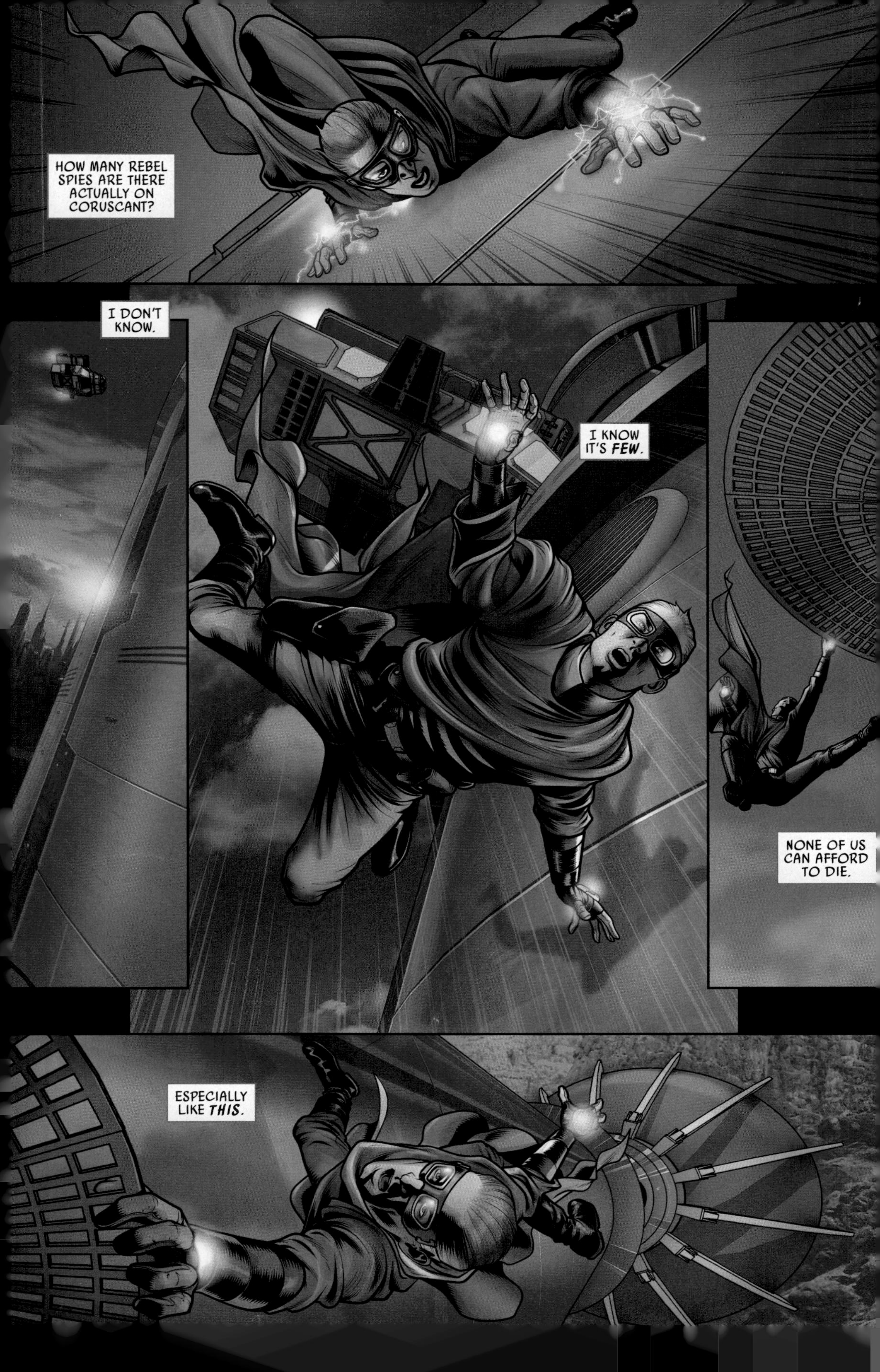
HOW MANY REBEL SPIES ARE THERE ACTUALLY ON CORUSCANT?
I DON'T KNOW.
I KNOW IT'S *FEW*.
NONE OF US CAN AFFORD TO DIE.
ESPECIALLY LIKE *THIS*.

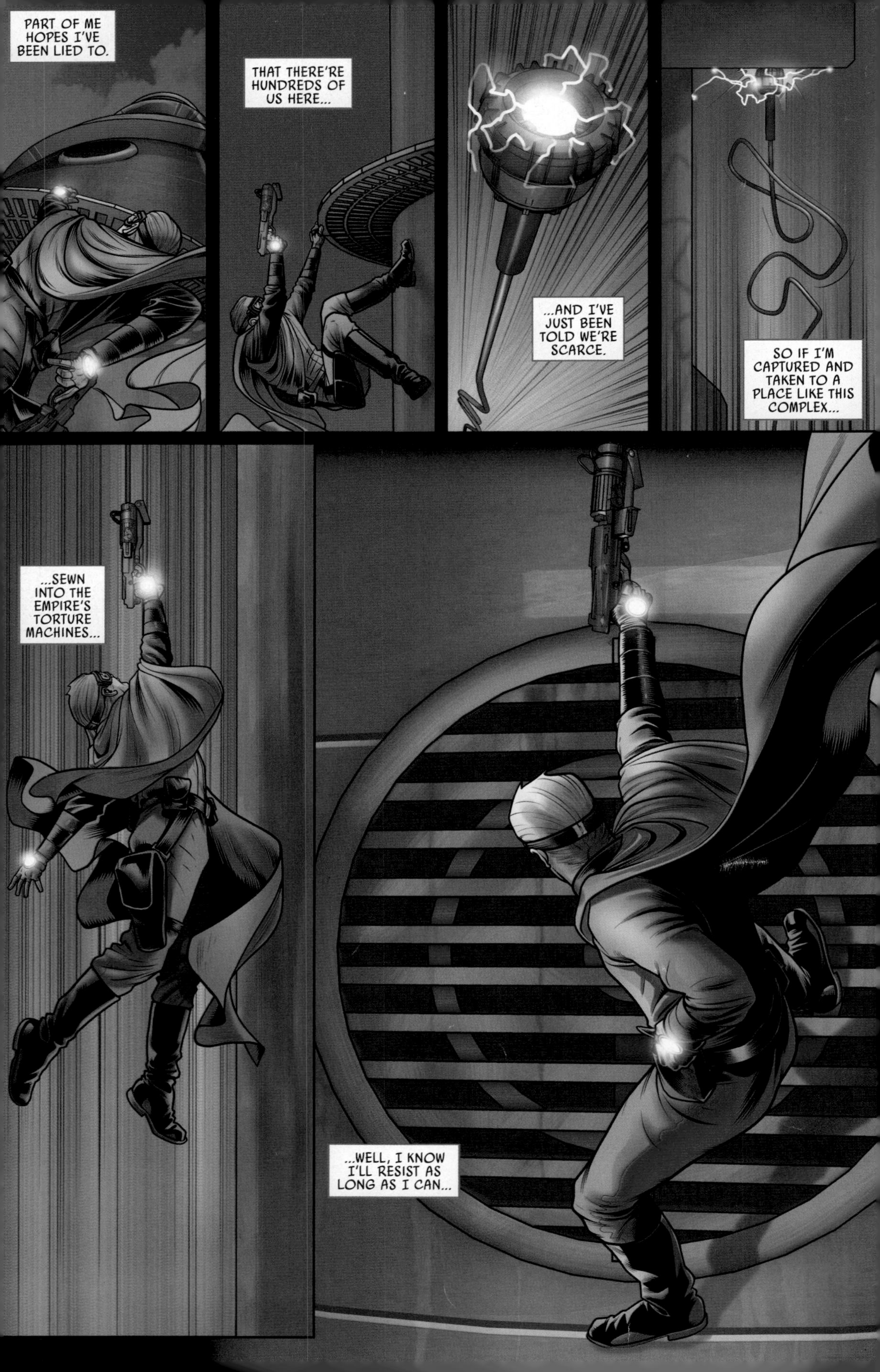
PART OF ME HOPES I'VE BEEN LIED TO.
THAT THERE'RE HUNDREDS OF US HERE...
...AND I'VE JUST BEEN TOLD WE'RE SCARCE.
SO IF I'M CAPTURED AND TAKEN TO A PLACE LIKE THIS COMPLEX...
...SEWN INTO THE EMPIRE'S TORTURE MACHINES...
...WELL, I KNOW I'LL RESIST AS LONG AS I CAN...

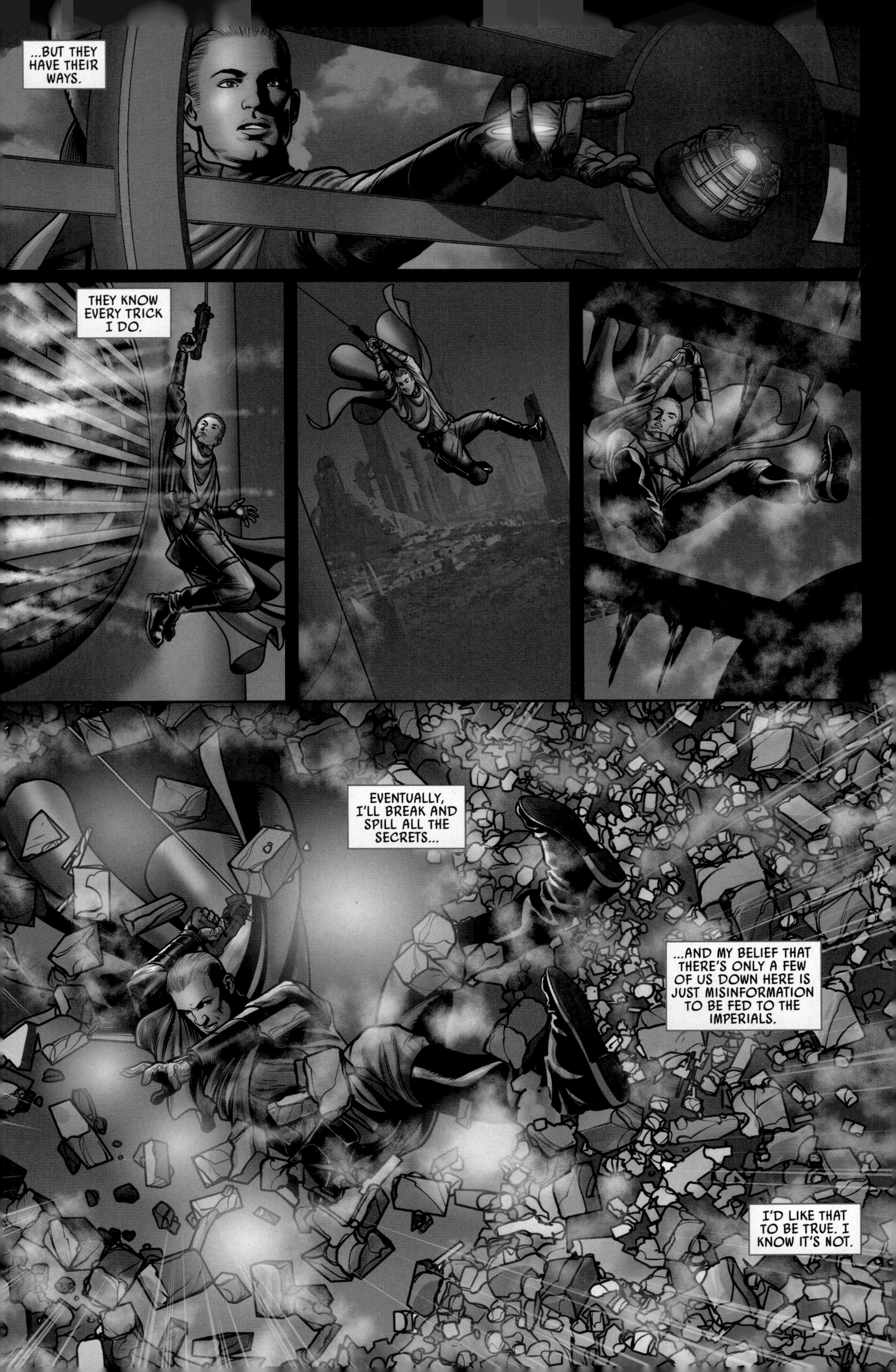
...BUT THEY HAVE THEIR WAYS.
THEY KNOW EVERY TRICK I DO.
EVENTUALLY, I'LL BREAK AND SPILL ALL THE SECRETS...
...AND MY BELIEF THAT THERE'S ONLY A FEW OF US DOWN HERE IS JUST MISINFORMATION TO BE FED TO THE IMPERIALS.
I'D LIKE THAT TO BE TRUE. I KNOW IT'S NOT.

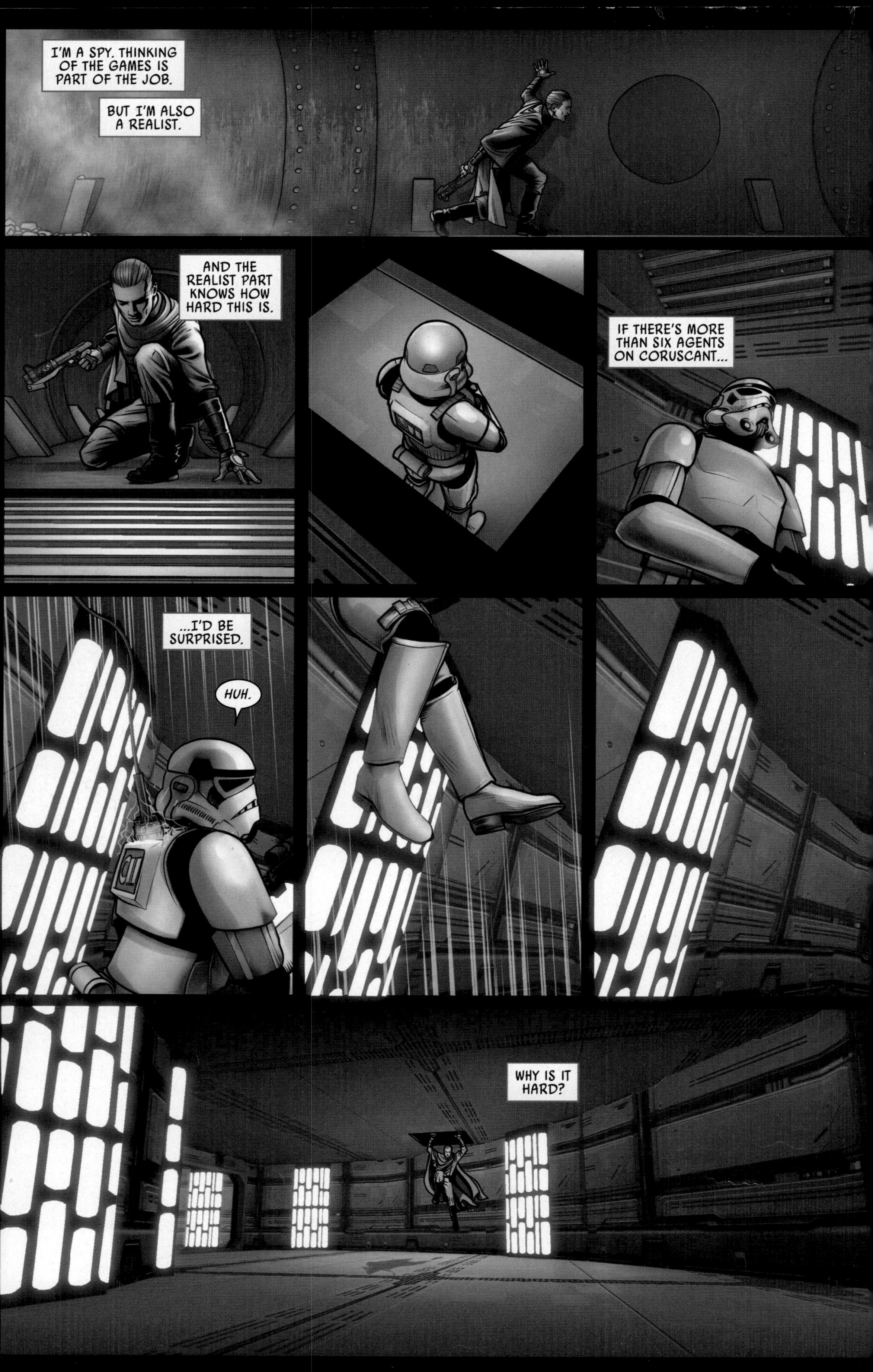
I'M A SPY. THINKING OF THE GAMES IS PART OF THE JOB.
BUT I'M ALSO A REALIST.
AND THE REALIST PART KNOWS HOW HARD THIS IS.
IF THERE'S MORE THAN SIX AGENTS ON CORUSCANT...
...I'D BE SURPRISED.
HUH.
WHY IS IT HARD?

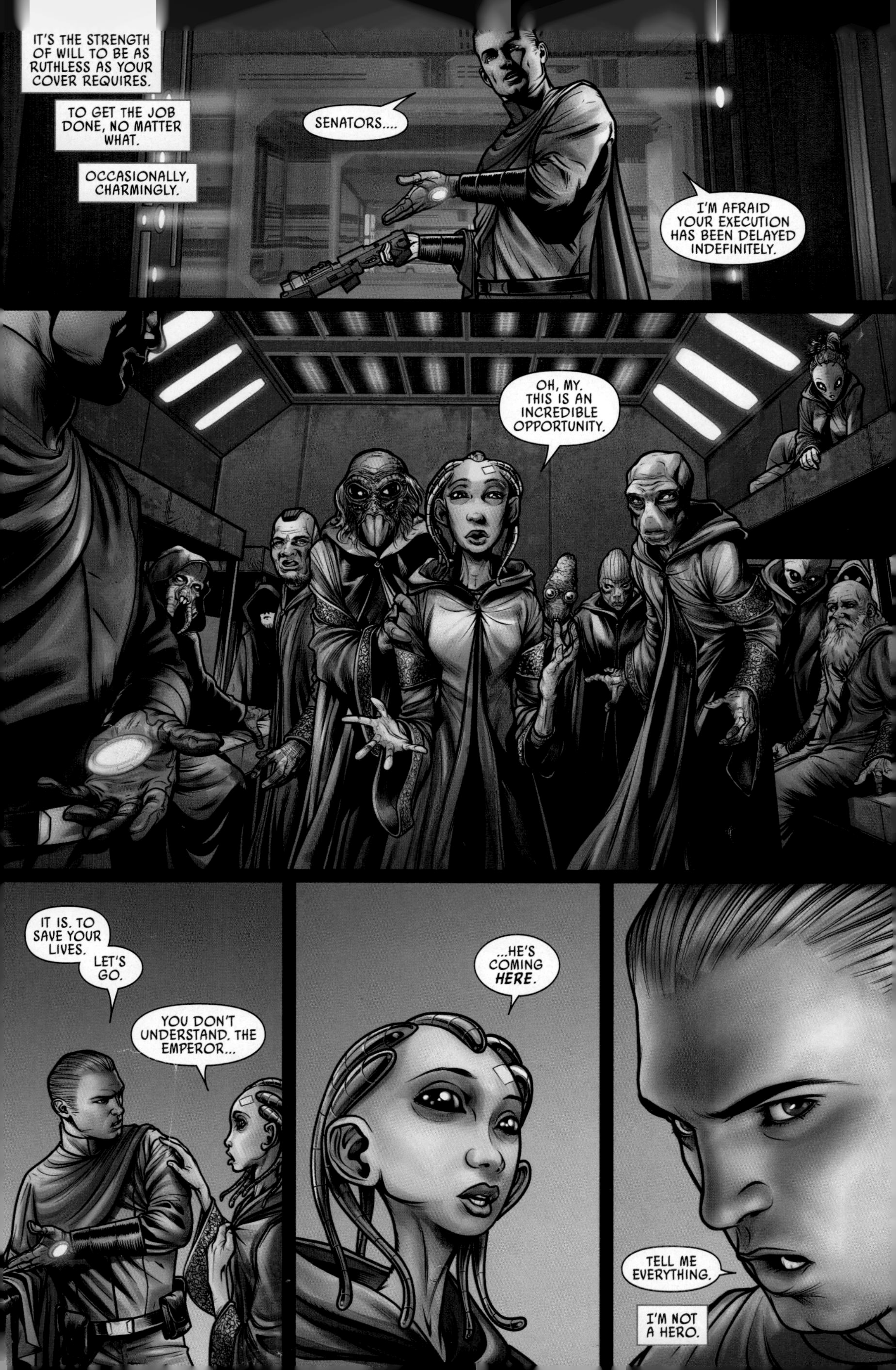
IT'S THE STRENGTH OF WILL TO BE AS RUTHLESS AS YOUR COVER REQUIRES.
TO GET THE JOB DONE, NO MATTER WHAT.
OCCASIONALLY, CHARMINGLY.
SENATORS....
I'M AFRAID YOUR EXECUTION HAS BEEN DELAYED INDEFINITELY.
OH, MY. THIS IS AN INCREDIBLE OPPORTUNITY.
IT IS. TO SAVE YOUR LIVES.
LET'S GO.
YOU DON'T UNDERSTAND. THE EMPEROR...
...HE'S COMING HERE.
TELL ME EVERYTHING.
I'M NOT A HERO.

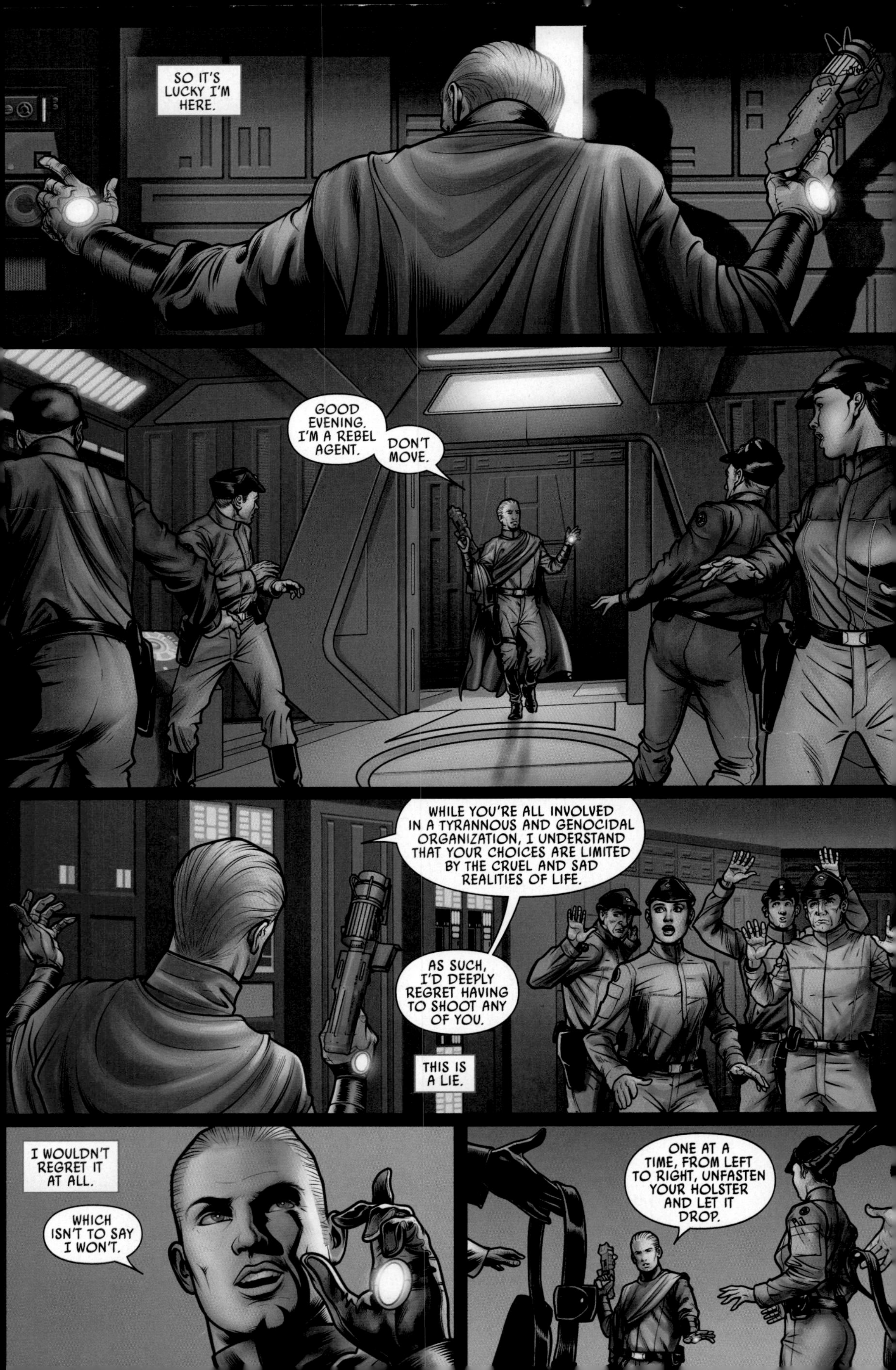
SO IT'S LUCKY I'M HERE.
GOOD EVENING. I'M A REBEL AGENT.
DON'T MOVE.
WHILE YOU'RE ALL INVOLVED IN A TYRANNOUS AND GENOCIDAL ORGANIZATION, I UNDERSTAND THAT YOUR CHOICES ARE LIMITED BY THE CRUEL AND SAD REALITIES OF LIFE.
AS SUCH, I'D DEEPLY REGRET HAVING TO SHOOT ANY OF YOU.
THIS IS A LIE.
I WOULDN'T REGRET IT AT ALL.
WHICH ISN'T TO SAY I WON'T.
ONE AT A TIME, FROM LEFT TO RIGHT, UNFASTEN YOUR HOLSTER AND LET IT DROP.

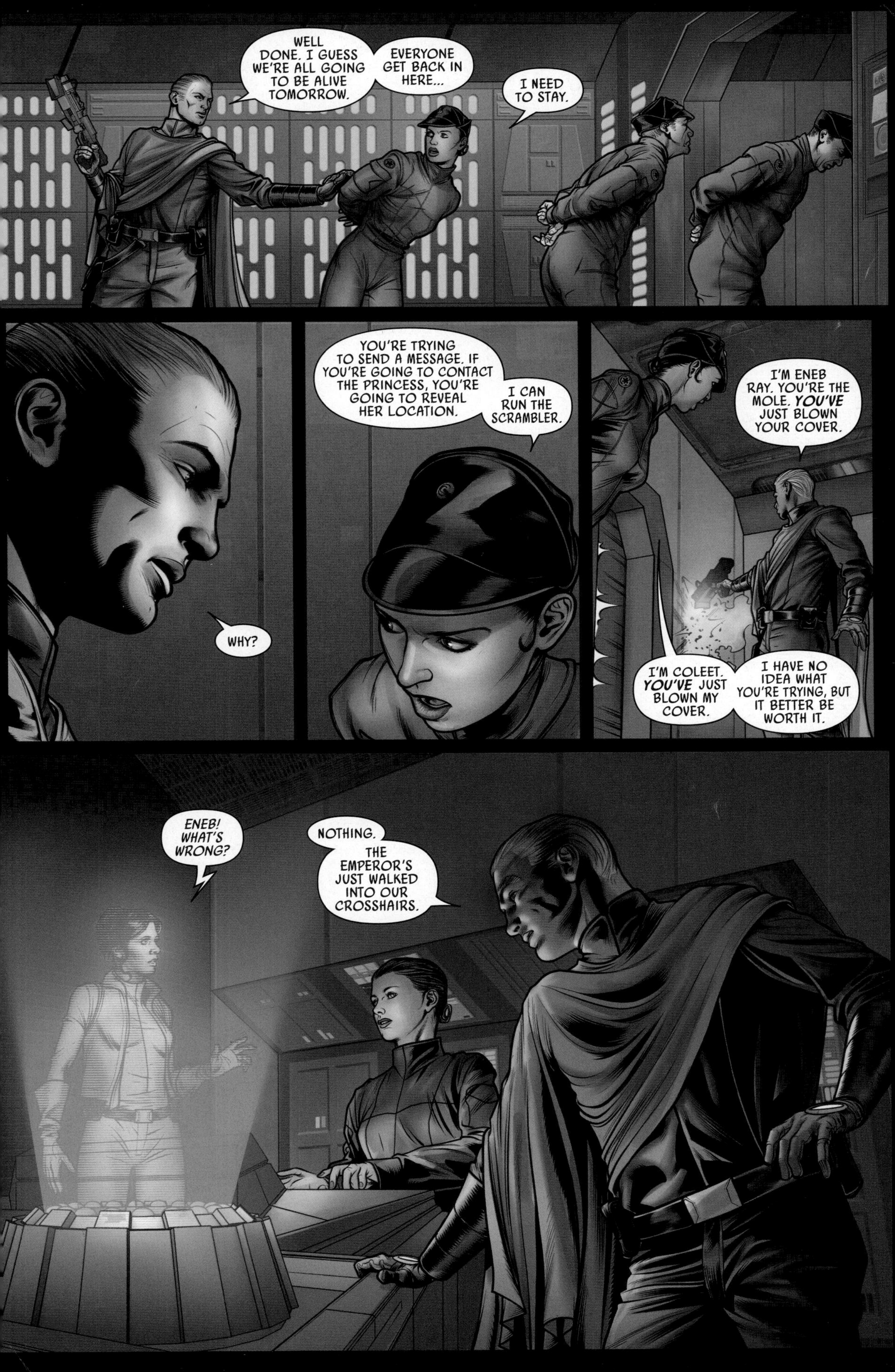
WELL DONE. I GUESS WE'RE ALL GOING TO BE ALIVE TOMORROW.
EVERYONE GET BACK IN HERE...
I NEED TO STAY.
WHY?
YOU'RE TRYING TO SEND A MESSAGE. IF YOU'RE GOING TO CONTACT THE PRINCESS, YOU'RE GOING TO REVEAL HER LOCATION.
I CAN RUN THE SCRAMBLER.
I'M ENEB RAY. YOU'RE THE MOLE. YOU'VE JUST BLOWN YOUR COVER.
I'M COLEET. YOU'VE JUST BLOWN MY COVER.
I HAVE NO IDEA WHAT YOU'RE TRYING, BUT IT BETTER BE WORTH IT.
ENEB! WHAT'S WRONG?
NOTHING.
THE EMPEROR'S JUST WALKED INTO OUR CROSSHAIRS.

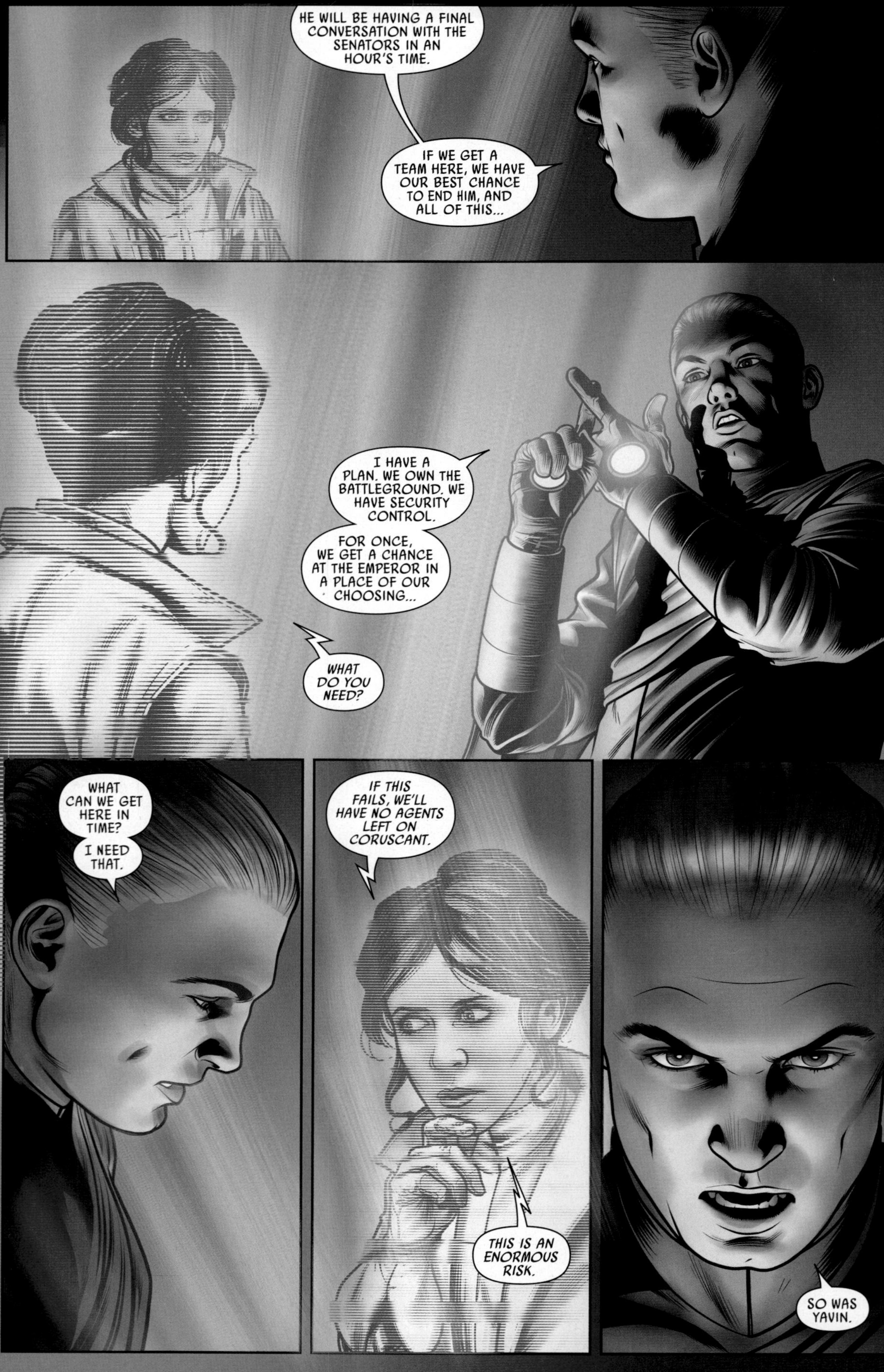
HE WILL BE HAVING A FINAL CONVERSATION WITH THE SENATORS IN AN HOUR'S TIME.
IF WE GET A TEAM HERE, WE HAVE OUR BEST CHANCE TO END HIM, AND ALL OF THIS...
I HAVE A PLAN. WE OWN THE BATTLEGROUND. WE HAVE SECURITY CONTROL.
FOR ONCE, WE GET A CHANCE AT THE EMPEROR IN A PLACE OF OUR CHOOSING...
WHAT DO YOU NEED?
WHAT CAN WE GET HERE IN TIME?
I NEED THAT.
IF THIS FAILS, WE'LL HAVE NO AGENTS LEFT ON CORUSCANT.
THIS IS AN ENORMOUS RISK.
SO WAS YAVIN.

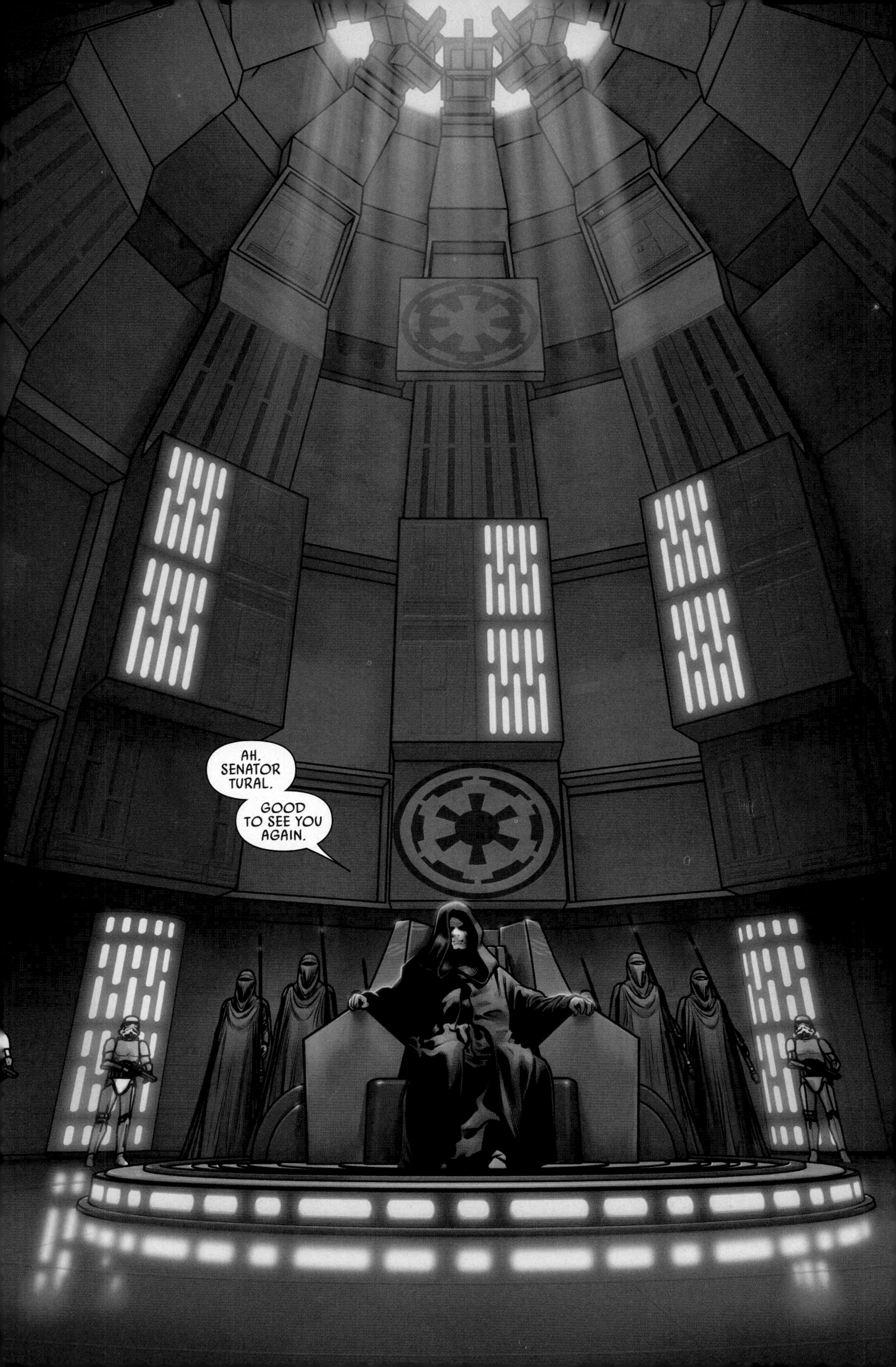
AH. SENATOR TURAL.
GOOD TO SEE YOU AGAIN.

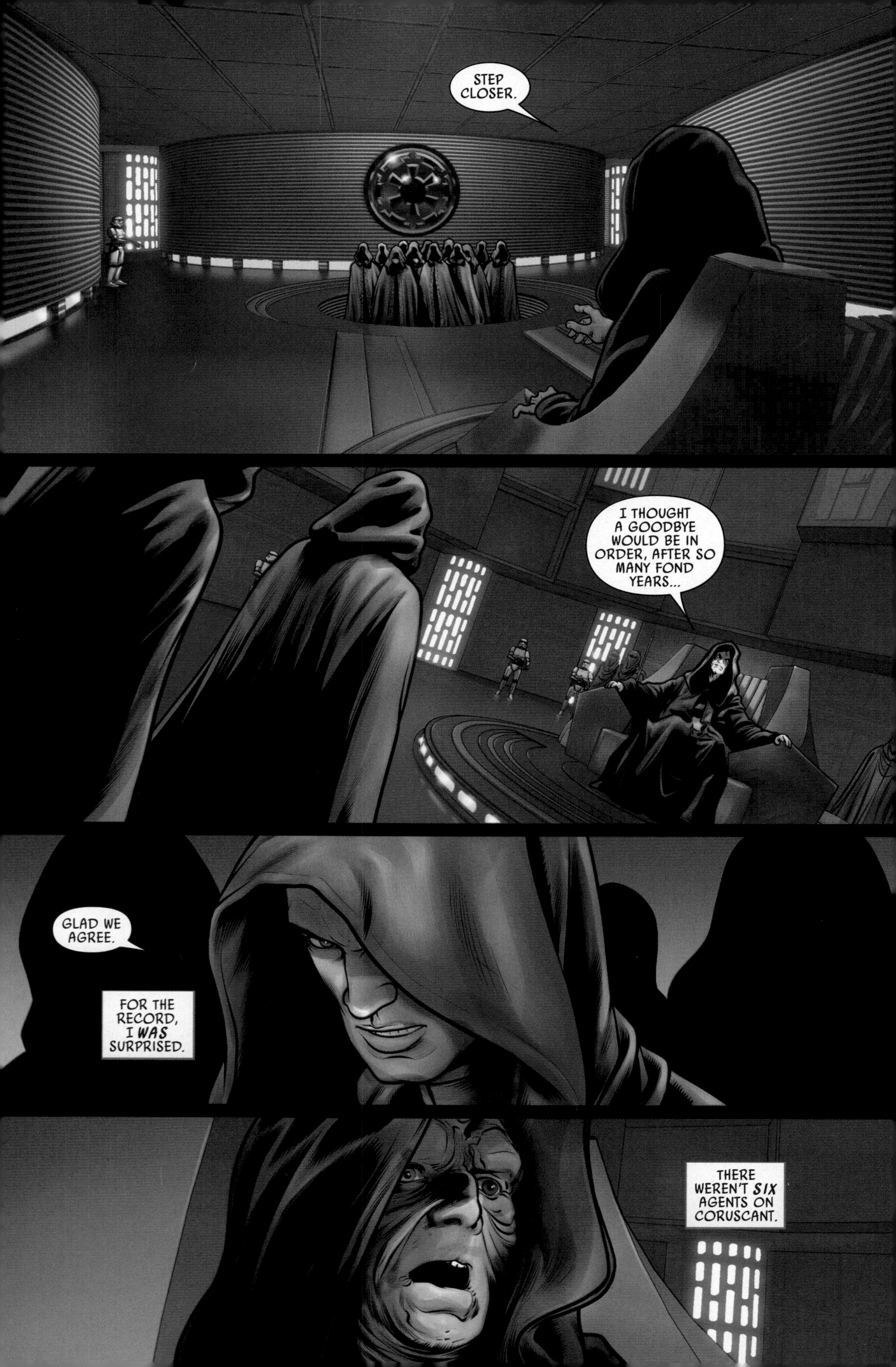
STEP CLOSER.
I THOUGHT A GOODBYE WOULD BE IN ORDER, AFTER SO MANY FOND YEARS...
GLAD WE AGREE.
FOR THE RECORD, I WAS SURPRISED.
THERE WEREN'T SIX AGENTS ON CORUSCANT.

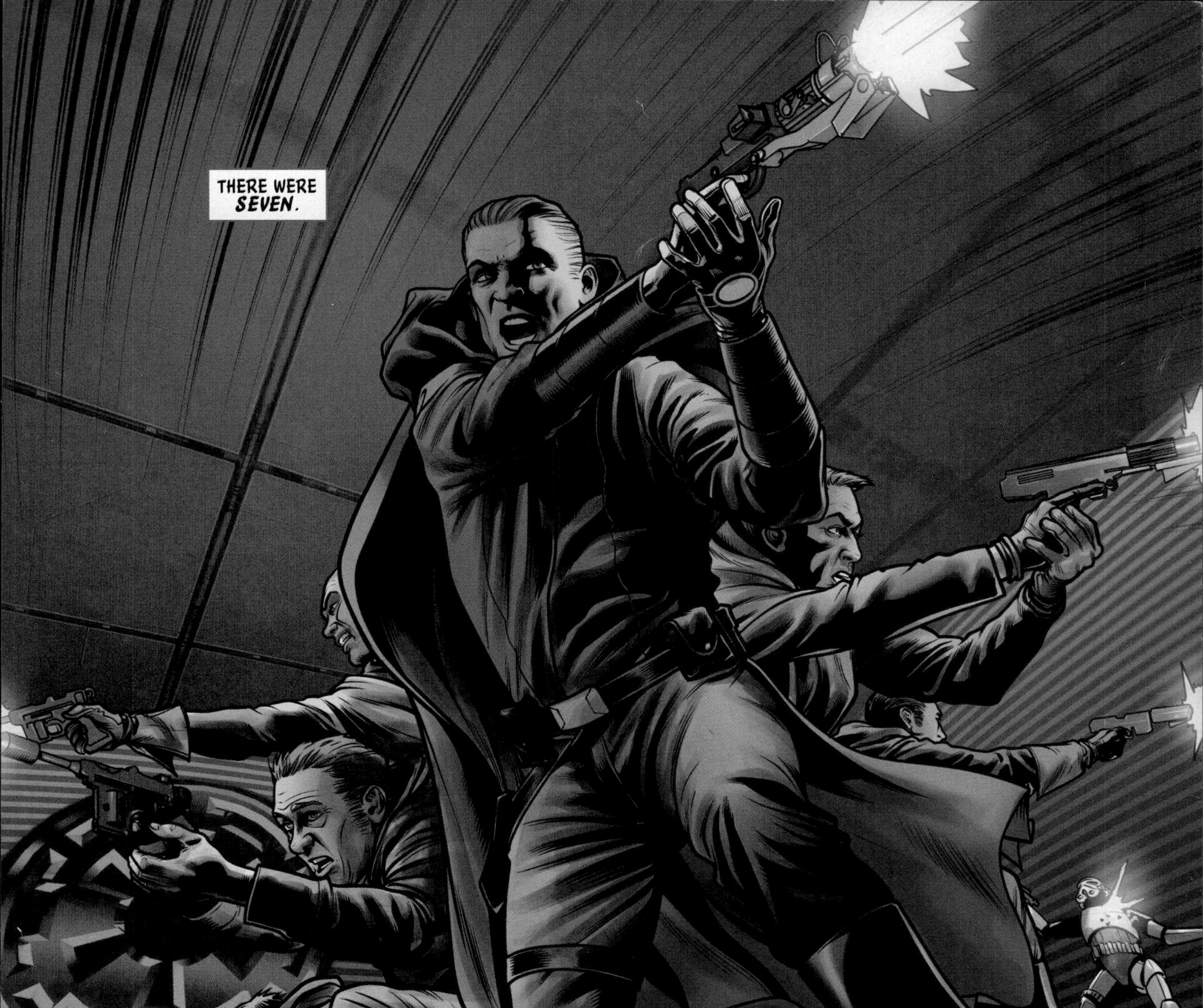
THERE WERE SEVEN.

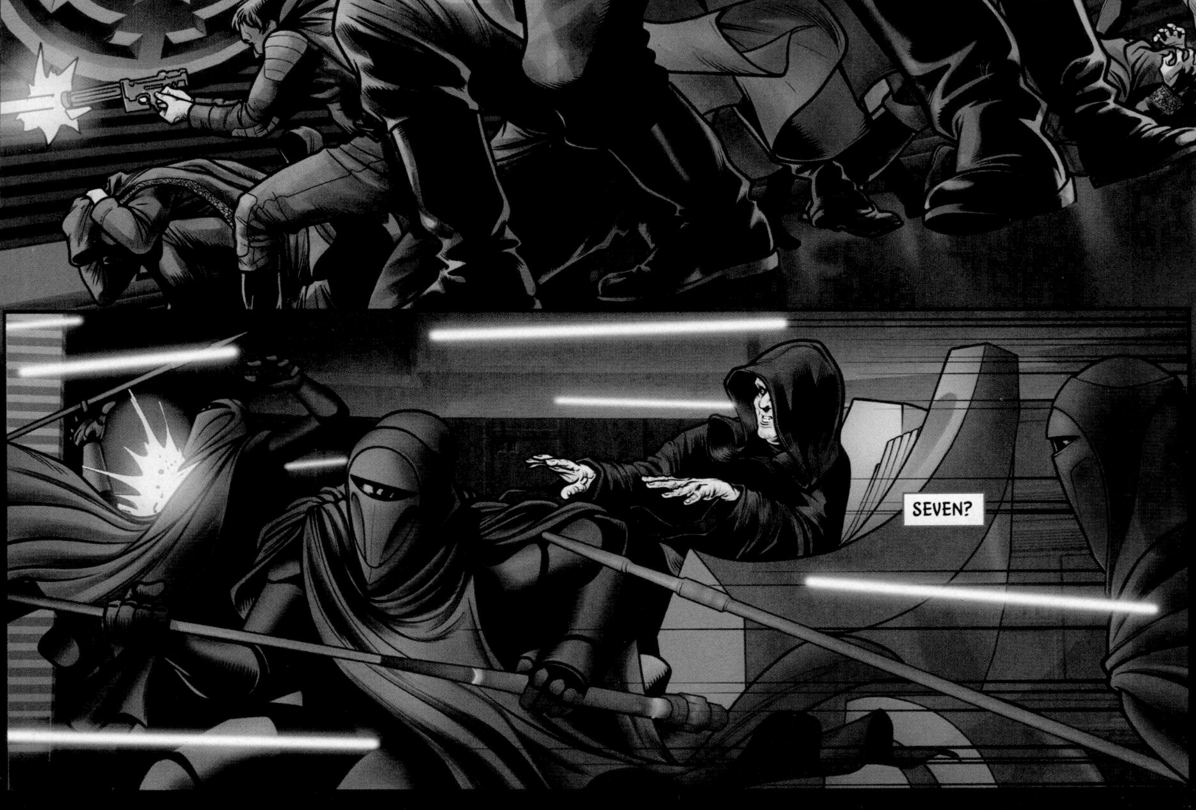
SEVEN?

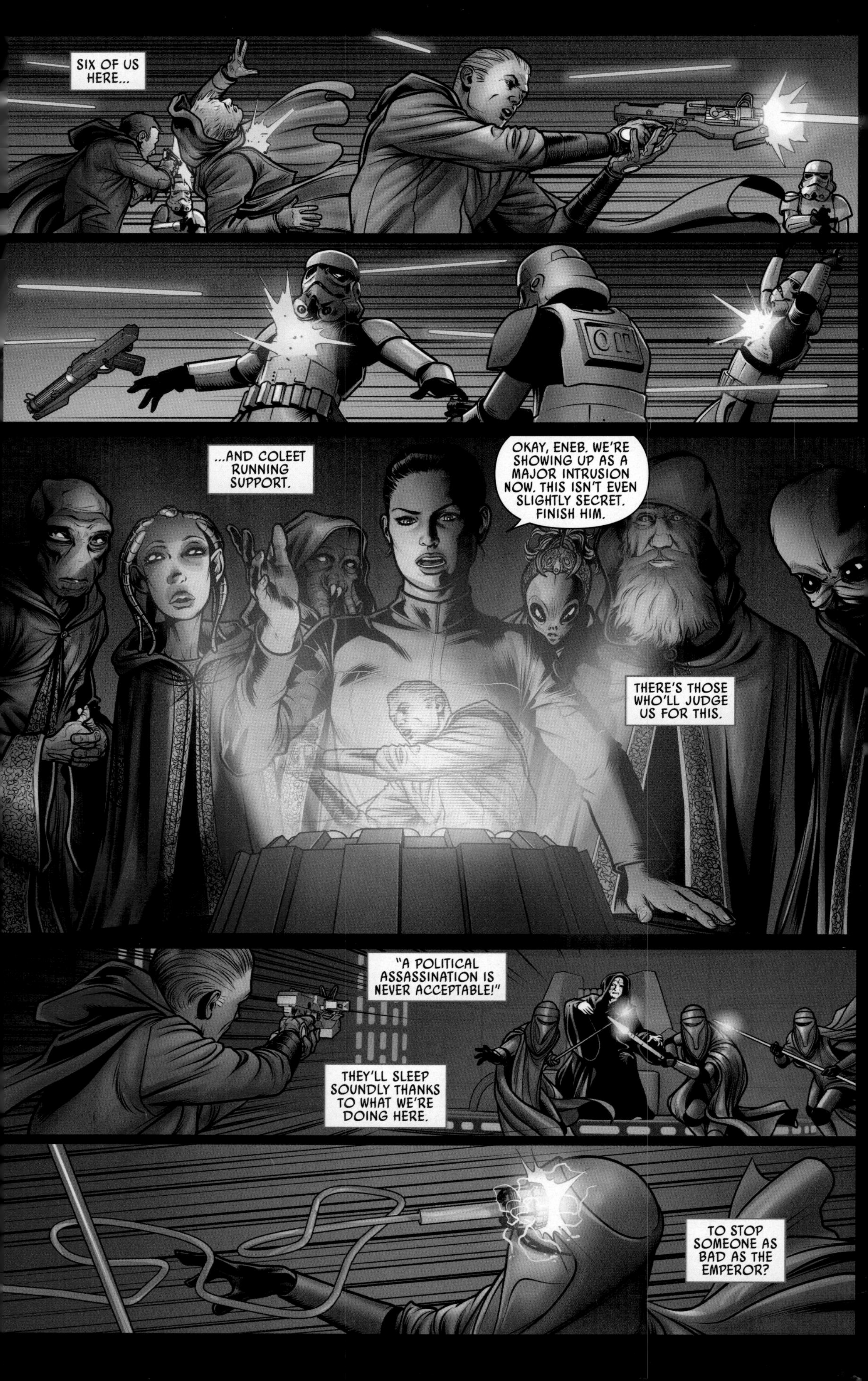
SIX OF US HERE...
...AND COLEET RUNNING SUPPORT.
OKAY, ENEB. WE'RE SHOWING UP AS A MAJOR INTRUSION NOW. THIS ISN'T EVEN SLIGHTLY SECRET. FINISH HIM.
THERE'S THOSE WHO'LL JUDGE US FOR THIS.
"A POLITICAL ASSASSINATION IS NEVER ACCEPTABLE!"
THEY'LL SLEEP SOUNDLY THANKS TO WHAT WE'RE DOING HERE.
TO STOP SOMEONE AS BAD AS THE EMPEROR?

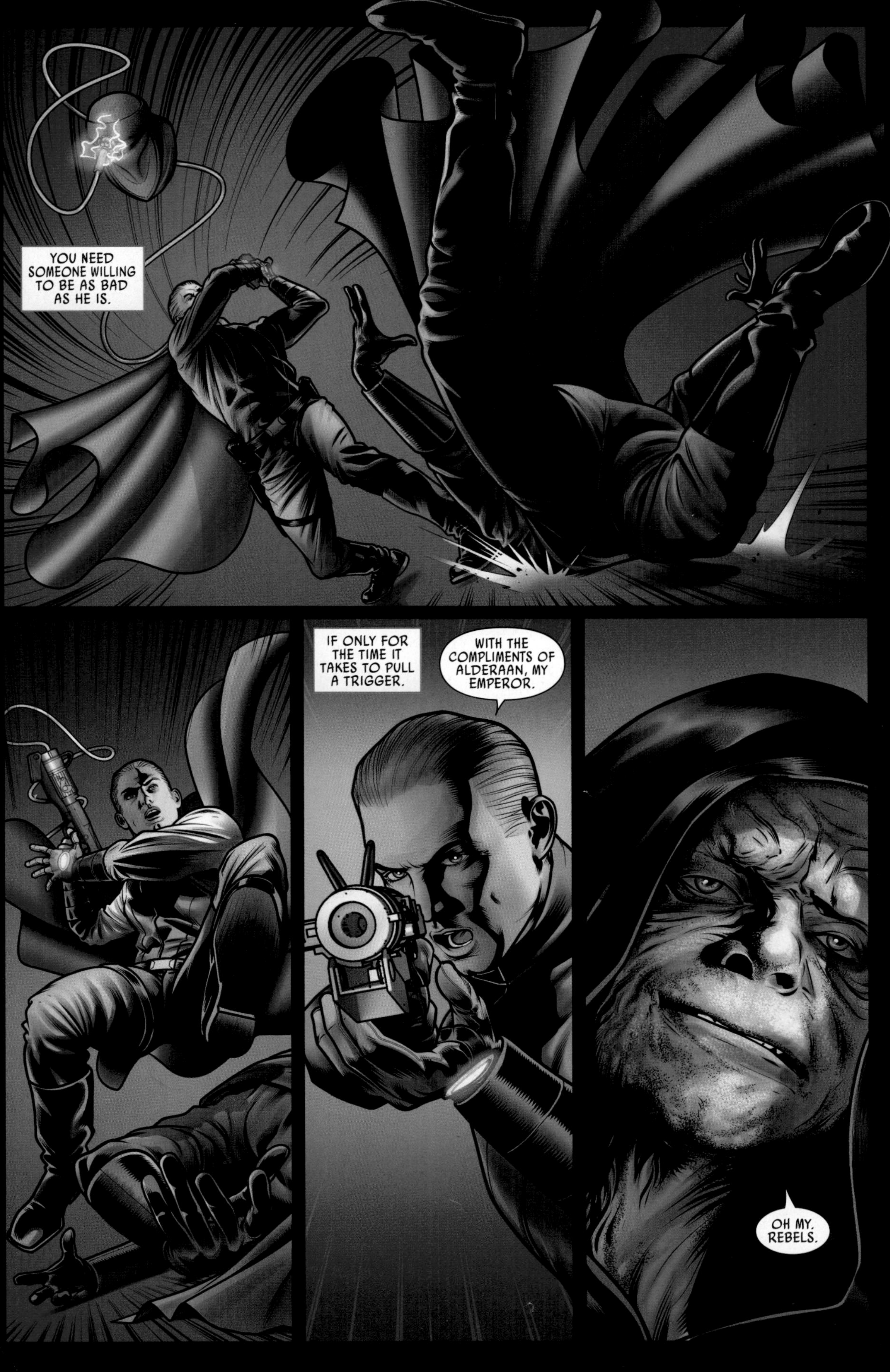
YOU NEED SOMEONE WILLING TO BE AS BAD AS HE IS.
IF ONLY FOR THE TIME IT TAKES TO PULL A TRIGGER.
WITH THE COMPLIMENTS OF ALDERAAN, MY EMPEROR.
OH MY. REBELS.

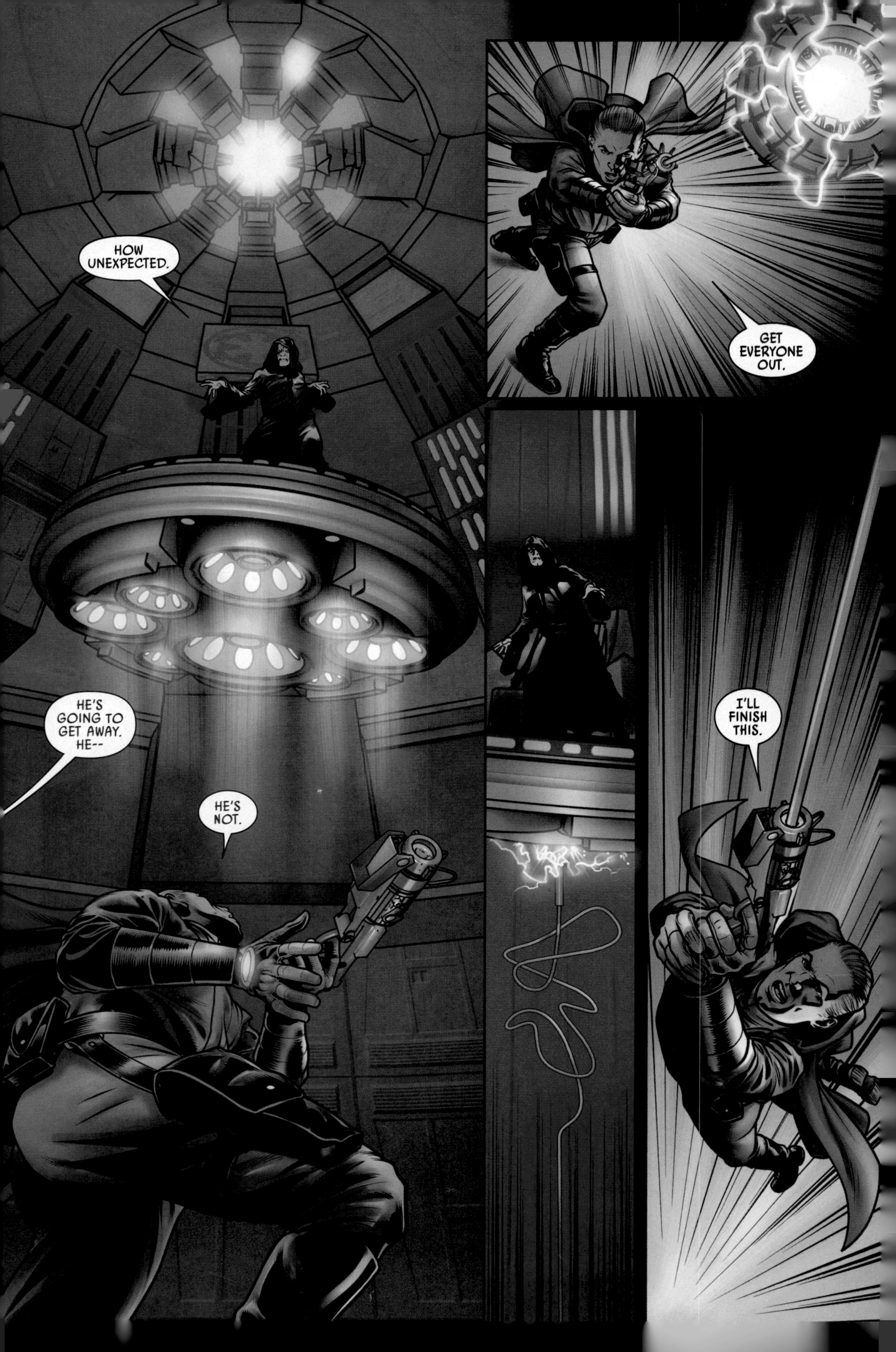
HOW UNEXPECTED.
HE'S GOING TO GET AWAY. HE--
HE'S NOT.
GET EVERYONE OUT.
I'LL FINISH THIS.

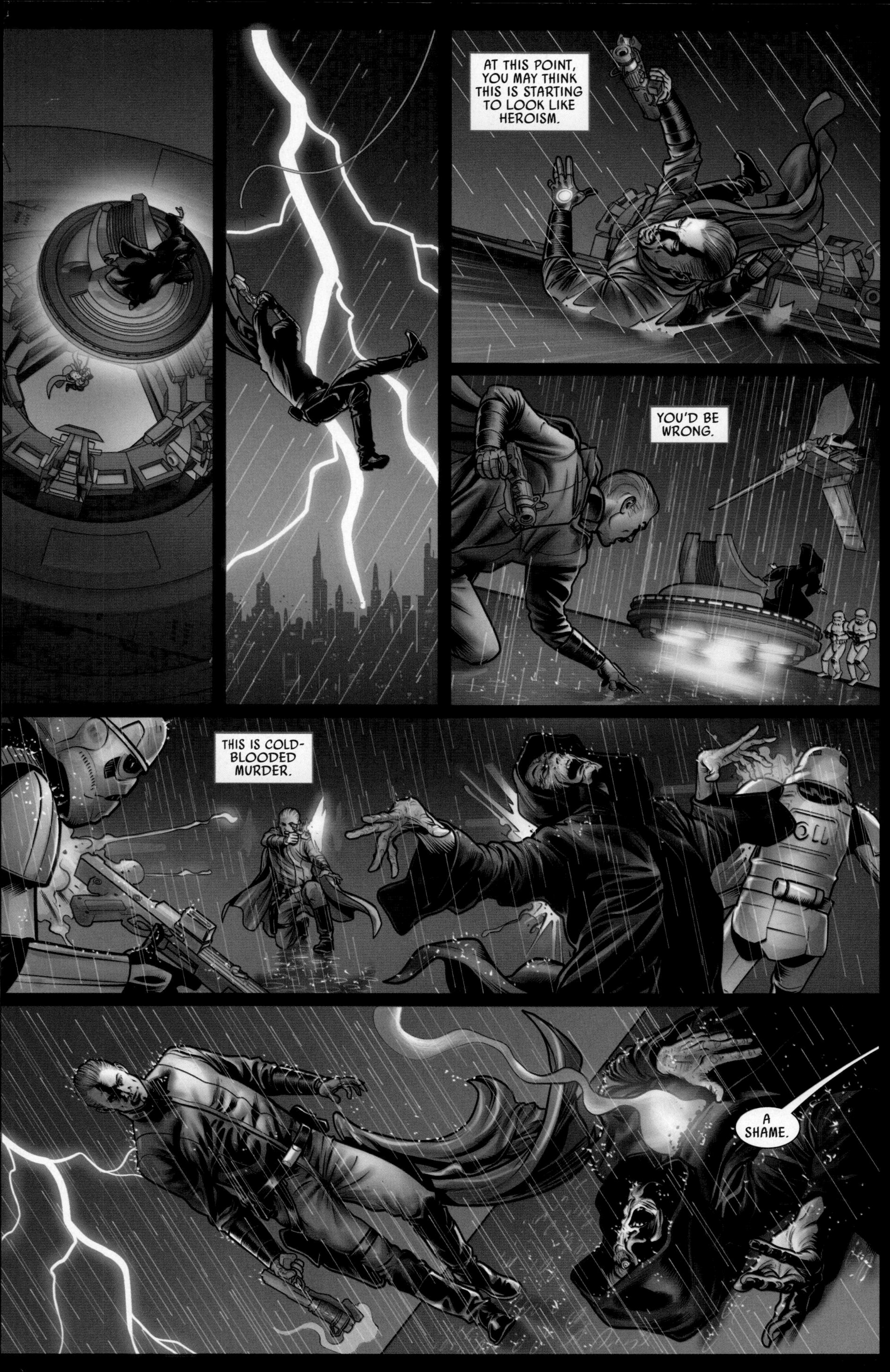
AT THIS POINT, YOU MAY THINK THIS IS STARTING TO LOOK LIKE HEROISM.
YOU'D BE WRONG.
THIS IS COLD-BLOODED MURDER.
A SHAME.

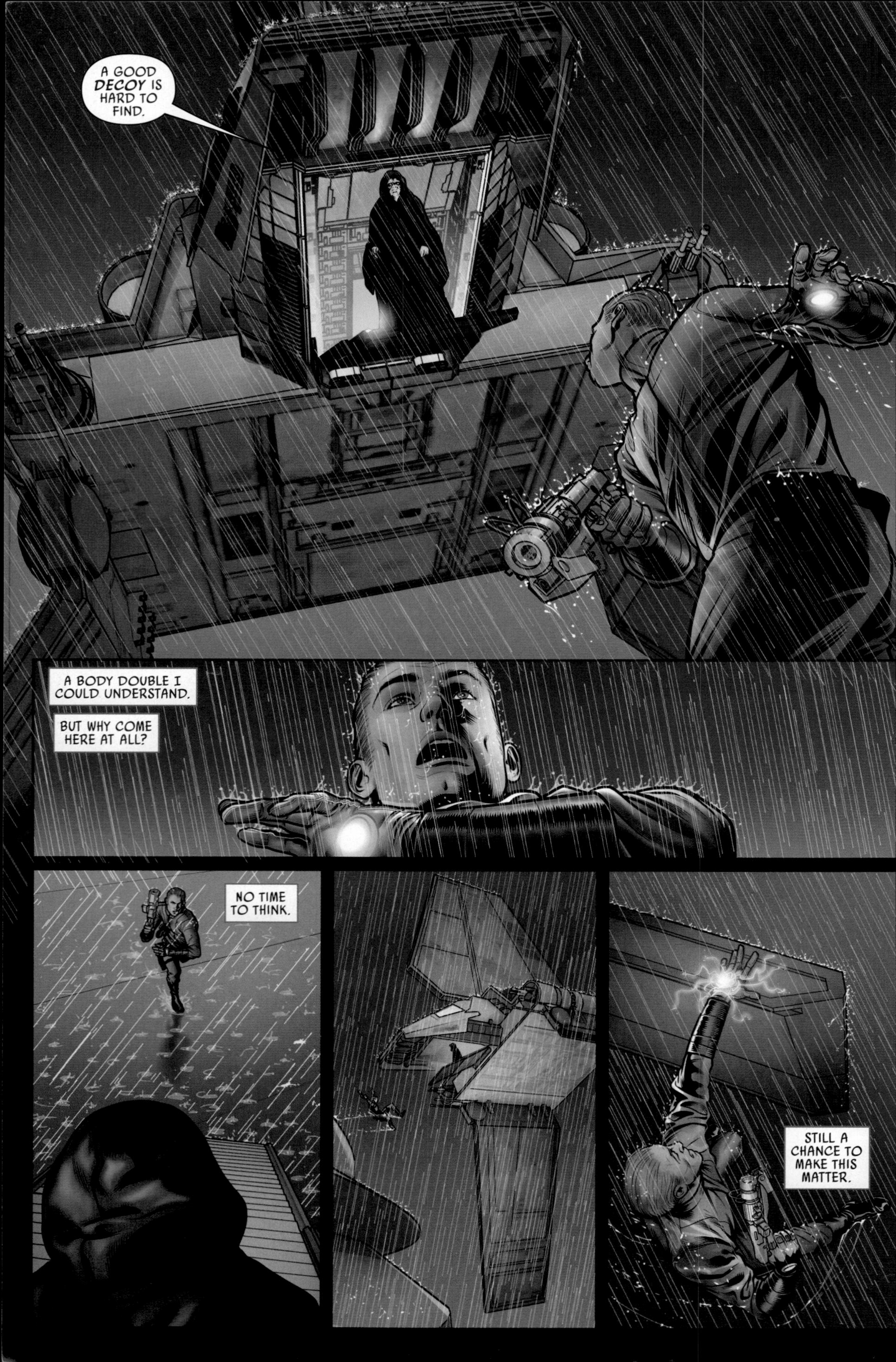
A GOOD DECOY IS HARD TO FIND.
A BODY DOUBLE I COULD UNDERSTAND.
BUT WHY COME HERE AT ALL?
NO TIME TO THINK.
STILL A CHANCE TO MAKE THIS MATTER.

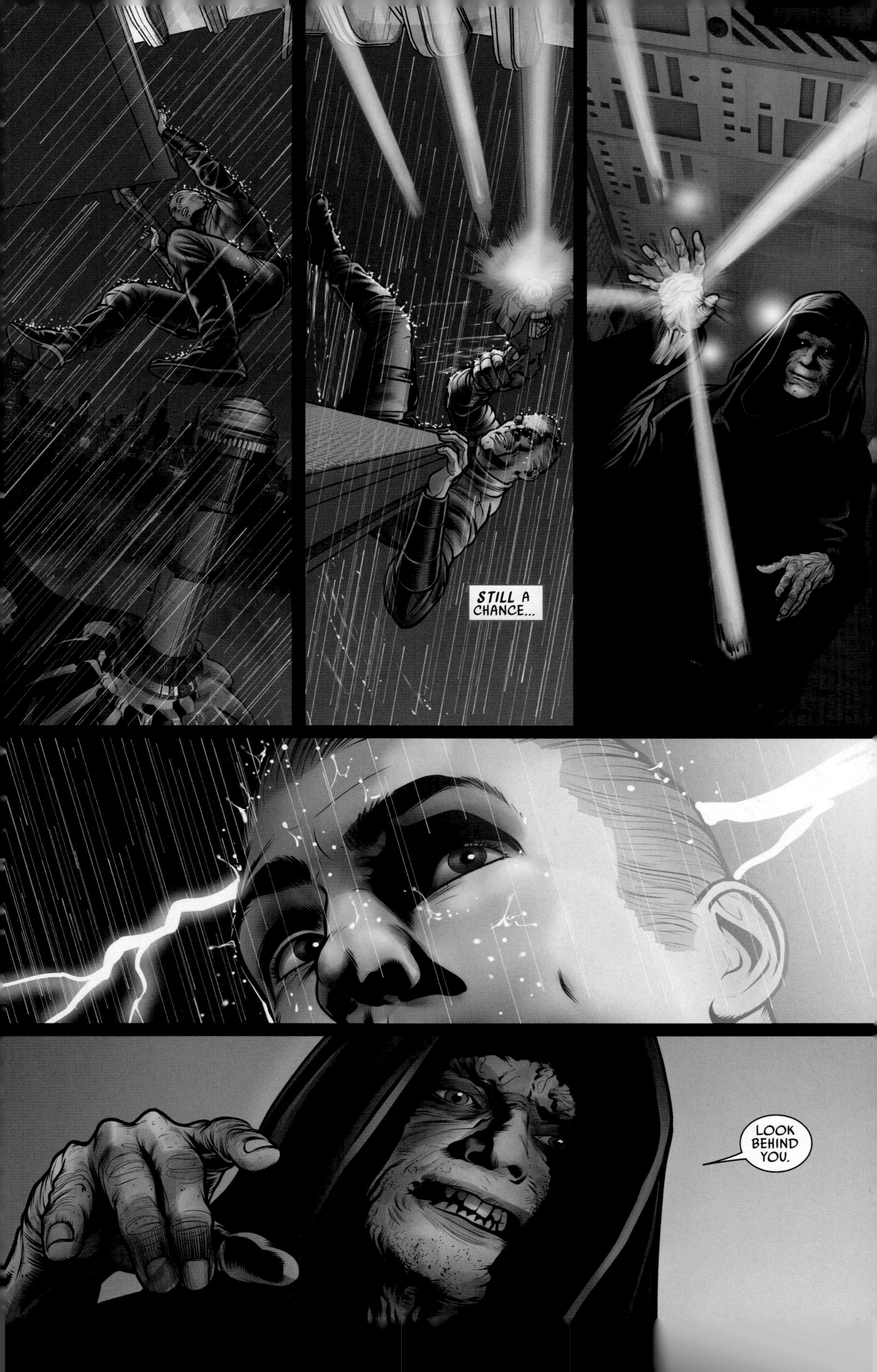
STILL A CHANCE...
LOOK BEHIND YOU.

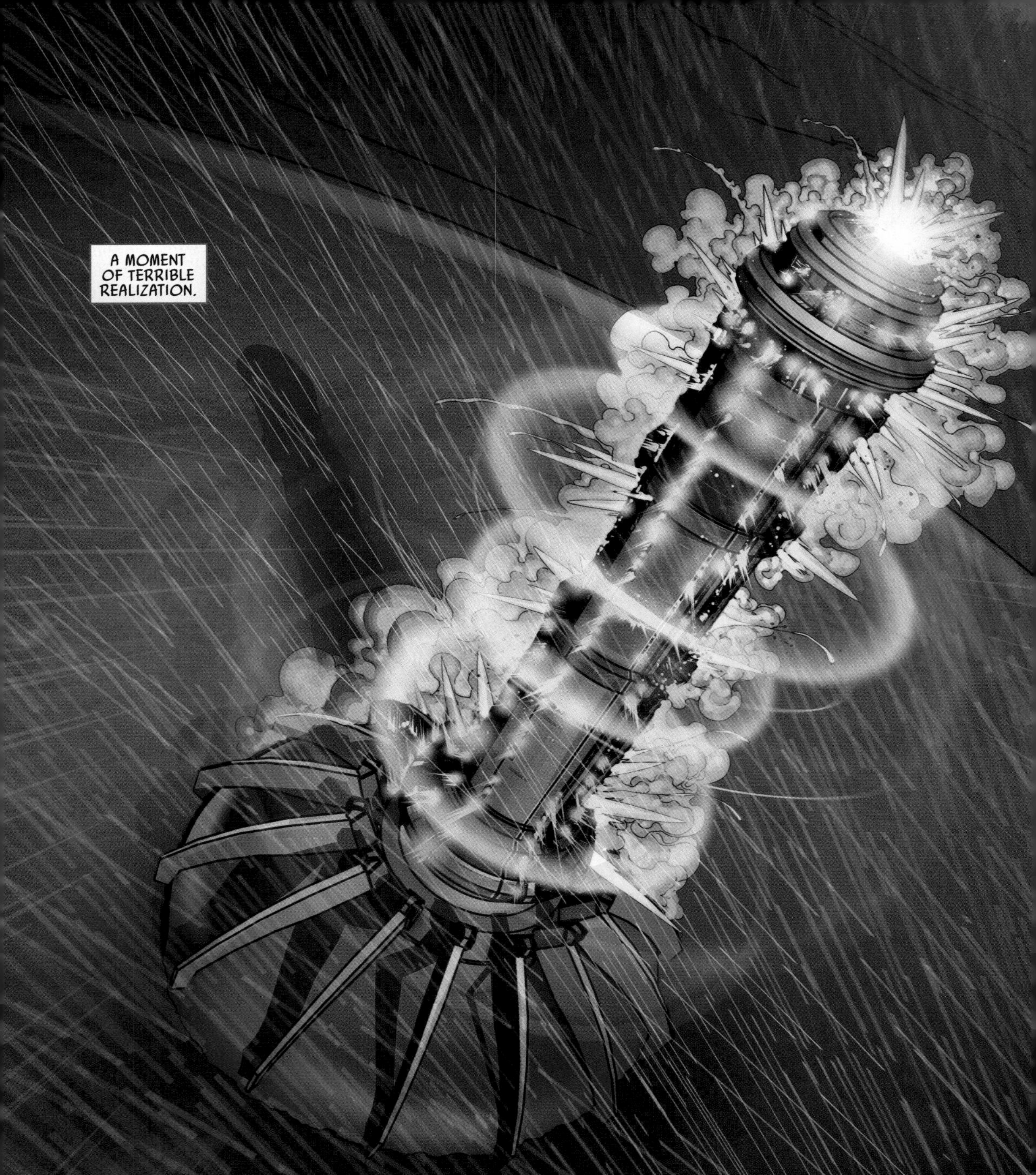
A MOMENT OF TERRIBLE REALIZATION.

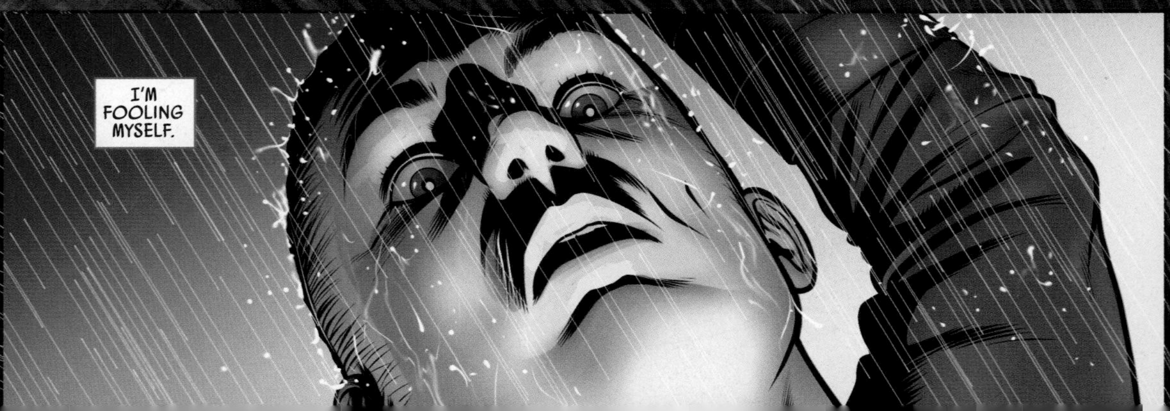
I'M FOOLING MYSELF.

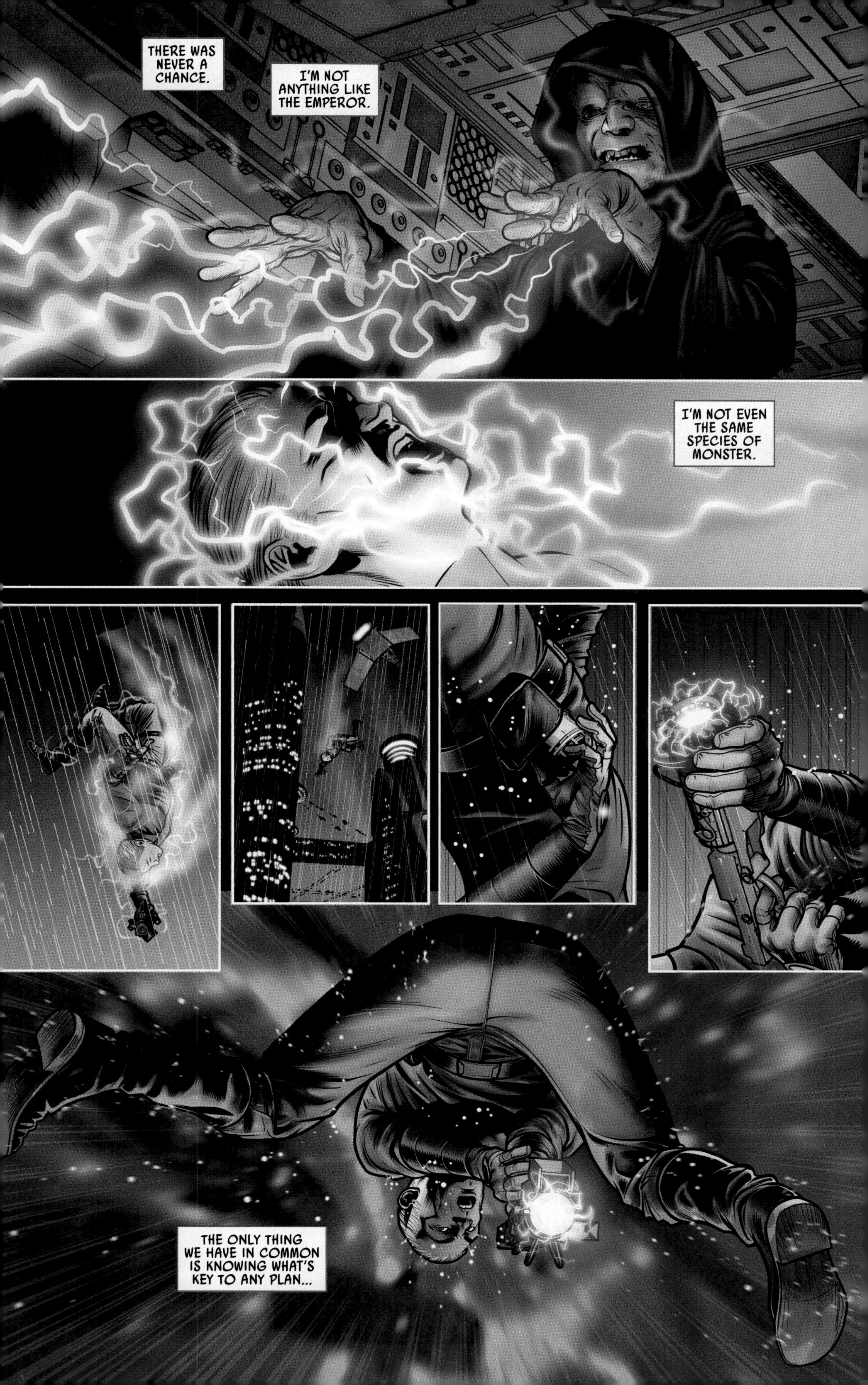
THERE WAS NEVER A CHANCE.
I'M NOT ANYTHING LIKE THE EMPEROR.
I'M NOT EVEN THE SAME SPECIES OF MONSTER.
THE ONLY THING WE HAVE IN COMMON IS KNOWING WHAT'S KEY TO ANY PLAN...

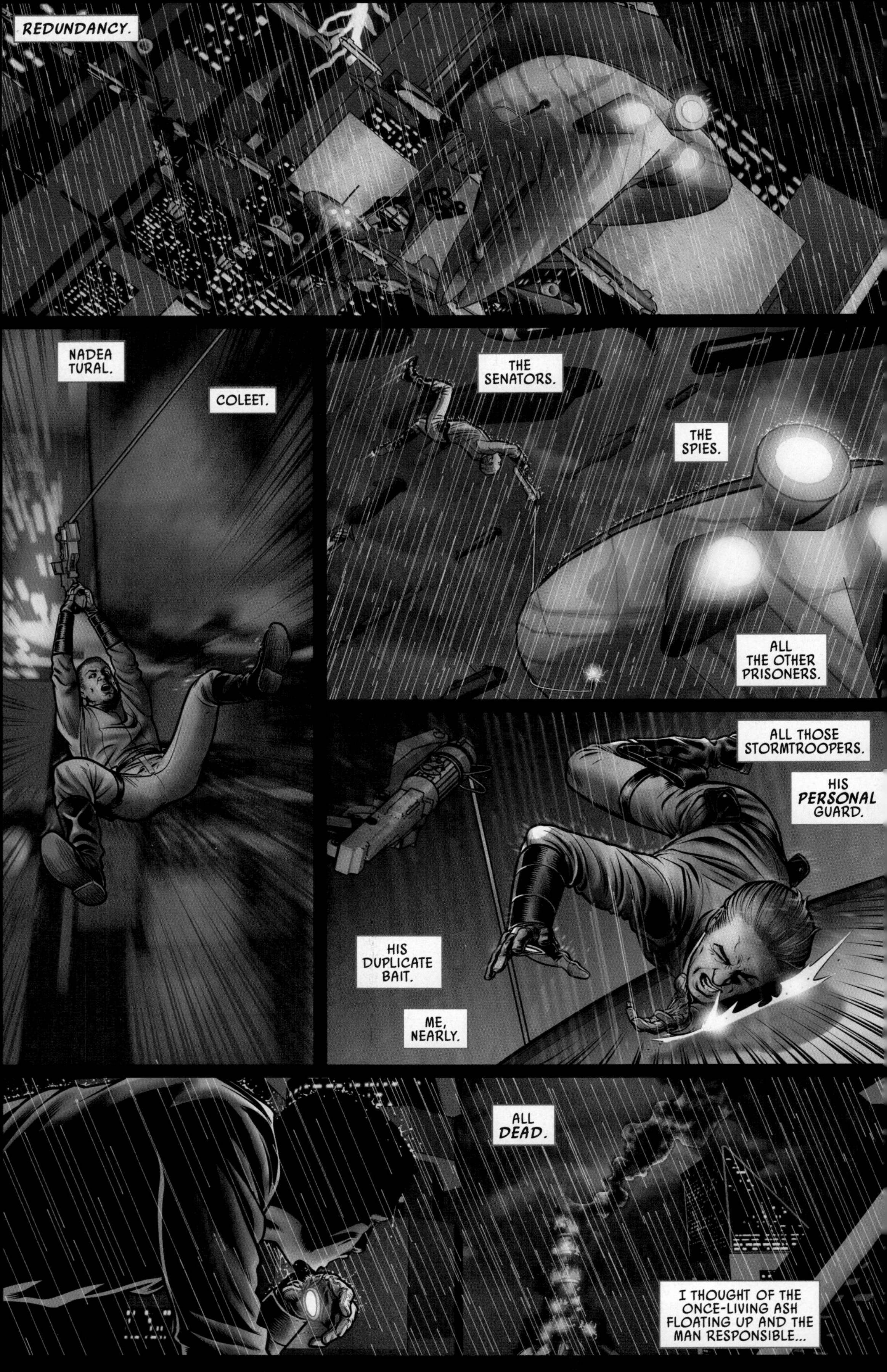

REDUNDANCY.
NADEA TURAL.
COLEET.
THE SENATORS.
THE SPIES.
ALL THE OTHER PRISONERS.
ALL THOSE STORMTROOPERS.
HIS *PERSONAL* GUARD.
HIS DUPLICATE BAIT.
ME, NEARLY.
ALL *DEAD*.
I THOUGHT OF THE ONCE-LIVING ASH FLOATING UP AND THE MAN RESPONSIBLE...

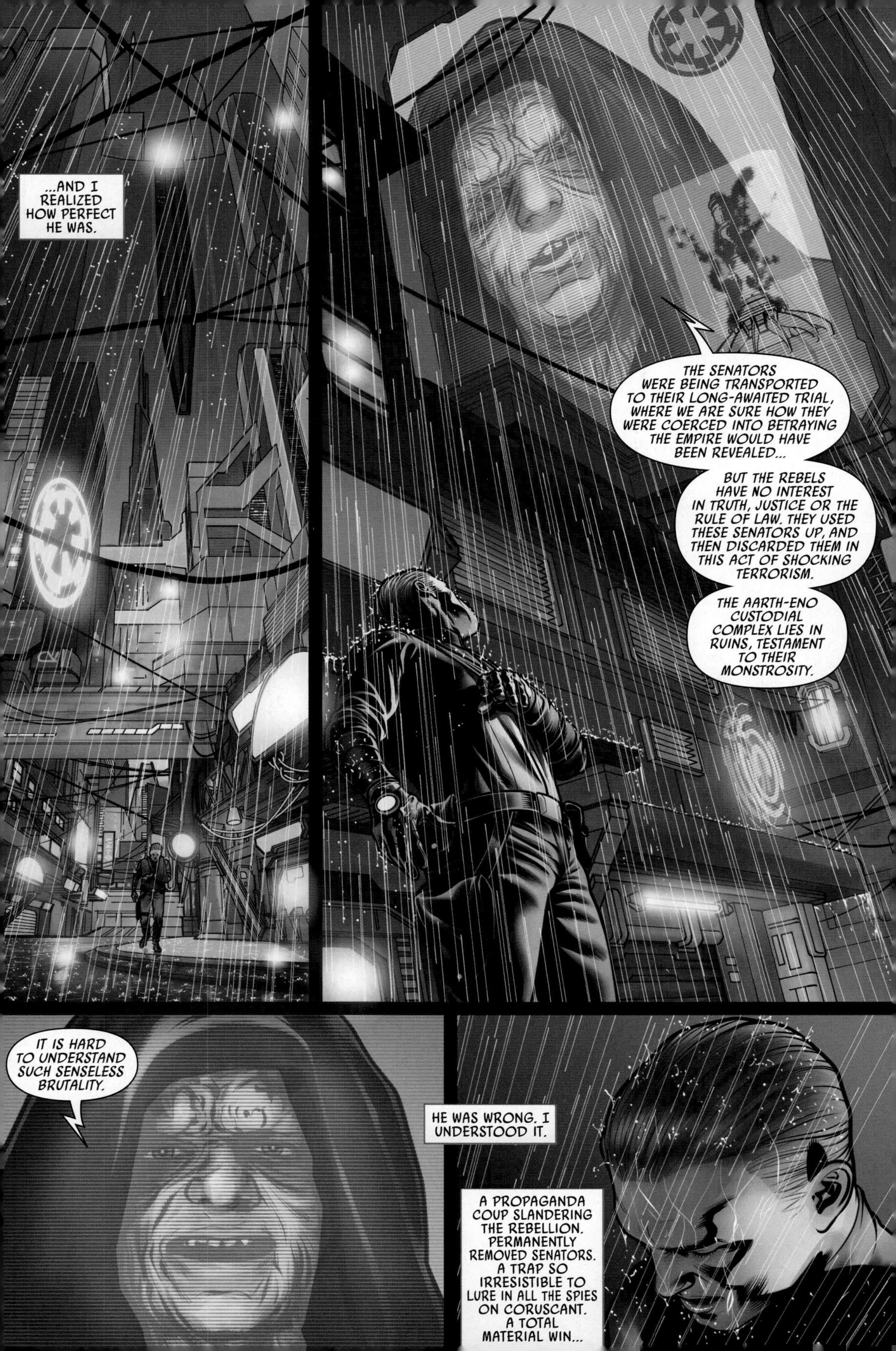
...AND I REALIZED HOW PERFECT HE WAS.
THE SENATORS WERE BEING TRANSPORTED TO THEIR LONG-AWAITED TRIAL, WHERE WE ARE SURE HOW THEY WERE COERCED INTO BETRAYING THE EMPIRE WOULD HAVE BEEN REVEALED...
BUT THE REBELS HAVE NO INTEREST IN TRUTH, JUSTICE OR THE RULE OF LAW. THEY USED THESE SENATORS UP, AND THEN DISCARDED THEM IN THIS ACT OF SHOCKING TERRORISM.
THE AARTH-ENO CUSTODIAL COMPLEX LIES IN RUINS, TESTAMENT TO THEIR MONSTROSITY.
IT IS HARD TO UNDERSTAND SUCH SENSELESS BRUTALITY.
HE WAS WRONG. I UNDERSTOOD IT.
A PROPAGANDA COUP SLANDERING THE REBELLION. PERMANENTLY REMOVED SENATORS. A TRAP SO IRRESISTIBLE TO LURE IN ALL THE SPIES ON CORUSCANT. A TOTAL MATERIAL WIN...

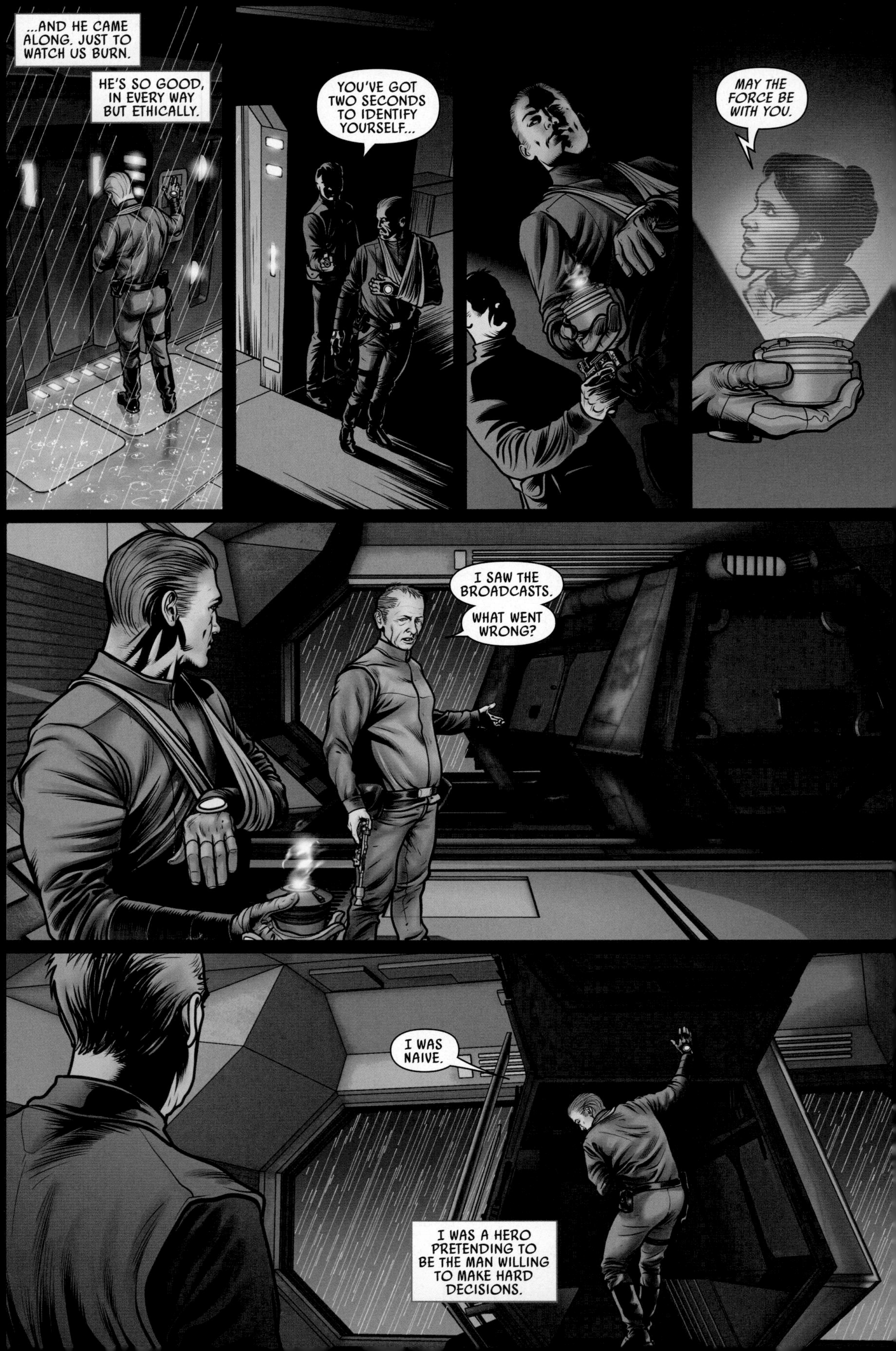
...AND HE CAME ALONG. JUST TO WATCH US BURN.
HE'S SO GOOD, IN EVERY WAY BUT ETHICALLY.
YOU'VE GOT TWO SECONDS TO IDENTIFY YOURSELF...
MAY THE FORCE BE WITH YOU.
I SAW THE BROADCASTS.
WHAT WENT WRONG?
I WAS NAIVE.
I WAS A HERO PRETENDING TO BE THE MAN WILLING TO MAKE HARD DECISIONS.

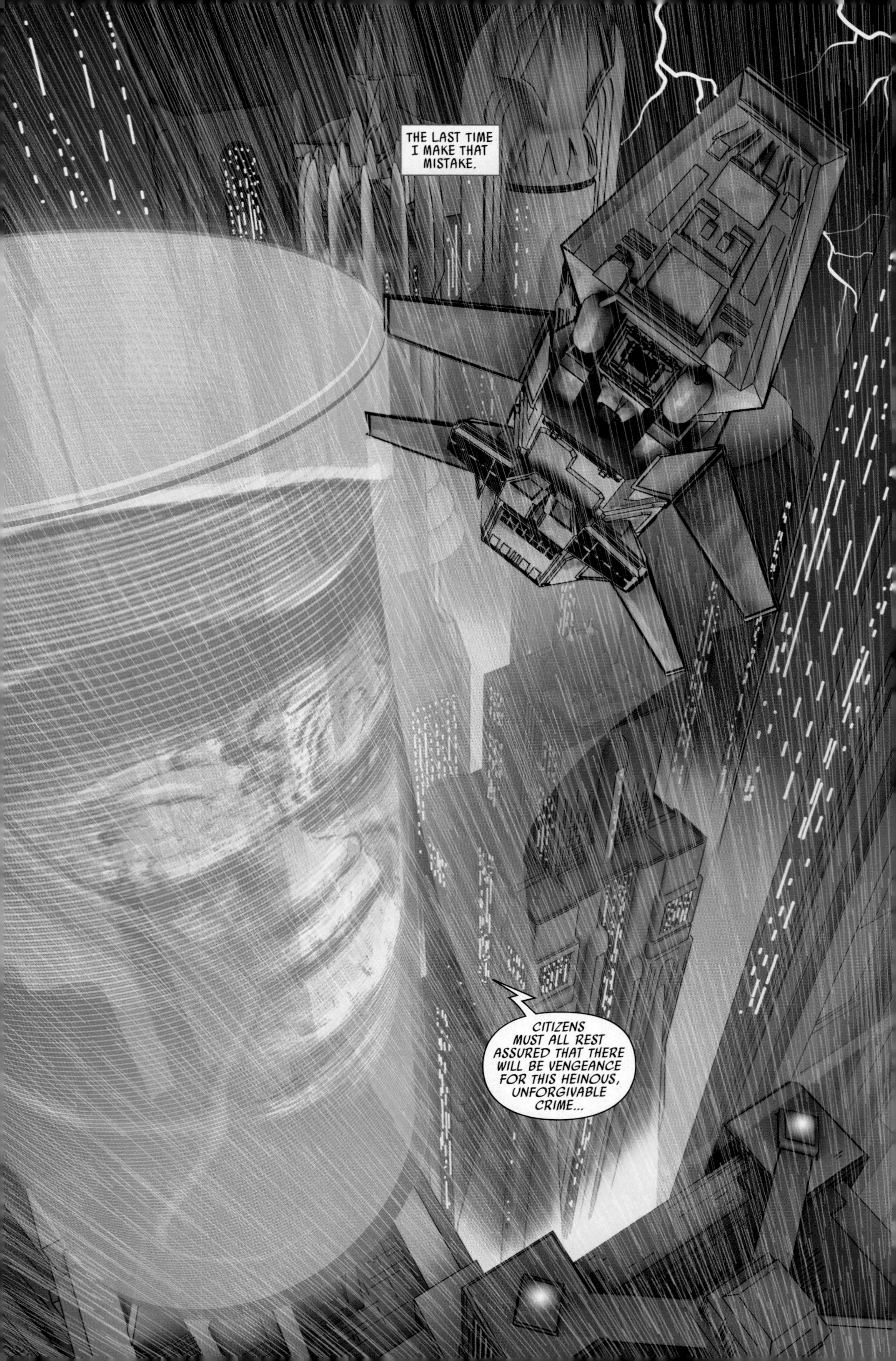
THE LAST TIME I MAKE THAT MISTAKE.
CITIZENS MUST ALL REST ASSURED THAT THERE WILL BE VENGEANCE FOR THIS HEINOUS, UNFORGIVABLE CRIME...

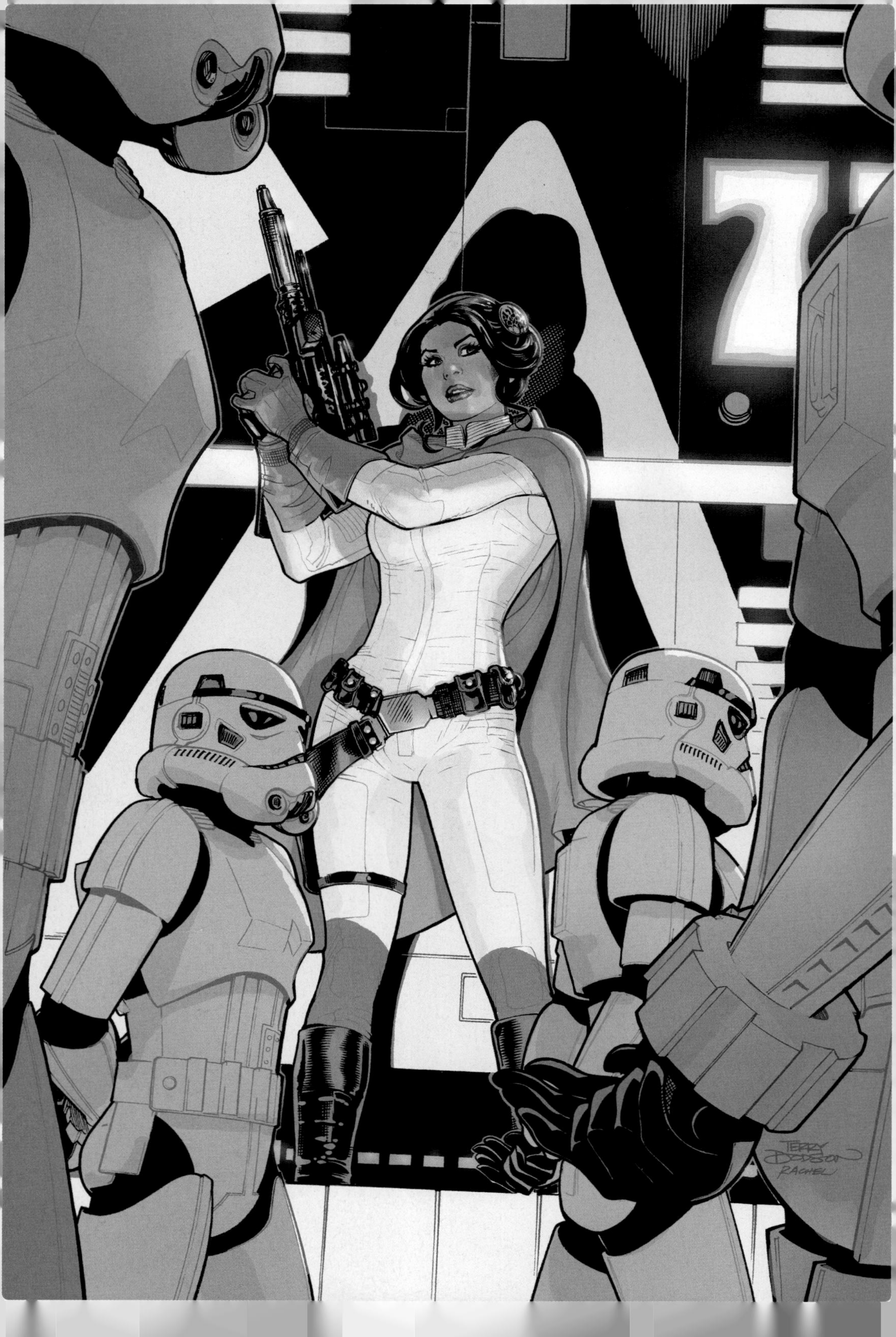
TERRY DODSON
RACHEL

REBEL JAIL

It is an era of renewed hope for the Rebellion.

After narrowly escaping another frightening encounter with Darth Vader, rebel heroes Luke Skywalker, Princess Leia, and Han Solo take the evil Sith Lord's secret ally, droid and weapon specialist Dr. Aphra, captive aboard the *Millennium Falcon.*

Now their mission to free the galaxy from the grasp of the Emperor continues as the Princess teams with smuggler Sana Starros, while Luke and Han pair together on a secret mission for the Rebellion....

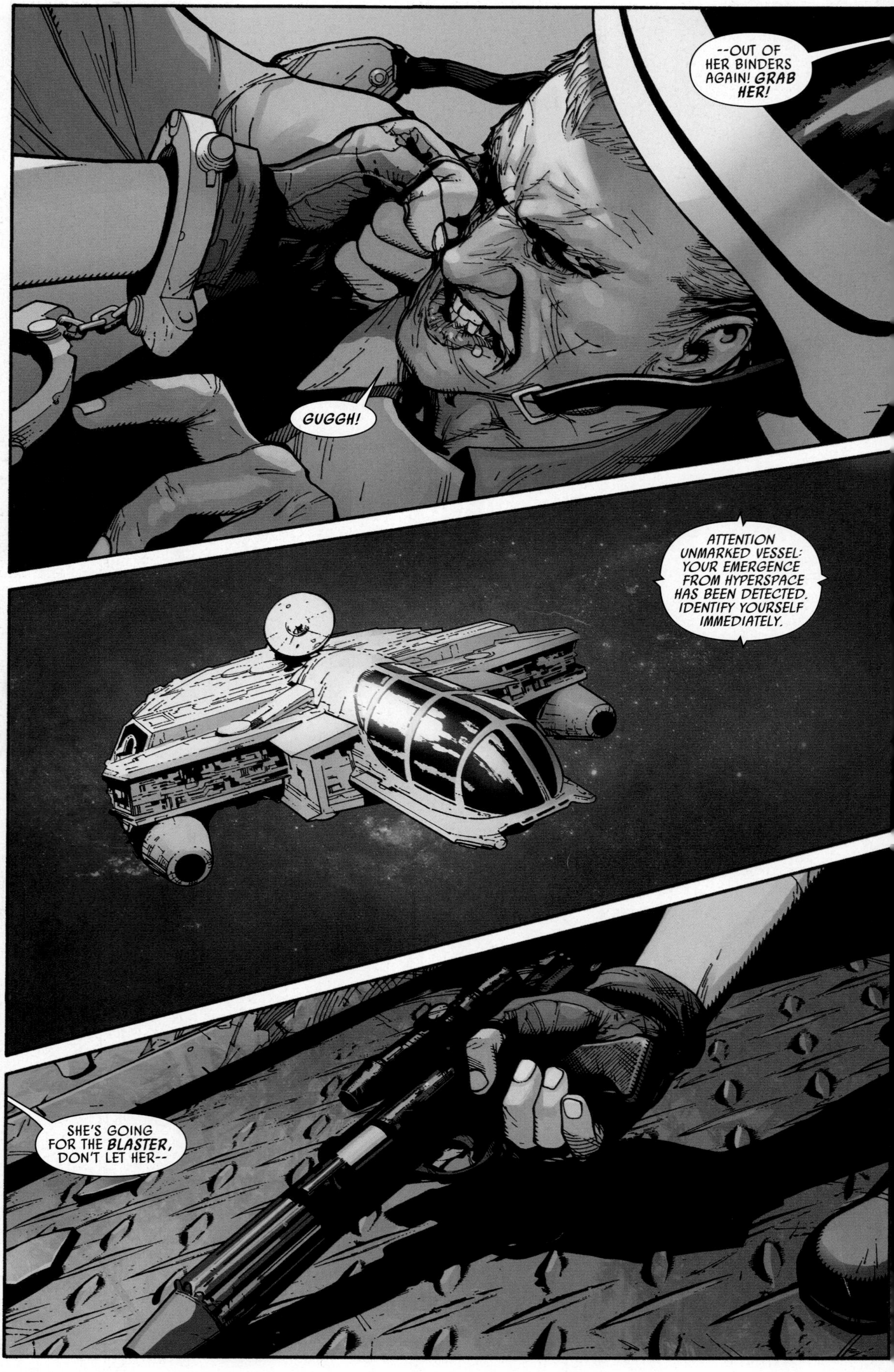
--OUT OF HER BINDERS AGAIN! GRAB HER!
GUGGH!
ATTENTION UNMARKED VESSEL: YOUR EMERGENCE FROM HYPERSPACE HAS BEEN DETECTED. IDENTIFY YOURSELF IMMEDIATELY.
SHE'S GOING FOR THE BLASTER, DON'T LET HER--

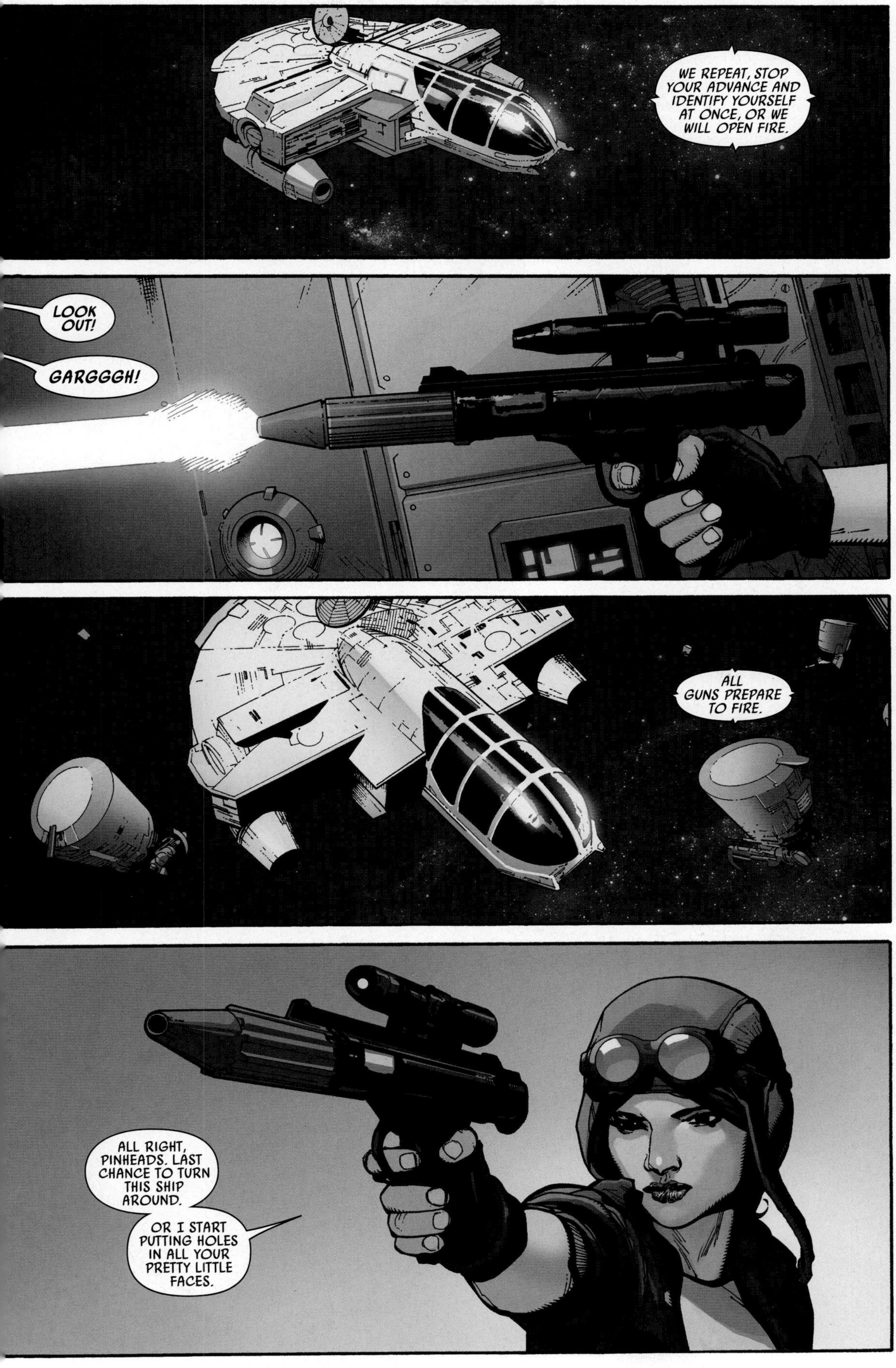
WE REPEAT, STOP YOUR ADVANCE AND IDENTIFY YOURSELF AT ONCE, OR WE WILL OPEN FIRE.
LOOK OUT!
GARGGGH!
ALL GUNS PREPARE TO FIRE.
ALL RIGHT, PINHEADS. LAST CHANCE TO TURN THIS SHIP AROUND.
OR I START PUTTING HOLES IN ALL YOUR PRETTY LITTLE FACES.

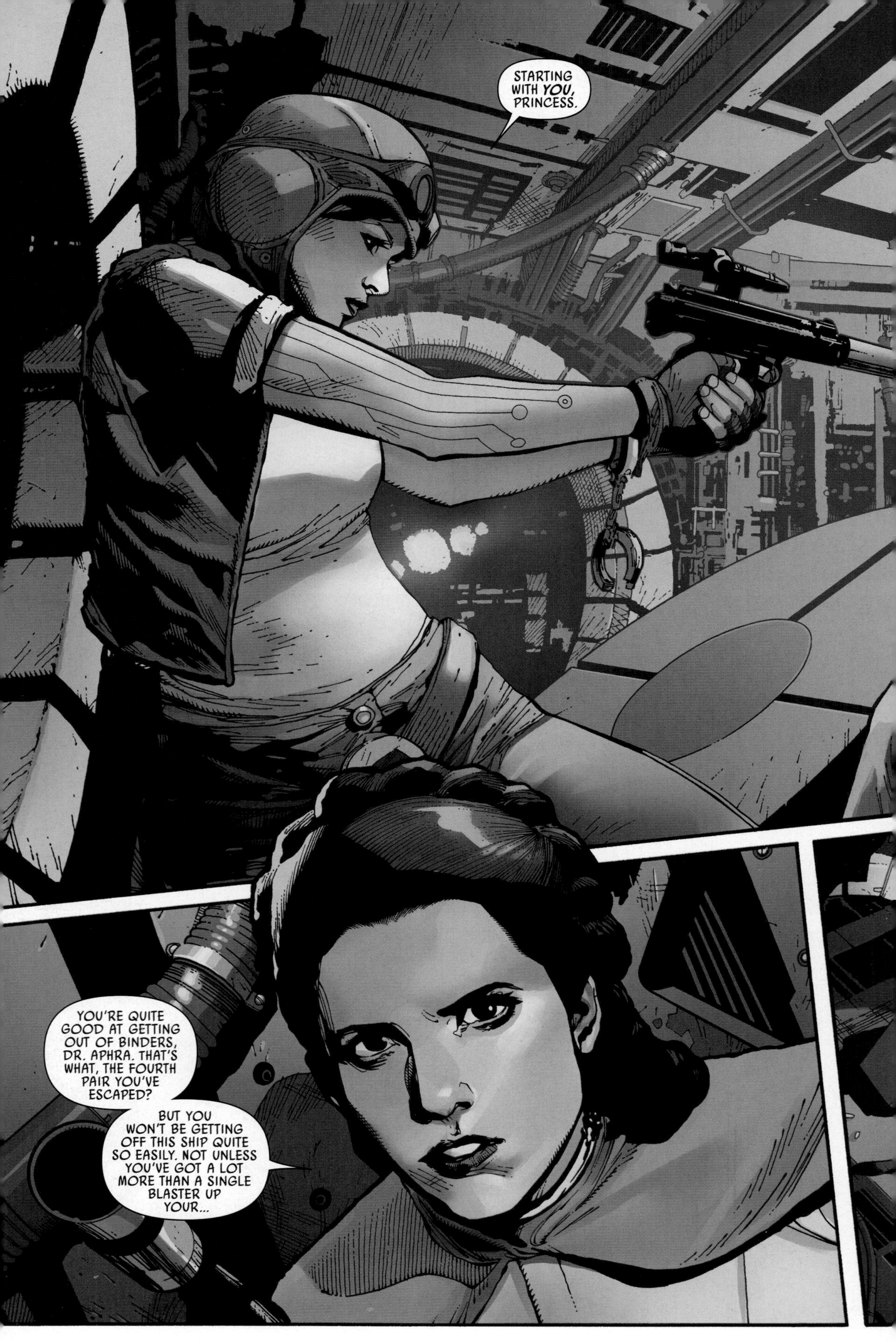
STARTING WITH YOU, PRINCESS.
YOU'RE QUITE GOOD AT GETTING OUT OF BINDERS, DR. APHRA. THAT'S WHAT, THE FOURTH PAIR YOU'VE ESCAPED?
BUT YOU WON'T BE GETTING OFF THIS SHIP QUITE SO EASILY. NOT UNLESS YOU'VE GOT A LOT MORE THAN A SINGLE BLASTER UP YOUR...

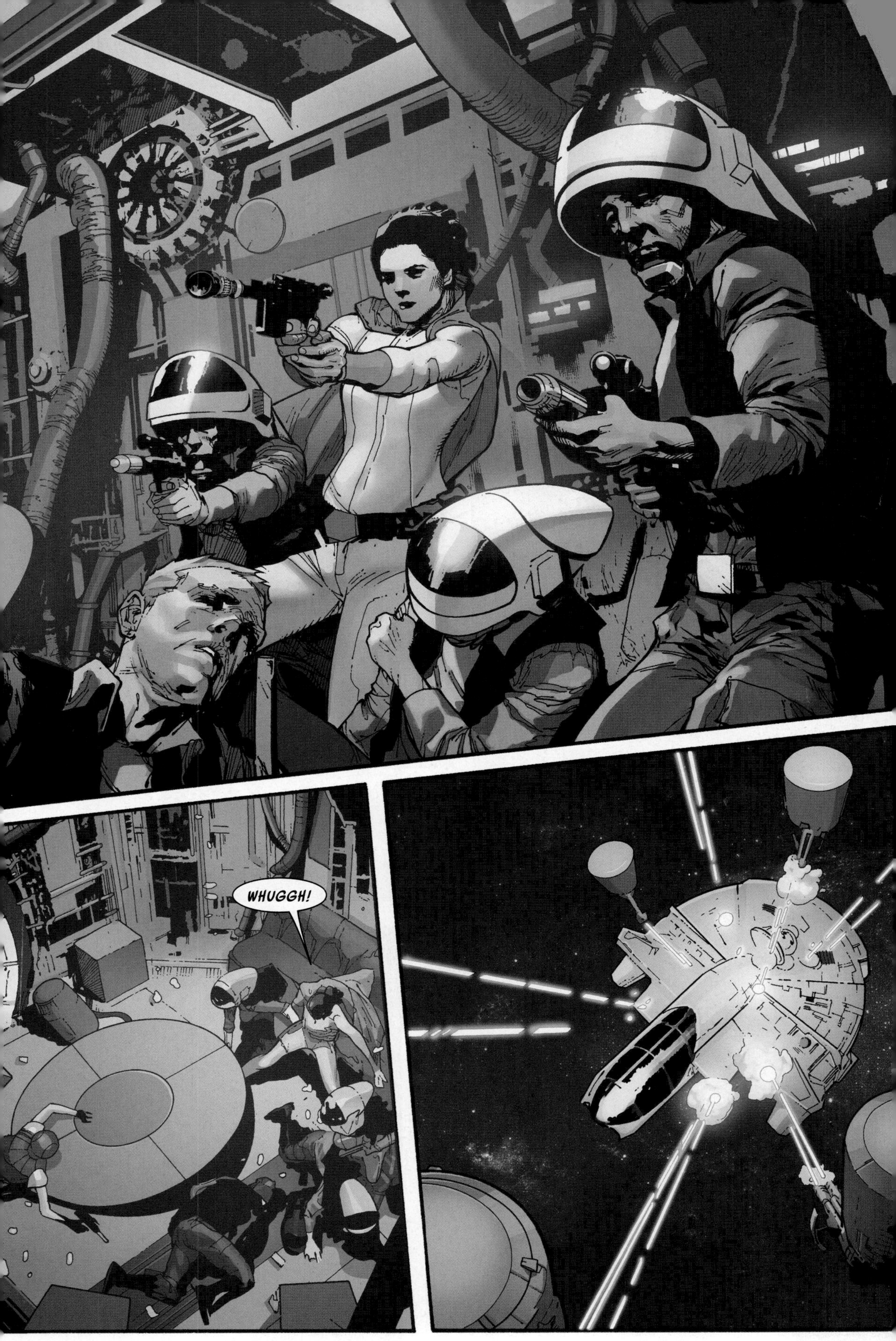
WHUGGH!

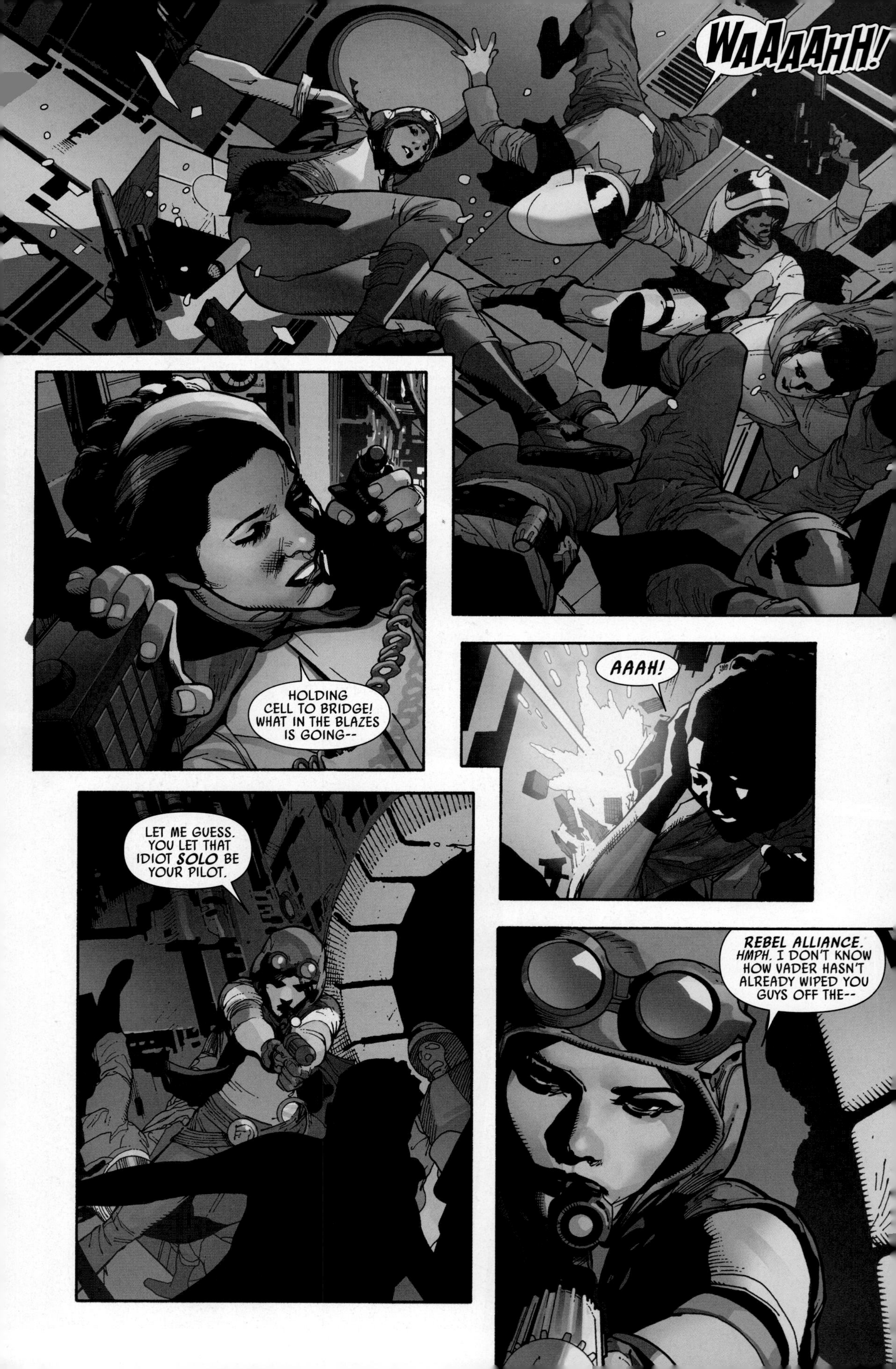
WAAAAHH!
HOLDING CELL TO BRIDGE! WHAT IN THE BLAZES IS GOING--
AAAH!
LET ME GUESS. YOU LET THAT IDIOT SOLO BE YOUR PILOT.
REBEL ALLIANCE. HMPH. I DON'T KNOW HOW VADER HASN'T ALREADY WIPED YOU GUYS OFF THE--

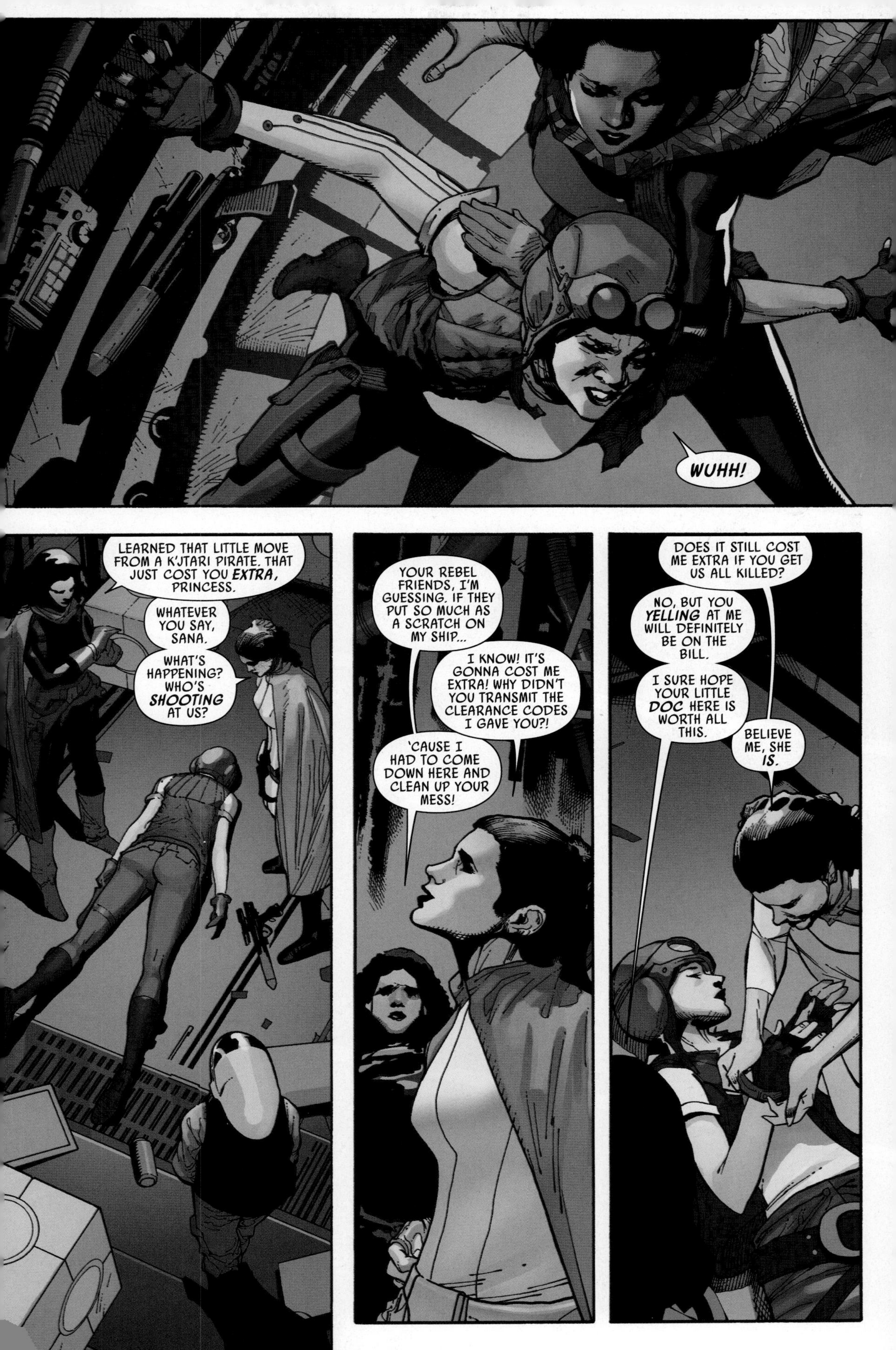
WUHH!
LEARNED THAT LITTLE MOVE FROM A K'JTARI PIRATE. THAT JUST COST YOU EXTRA, PRINCESS.
WHATEVER YOU SAY, SANA.
WHAT'S HAPPENING? WHO'S SHOOTING AT US?
YOUR REBEL FRIENDS, I'M GUESSING. IF THEY PUT SO MUCH AS A SCRATCH ON MY SHIP...
I KNOW! IT'S GONNA COST ME EXTRA! WHY DIDN'T YOU TRANSMIT THE CLEARANCE CODES I GAVE YOU?!
'CAUSE I HAD TO COME DOWN HERE AND CLEAN UP YOUR MESS!
DOES IT STILL COST ME EXTRA IF YOU GET US ALL KILLED?
NO, BUT YOU YELLING AT ME WILL DEFINITELY BE ON THE BILL.
I SURE HOPE YOUR LITTLE DOC HERE IS WORTH ALL THIS.
BELIEVE ME, SHE IS.

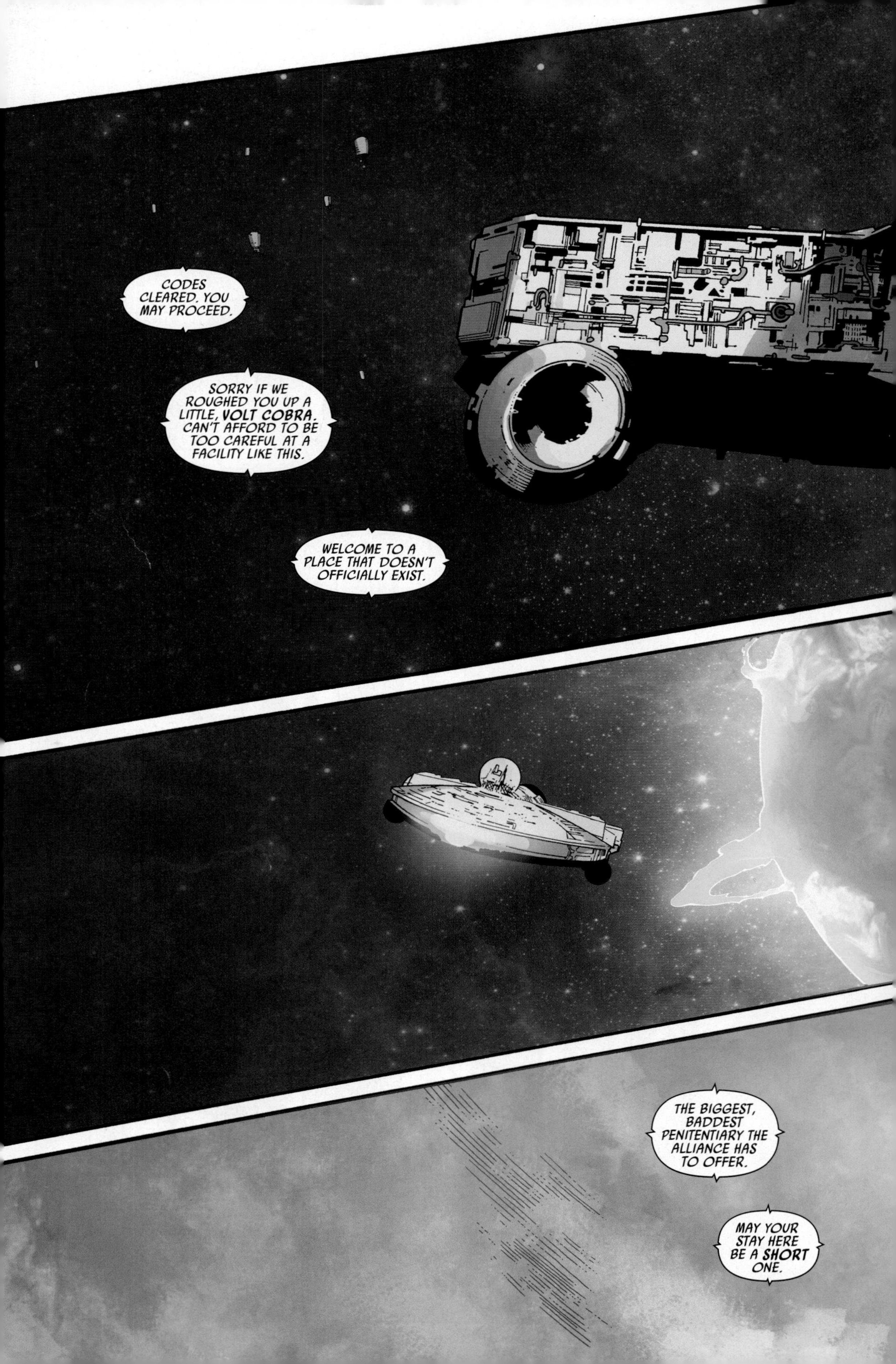
CODES CLEARED. YOU MAY PROCEED.
SORRY IF WE ROUGHED YOU UP A LITTLE, VOLT COBRA. CAN'T AFFORD TO BE TOO CAREFUL AT A FACILITY LIKE THIS.
WELCOME TO A PLACE THAT DOESN'T OFFICIALLY EXIST.
THE BIGGEST, BADDEST PENITENTIARY THE ALLIANCE HAS TO OFFER.
MAY YOUR STAY HERE BE A SHORT ONE.

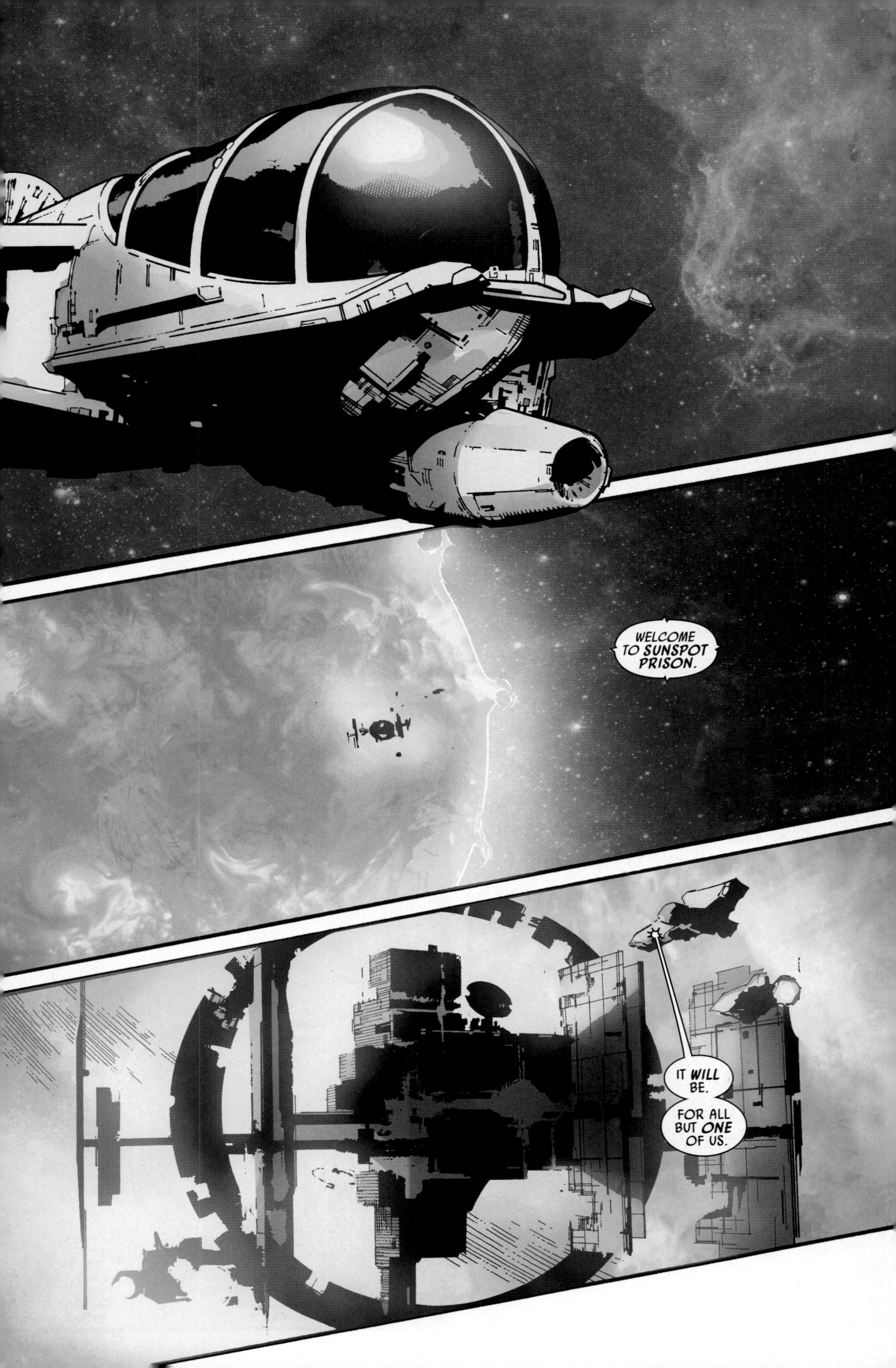
WELCOME TO SUNSPOT PRISON.
IT WILL BE.
FOR ALL BUT ONE OF US.

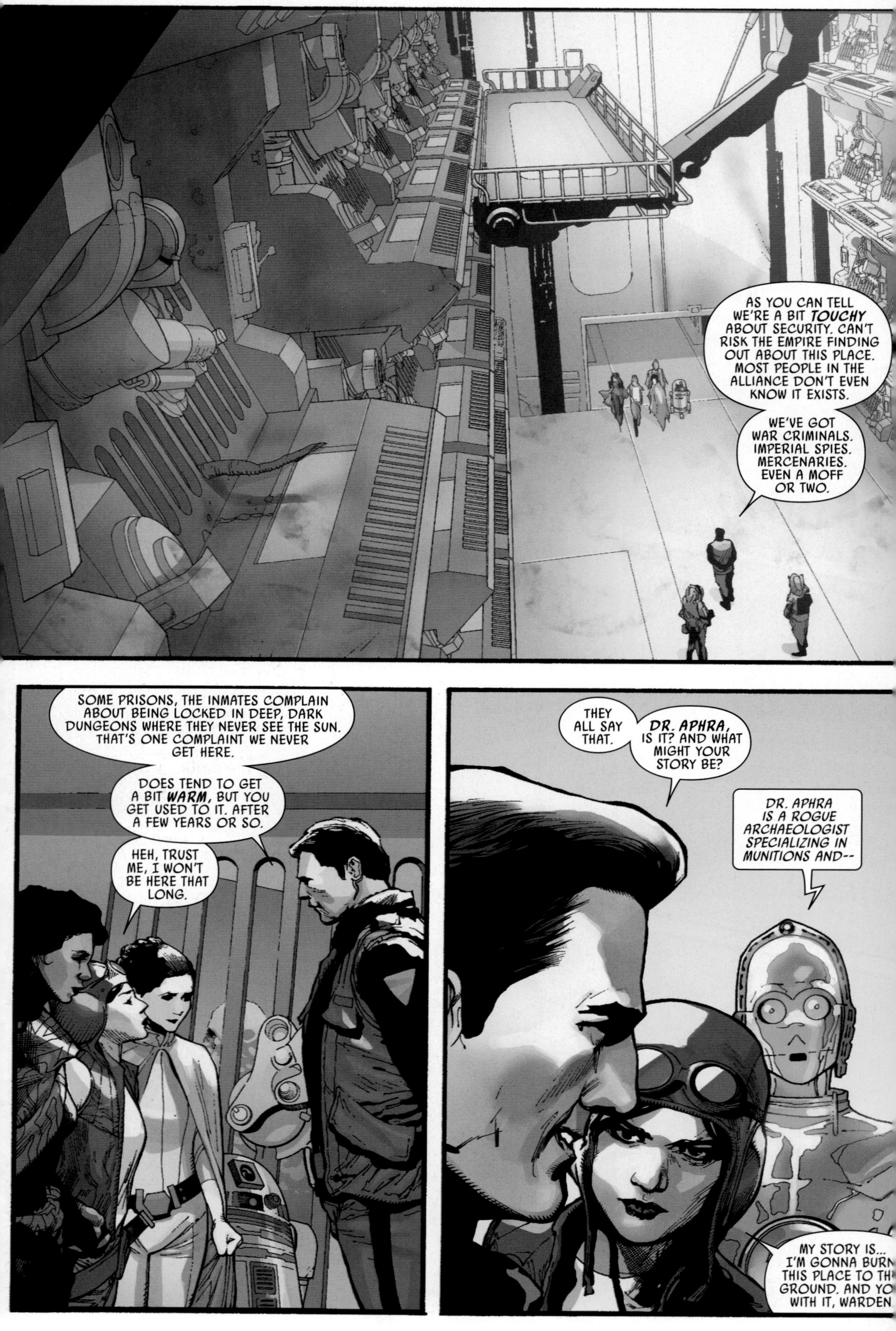
AS YOU CAN TELL WE'RE A BIT TOUCHY ABOUT SECURITY. CAN'T RISK THE EMPIRE FINDING OUT ABOUT THIS PLACE. MOST PEOPLE IN THE ALLIANCE DON'T EVEN KNOW IT EXISTS.
WE'VE GOT WAR CRIMINALS. IMPERIAL SPIES. MERCENARIES. EVEN A MOFF OR TWO.
SOME PRISONS, THE INMATES COMPLAIN ABOUT BEING LOCKED IN DEEP, DARK DUNGEONS WHERE THEY NEVER SEE THE SUN. THAT'S ONE COMPLAINT WE NEVER GET HERE.
DOES TEND TO GET A BIT WARM, BUT YOU GET USED TO IT. AFTER A FEW YEARS OR SO.
HEH, TRUST ME, I WON'T BE HERE THAT LONG.
THEY ALL SAY THAT.
DR. APHRA, IS IT? AND WHAT MIGHT YOUR STORY BE?
DR. APHRA IS A ROGUE ARCHAEOLOGIST SPECIALIZING IN MUNITIONS AND--
MY STORY IS... I'M GONNA BURN THIS PLACE TO TH GROUND. AND YO WITH IT, WARDEN

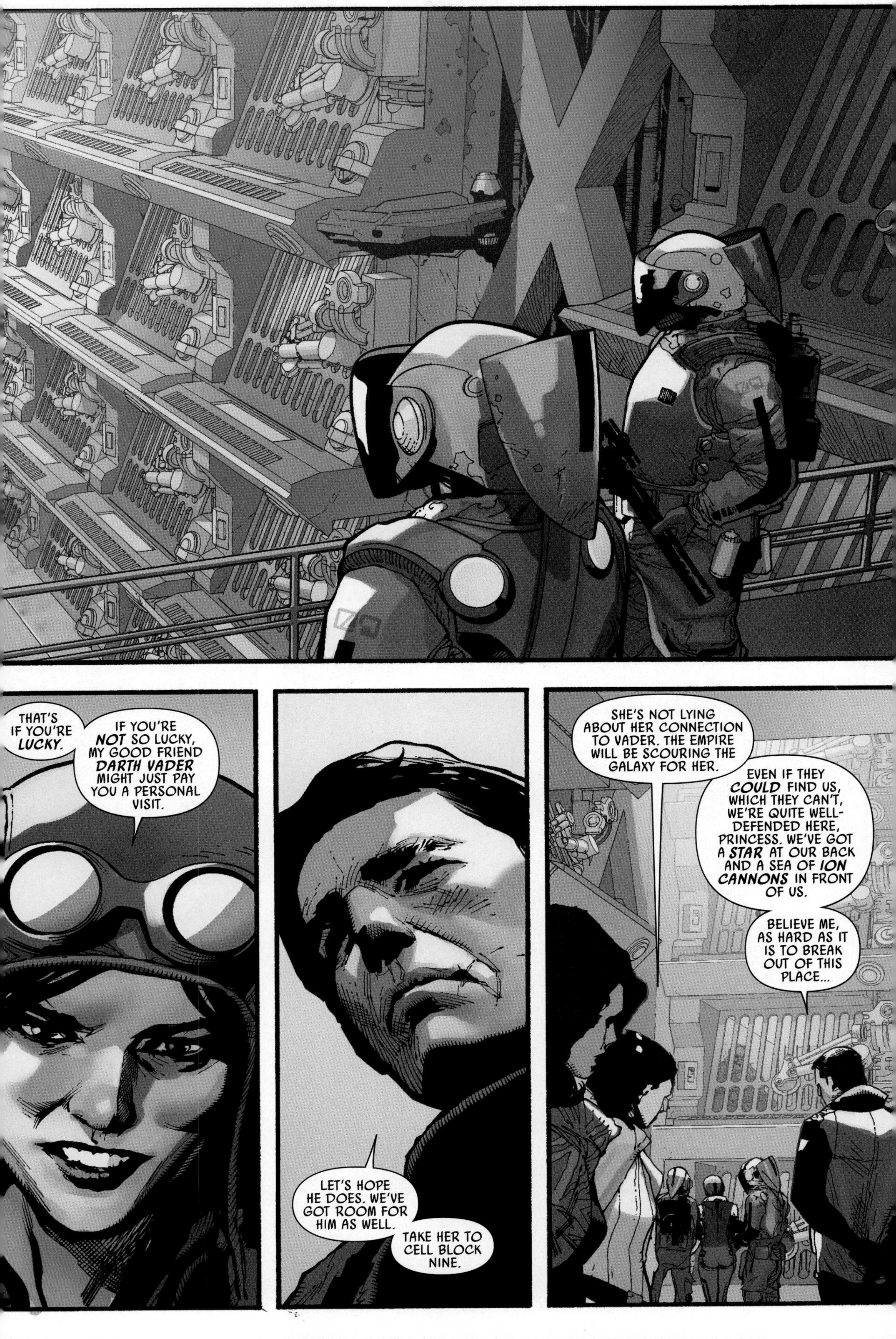
THAT'S IF YOU'RE LUCKY.
IF YOU'RE NOT SO LUCKY, MY GOOD FRIEND DARTH VADER MIGHT JUST PAY YOU A PERSONAL VISIT.
LET'S HOPE HE DOES. WE'VE GOT ROOM FOR HIM AS WELL.
TAKE HER TO CELL BLOCK NINE.
SHE'S NOT LYING ABOUT HER CONNECTION TO VADER. THE EMPIRE WILL BE SCOURING THE GALAXY FOR HER.
EVEN IF THEY COULD FIND US, WHICH THEY CAN'T, WE'RE QUITE WELL-DEFENDED HERE, PRINCESS. WE'VE GOT A STAR AT OUR BACK AND A SEA OF ION CANNONS IN FRONT OF US.
BELIEVE ME, AS HARD AS IT IS TO BREAK OUT OF THIS PLACE...

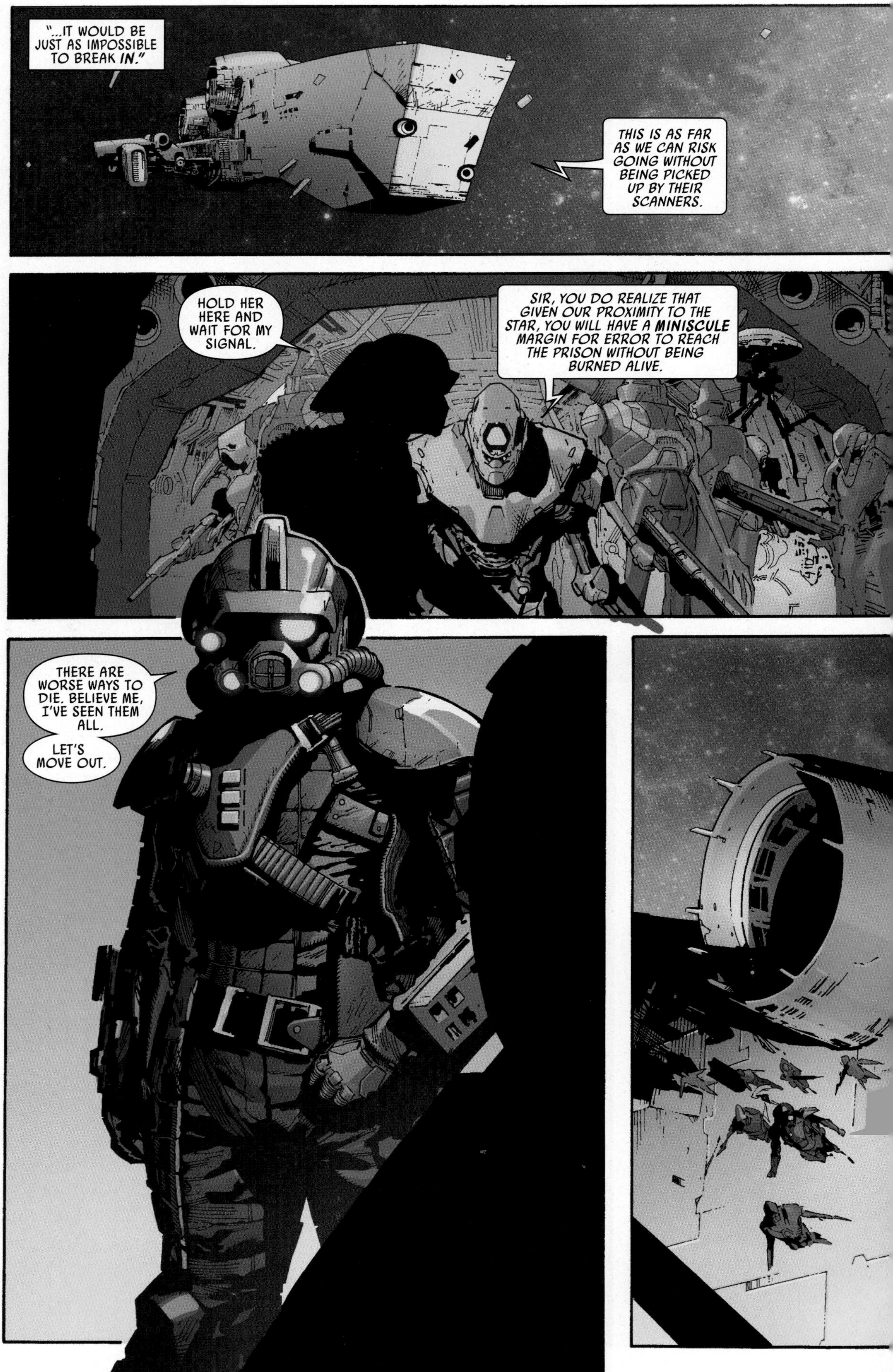
"...IT WOULD BE JUST AS IMPOSSIBLE TO BREAK IN."
THIS IS AS FAR AS WE CAN RISK GOING WITHOUT BEING PICKED UP BY THEIR SCANNERS.
HOLD HER HERE AND WAIT FOR MY SIGNAL.
SIR, YOU DO REALIZE THAT GIVEN OUR PROXIMITY TO THE STAR, YOU WILL HAVE A MINISCULE MARGIN FOR ERROR TO REACH THE PRISON WITHOUT BEING BURNED ALIVE.
THERE ARE WORSE WAYS TO DIE. BELIEVE ME, I'VE SEEN THEM ALL.
LET'S MOVE OUT.

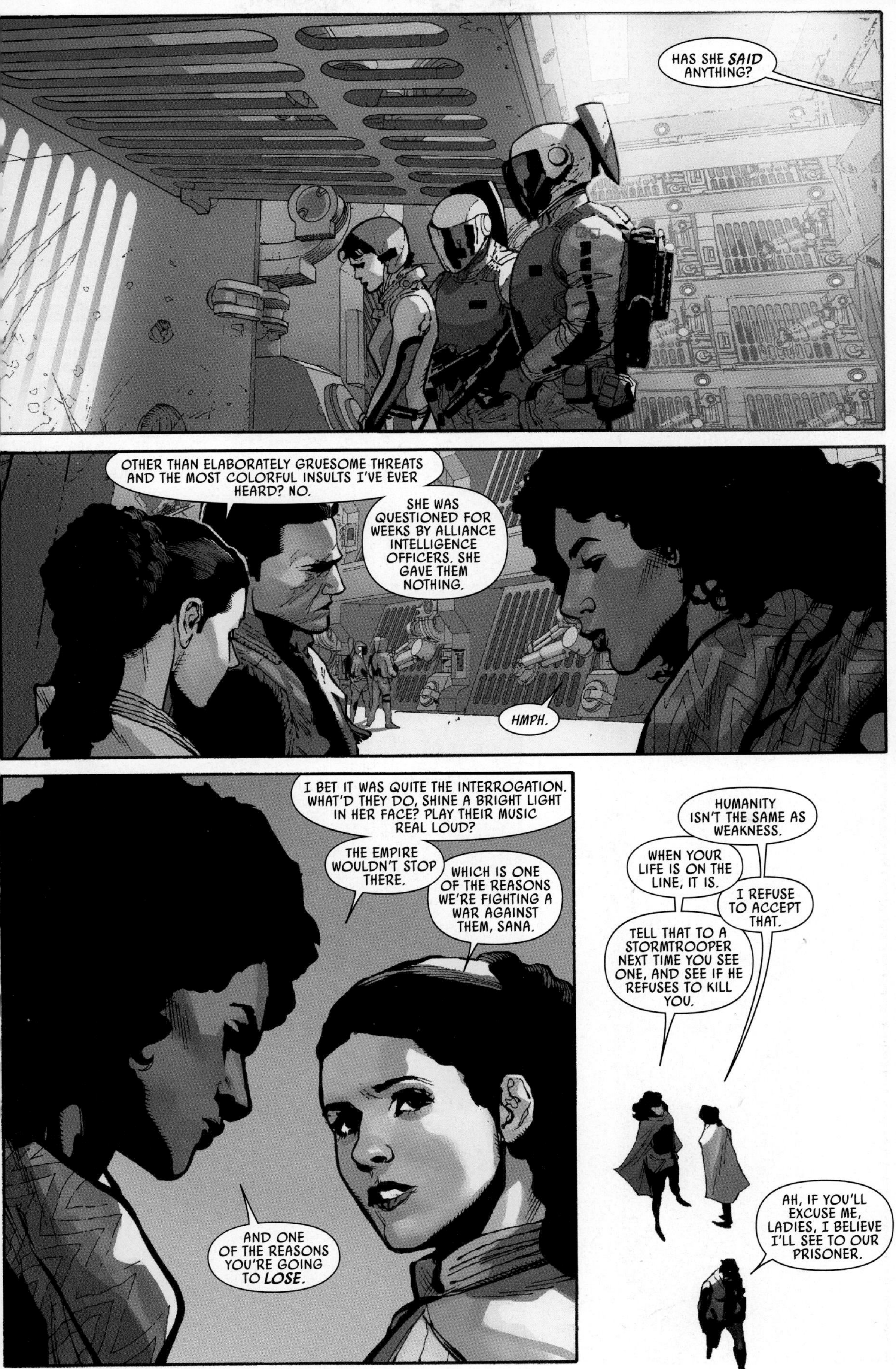
HAS SHE *SAID* ANYTHING?
OTHER THAN ELABORATELY GRUESOME THREATS AND THE MOST COLORFUL INSULTS I'VE EVER HEARD? NO.
SHE WAS QUESTIONED FOR WEEKS BY ALLIANCE INTELLIGENCE OFFICERS. SHE GAVE THEM NOTHING.
HMPH.
I BET IT WAS QUITE THE INTERROGATION. WHAT'D THEY DO, SHINE A BRIGHT LIGHT IN HER FACE? PLAY THEIR MUSIC REAL LOUD?
THE EMPIRE WOULDN'T STOP THERE.
WHICH IS ONE OF THE REASONS WE'RE FIGHTING A WAR AGAINST THEM, SANA.
AND ONE OF THE REASONS YOU'RE GOING TO *LOSE*.
HUMANITY ISN'T THE SAME AS WEAKNESS.
WHEN YOUR LIFE IS ON THE LINE, IT IS.
I REFUSE TO ACCEPT THAT.
TELL THAT TO A STORMTROOPER NEXT TIME YOU SEE ONE, AND SEE IF HE REFUSES TO KILL YOU.
AH, IF YOU'LL EXCUSE ME, LADIES, I BELIEVE I'LL SEE TO OUR PRISONER.

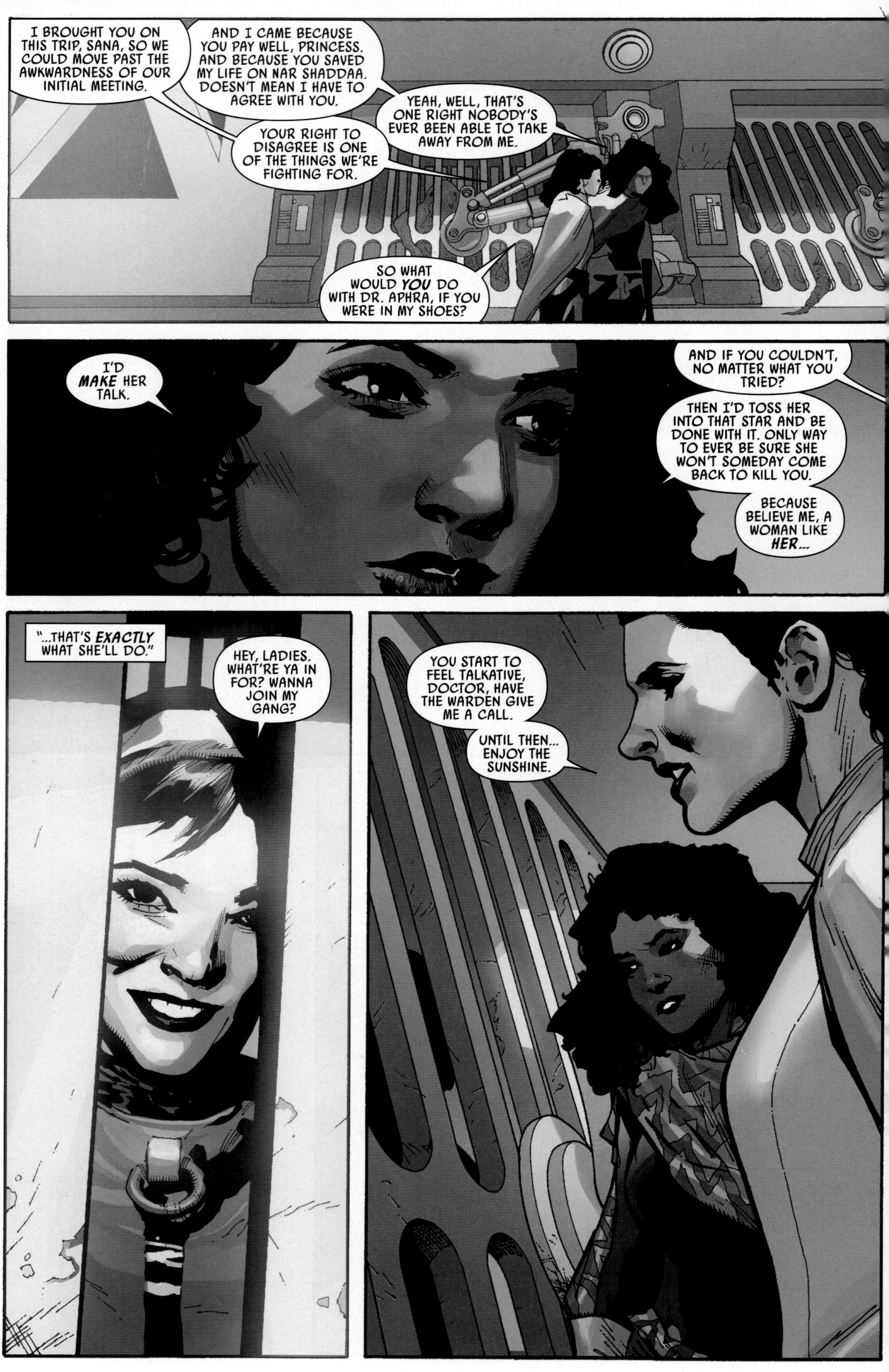
I BROUGHT YOU ON THIS TRIP, SANA, SO WE COULD MOVE PAST THE AWKWARDNESS OF OUR INITIAL MEETING.
AND I CAME BECAUSE YOU PAY WELL, PRINCESS. AND BECAUSE YOU SAVED MY LIFE ON NAR SHADDAA. DOESN'T MEAN I HAVE TO AGREE WITH YOU.
YOUR RIGHT TO DISAGREE IS ONE OF THE THINGS WE'RE FIGHTING FOR.
YEAH, WELL, THAT'S ONE RIGHT NOBODY'S EVER BEEN ABLE TO TAKE AWAY FROM ME.
SO WHAT WOULD YOU DO WITH DR. APHRA, IF YOU WERE IN MY SHOES?
I'D MAKE HER TALK.
AND IF YOU COULDN'T, NO MATTER WHAT YOU TRIED?
THEN I'D TOSS HER INTO THAT STAR AND BE DONE WITH IT. ONLY WAY TO EVER BE SURE SHE WON'T SOMEDAY COME BACK TO KILL YOU.
BECAUSE BELIEVE ME, A WOMAN LIKE HER...
"...THAT'S EXACTLY WHAT SHE'LL DO."
HEY, LADIES. WHAT'RE YA IN FOR? WANNA JOIN MY GANG?
YOU START TO FEEL TALKATIVE, DOCTOR, HAVE THE WARDEN GIVE ME A CALL.
UNTIL THEN... ENJOY THE SUNSHINE.

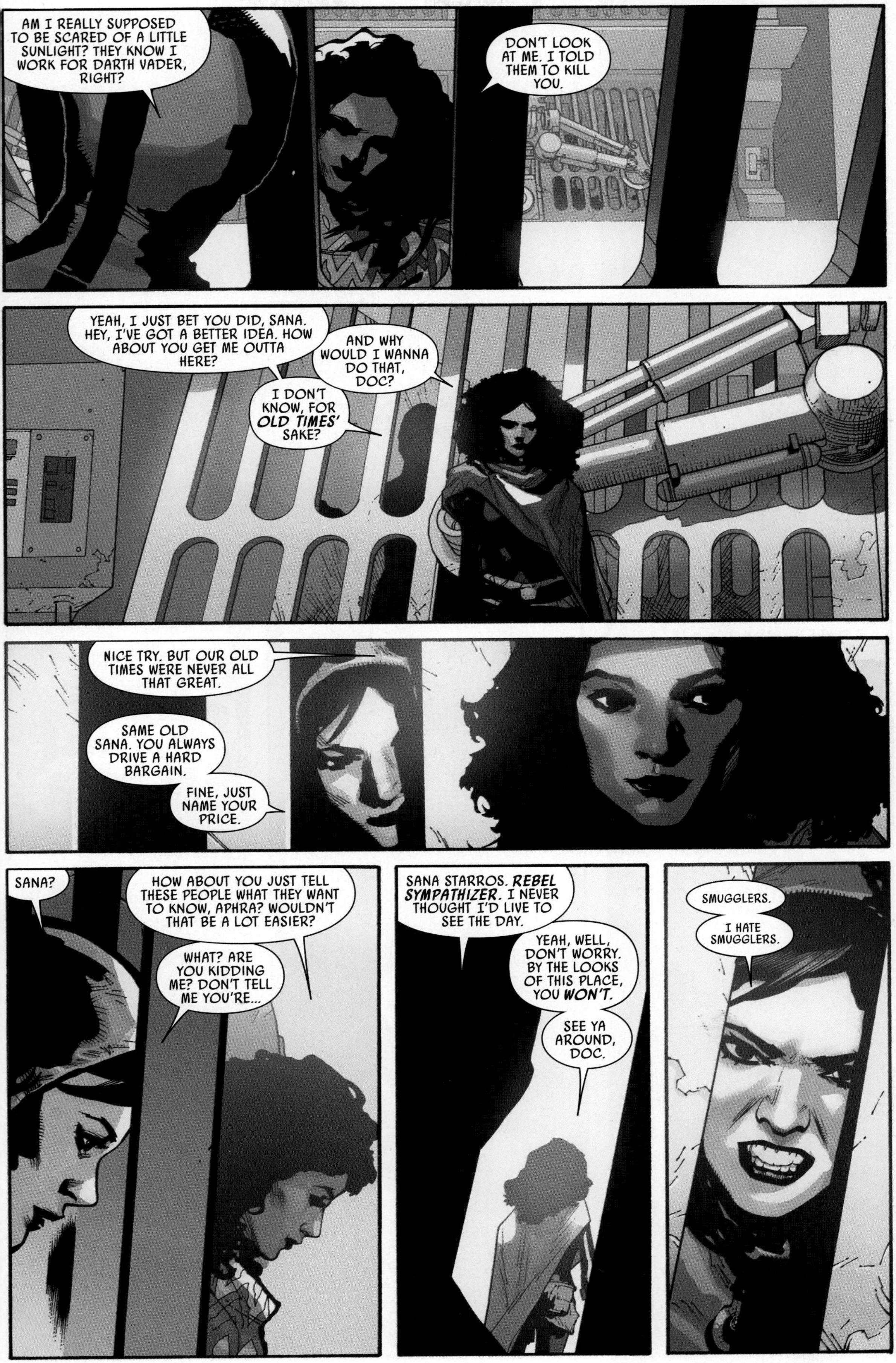
AM I REALLY SUPPOSED TO BE SCARED OF A LITTLE SUNLIGHT? THEY KNOW I WORK FOR DARTH VADER, RIGHT?
DON'T LOOK AT ME. I TOLD THEM TO KILL YOU.
YEAH, I JUST BET YOU DID, SANA. HEY, I'VE GOT A BETTER IDEA. HOW ABOUT YOU GET ME OUTTA HERE?
AND WHY WOULD I WANNA DO THAT, DOC?
I DON'T KNOW, FOR OLD TIMES' SAKE?
NICE TRY. BUT OUR OLD TIMES WERE NEVER ALL THAT GREAT.
SAME OLD SANA. YOU ALWAYS DRIVE A HARD BARGAIN.
FINE, JUST NAME YOUR PRICE.
SANA?
HOW ABOUT YOU JUST TELL THESE PEOPLE WHAT THEY WANT TO KNOW, APHRA? WOULDN'T THAT BE A LOT EASIER?
WHAT? ARE YOU KIDDING ME? DON'T TELL ME YOU'RE...
SANA STARROS. REBEL SYMPATHIZER. I NEVER THOUGHT I'D LIVE TO SEE THE DAY.
YEAH, WELL, DON'T WORRY. BY THE LOOKS OF THIS PLACE, YOU WON'T.
SEE YA AROUND, DOC.
SMUGGLERS.
I HATE SMUGGLERS.

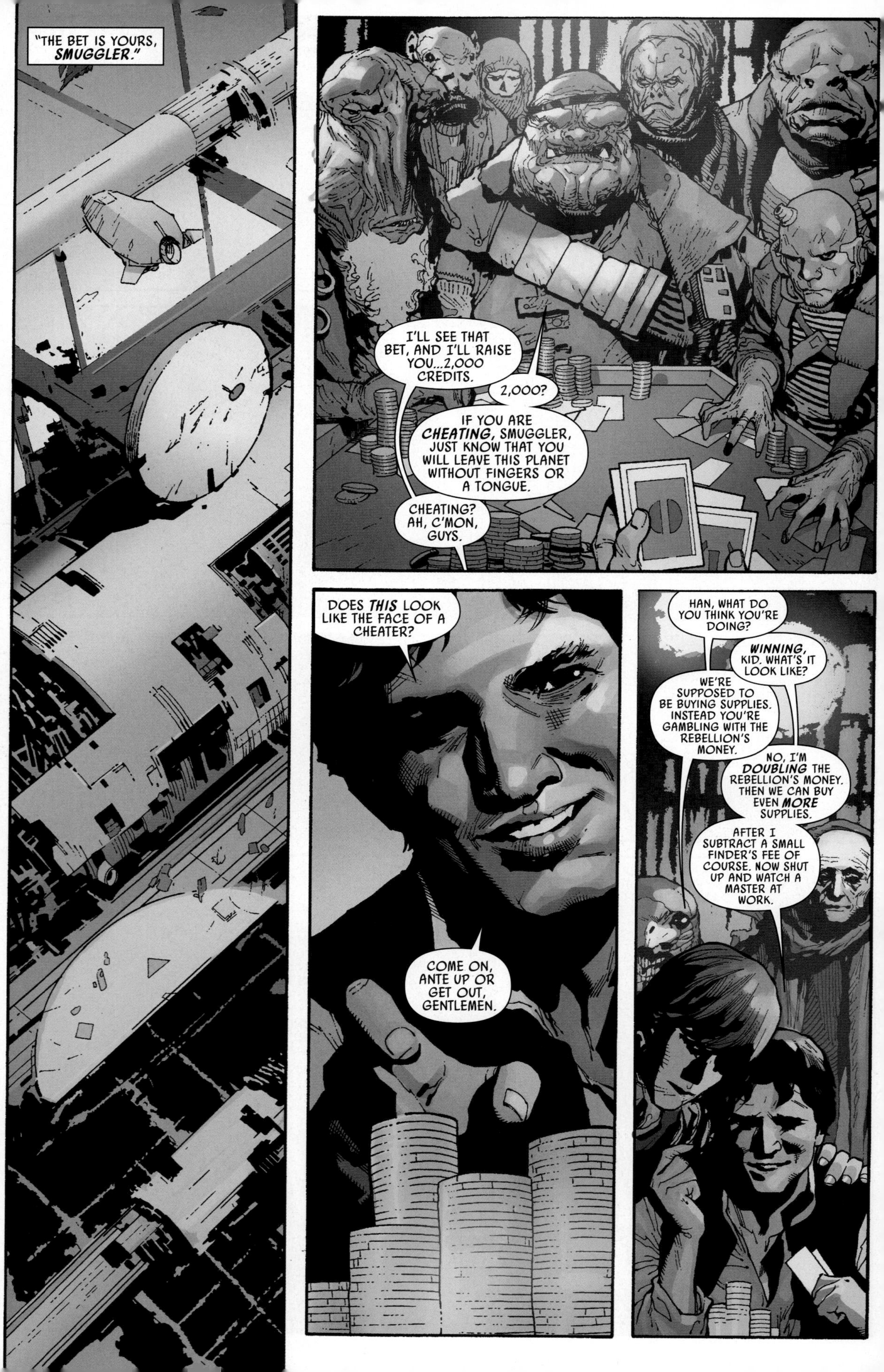
"THE BET IS YOURS, SMUGGLER."
I'LL SEE THAT BET, AND I'LL RAISE YOU...2,000 CREDITS.
2,000?
IF YOU ARE CHEATING, SMUGGLER, JUST KNOW THAT YOU WILL LEAVE THIS PLANET WITHOUT FINGERS OR A TONGUE.
CHEATING? AH, C'MON, GUYS.
DOES THIS LOOK LIKE THE FACE OF A CHEATER?
COME ON, ANTE UP OR GET OUT, GENTLEMEN.
HAN, WHAT DO YOU THINK YOU'RE DOING?
WINNING, KID. WHAT'S IT LOOK LIKE?
WE'RE SUPPOSED TO BE BUYING SUPPLIES. INSTEAD YOU'RE GAMBLING WITH THE REBELLION'S MONEY.
NO, I'M DOUBLING THE REBELLION'S MONEY. THEN WE CAN BUY EVEN MORE SUPPLIES.
AFTER I SUBTRACT A SMALL FINDER'S FEE OF COURSE. NOW SHUT UP AND WATCH A MASTER AT WORK.

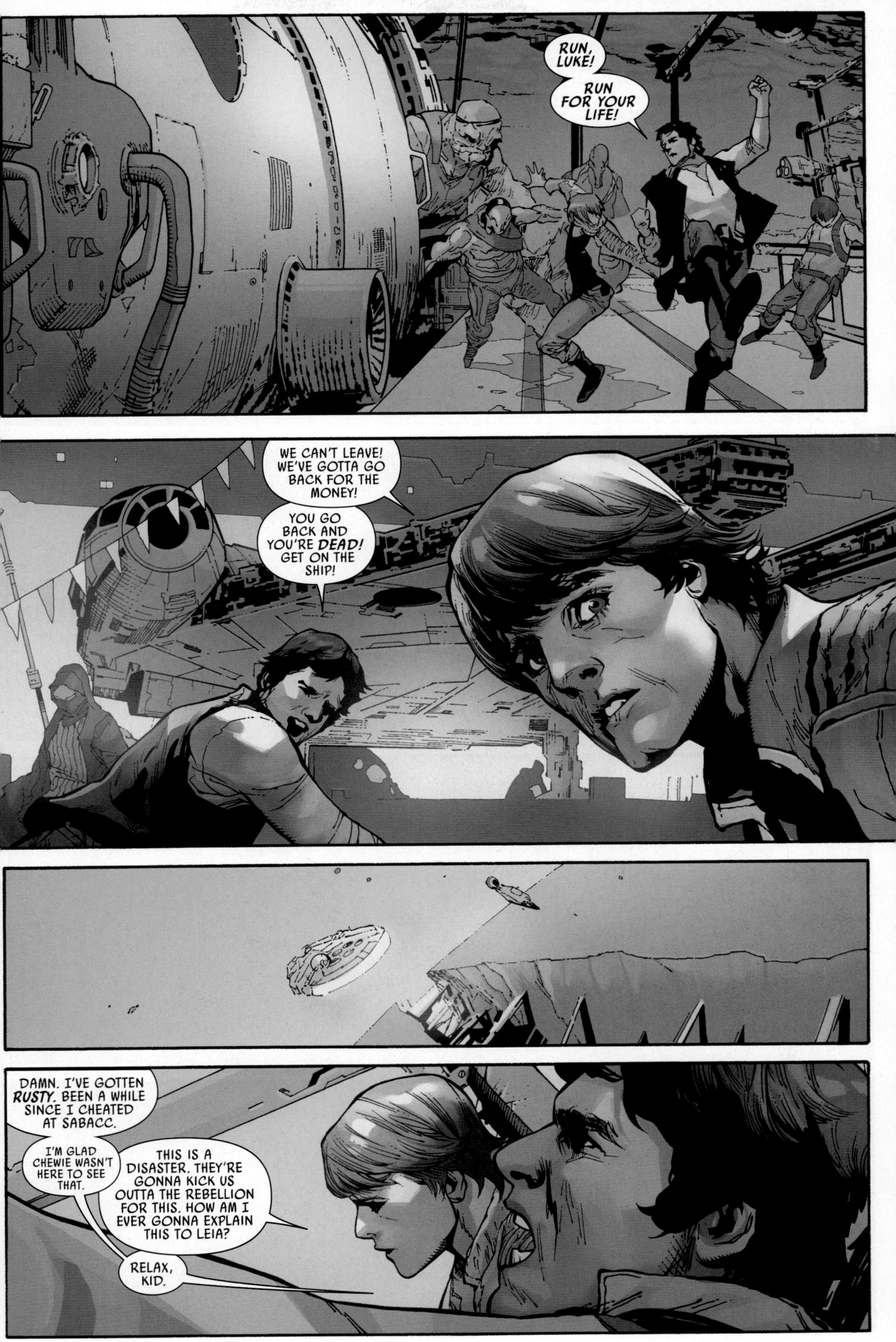
RUN, LUKE!
RUN FOR YOUR LIFE!
WE CAN'T LEAVE! WE'VE GOTTA GO BACK FOR THE MONEY!
YOU GO BACK AND YOU'RE *DEAD!* GET ON THE SHIP!
DAMN. I'VE GOTTEN *RUSTY.* BEEN A WHILE SINCE I CHEATED AT SABACC.
I'M GLAD CHEWIE WASN'T HERE TO SEE THAT.
THIS IS A DISASTER. THEY'RE GONNA KICK US OUTTA THE REBELLION FOR THIS. HOW AM I EVER GONNA EXPLAIN THIS TO LEIA?
RELAX, KID.

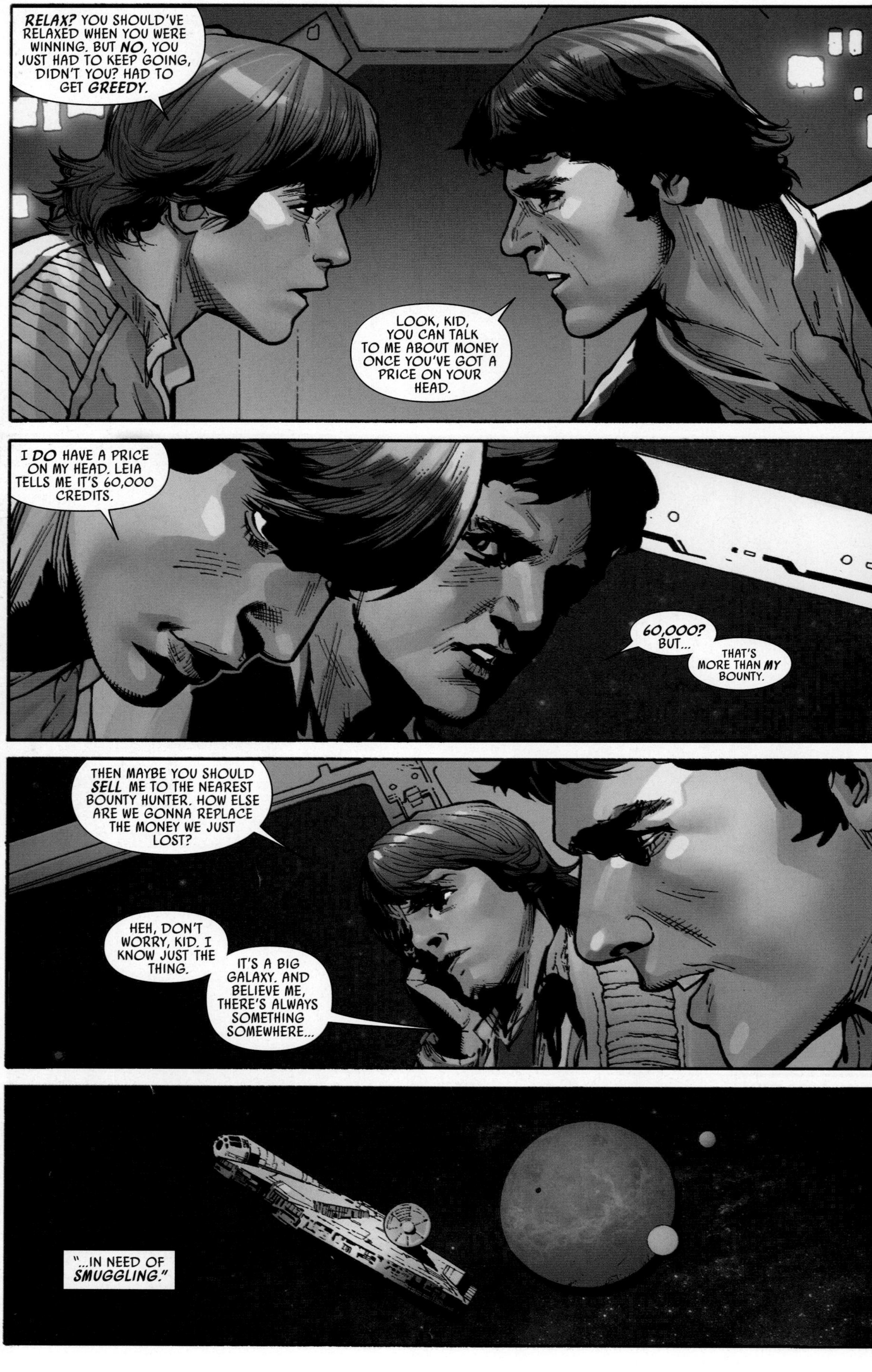
RELAX? YOU SHOULD'VE RELAXED WHEN YOU WERE WINNING. BUT NO, YOU JUST HAD TO KEEP GOING, DIDN'T YOU? HAD TO GET GREEDY.
LOOK, KID, YOU CAN TALK TO ME ABOUT MONEY ONCE YOU'VE GOT A PRICE ON YOUR HEAD.
I DO HAVE A PRICE ON MY HEAD. LEIA TELLS ME IT'S 60,000 CREDITS.
60,000? BUT...
THAT'S MORE THAN MY BOUNTY.
THEN MAYBE YOU SHOULD SELL ME TO THE NEAREST BOUNTY HUNTER. HOW ELSE ARE WE GONNA REPLACE THE MONEY WE JUST LOST?
HEH, DON'T WORRY, KID. I KNOW JUST THE THING.
IT'S A BIG GALAXY. AND BELIEVE ME, THERE'S ALWAYS SOMETHING SOMEWHERE...
"...IN NEED OF SMUGGLING."

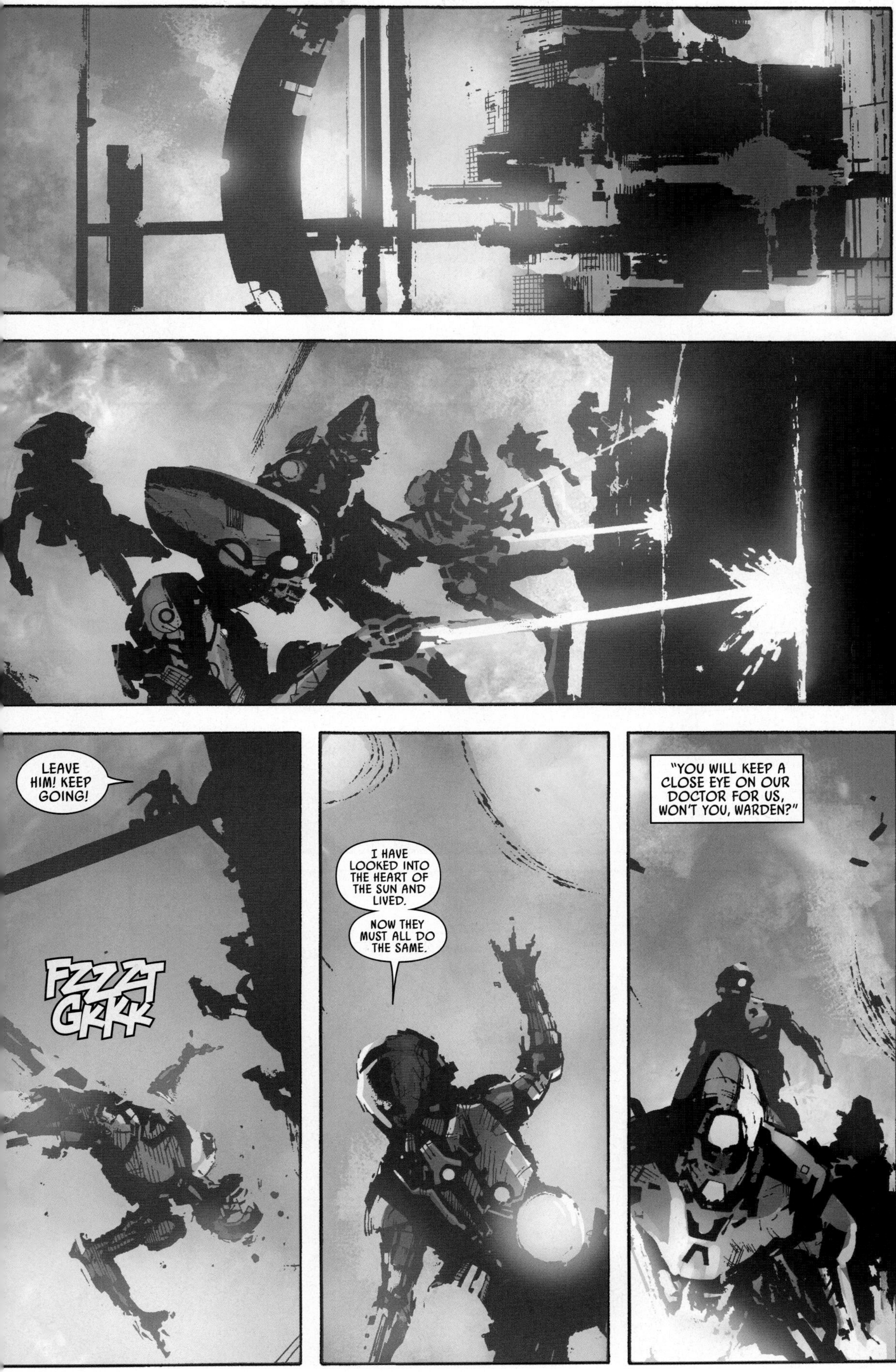
LEAVE HIM! KEEP GOING!
FZZZT GKKK
I HAVE LOOKED INTO THE HEART OF THE SUN AND LIVED.
NOW THEY MUST ALL DO THE SAME.
"YOU WILL KEEP A CLOSE EYE ON OUR DOCTOR FOR US, WON'T YOU, WARDEN?"

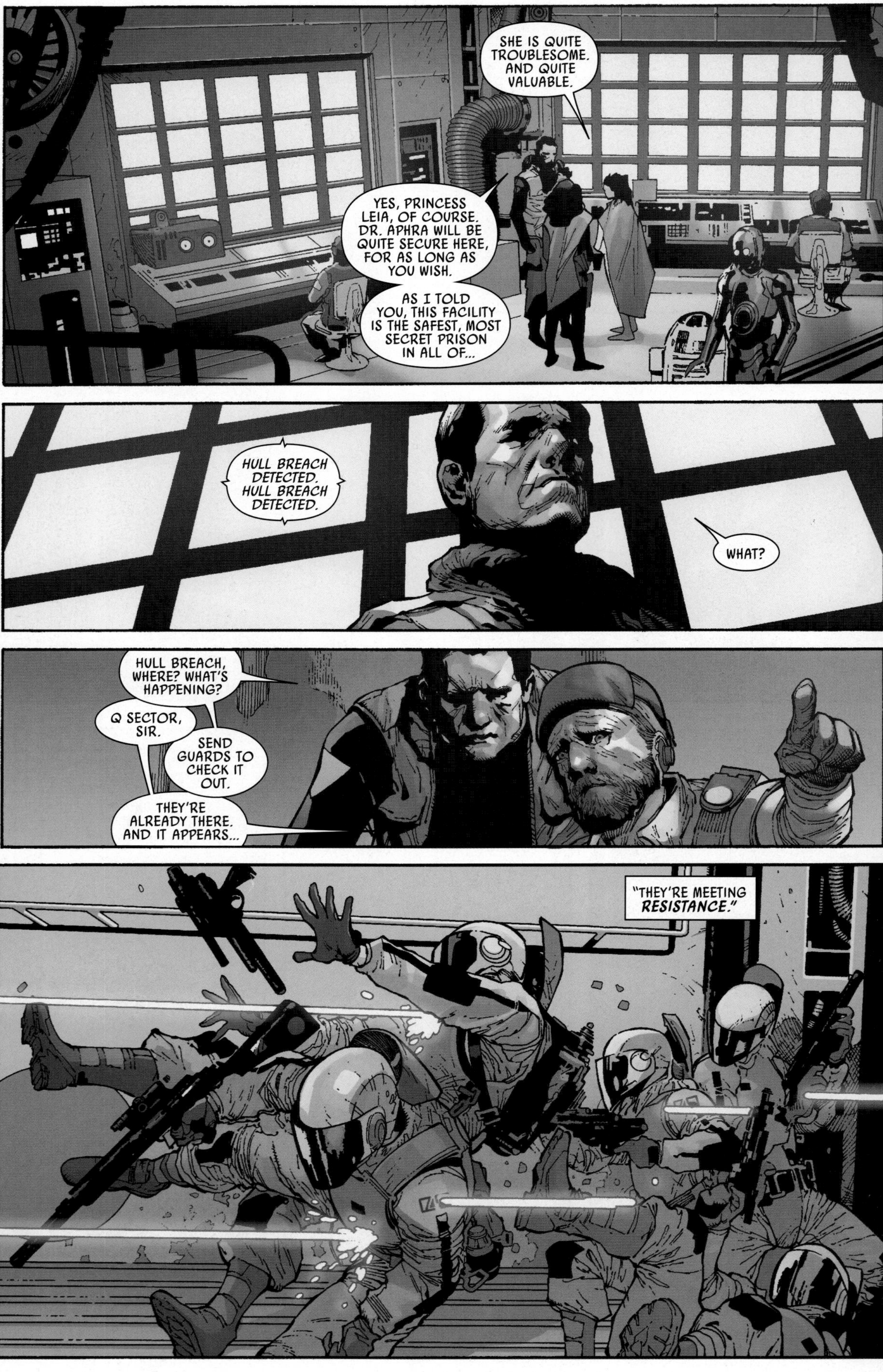
SHE IS QUITE TROUBLESOME. AND QUITE VALUABLE.
YES, PRINCESS LEIA, OF COURSE. DR. APHRA WILL BE QUITE SECURE HERE, FOR AS LONG AS YOU WISH.
AS I TOLD YOU, THIS FACILITY IS THE SAFEST, MOST SECRET PRISON IN ALL OF...
HULL BREACH DETECTED. HULL BREACH DETECTED.
WHAT?
HULL BREACH, WHERE? WHAT'S HAPPENING?
Q SECTOR, SIR.
SEND GUARDS TO CHECK IT OUT.
THEY'RE ALREADY THERE. AND IT APPEARS...
"THEY'RE MEETING RESISTANCE."

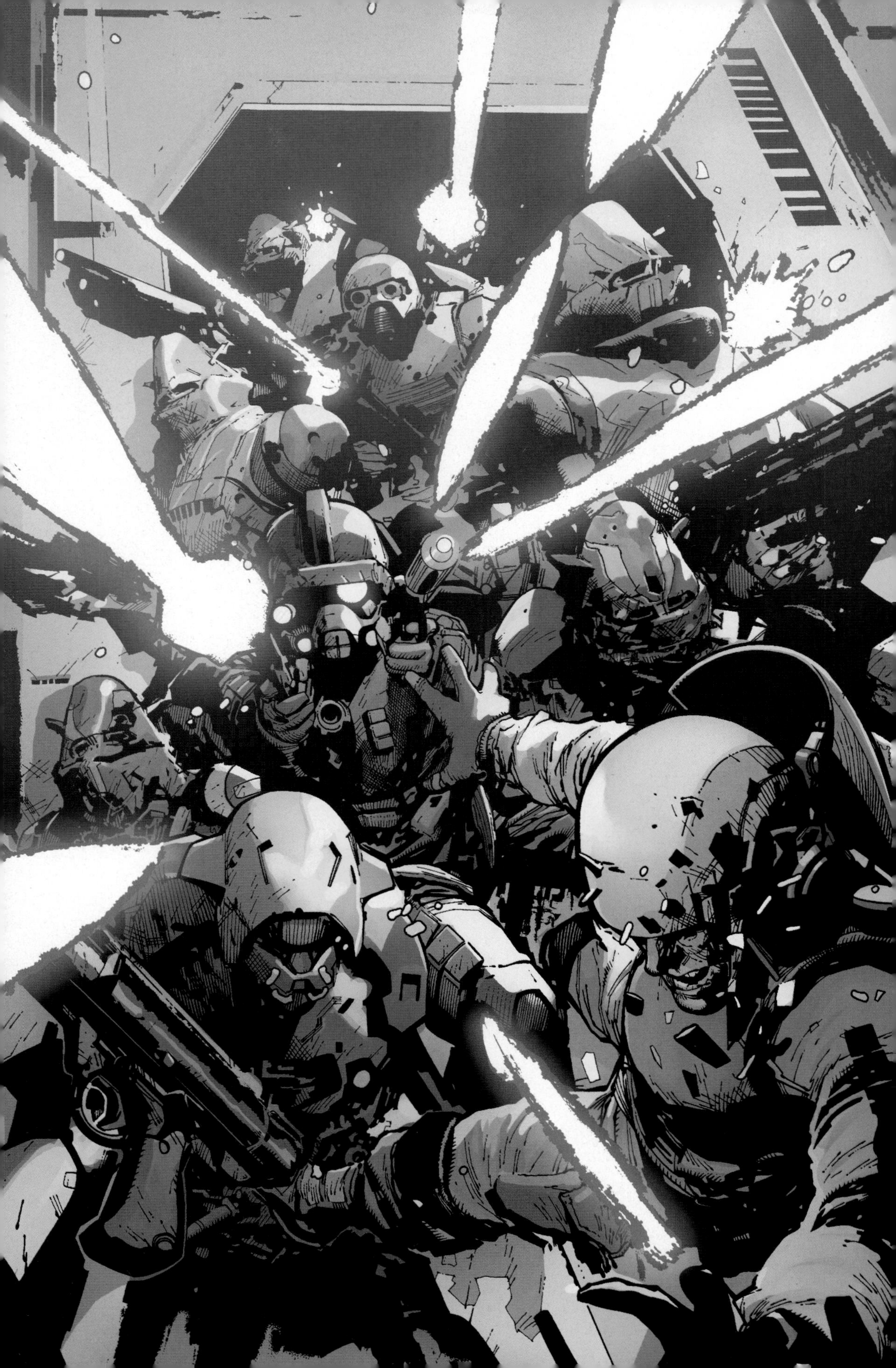

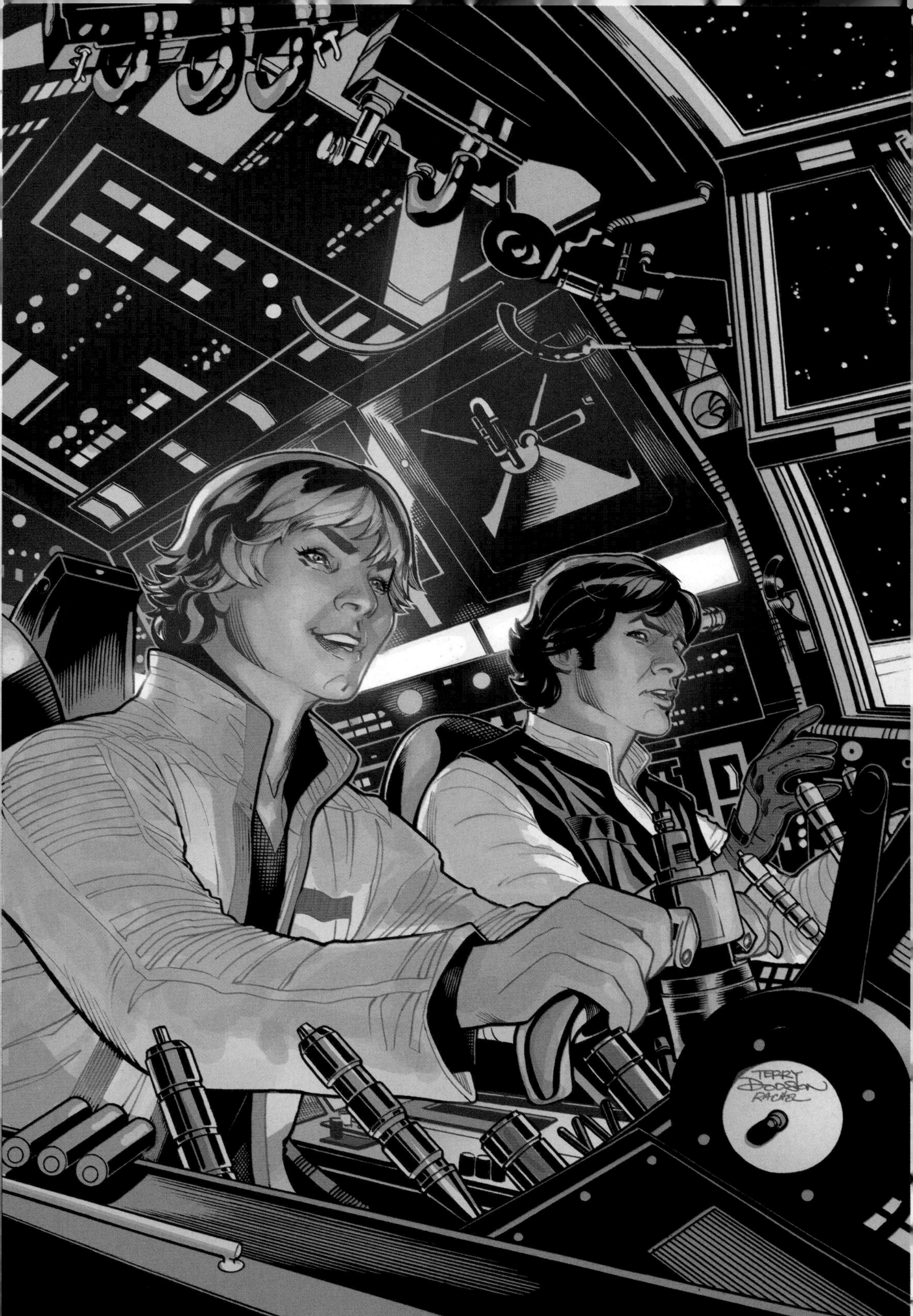
TERRY
DODSON
RACHEL

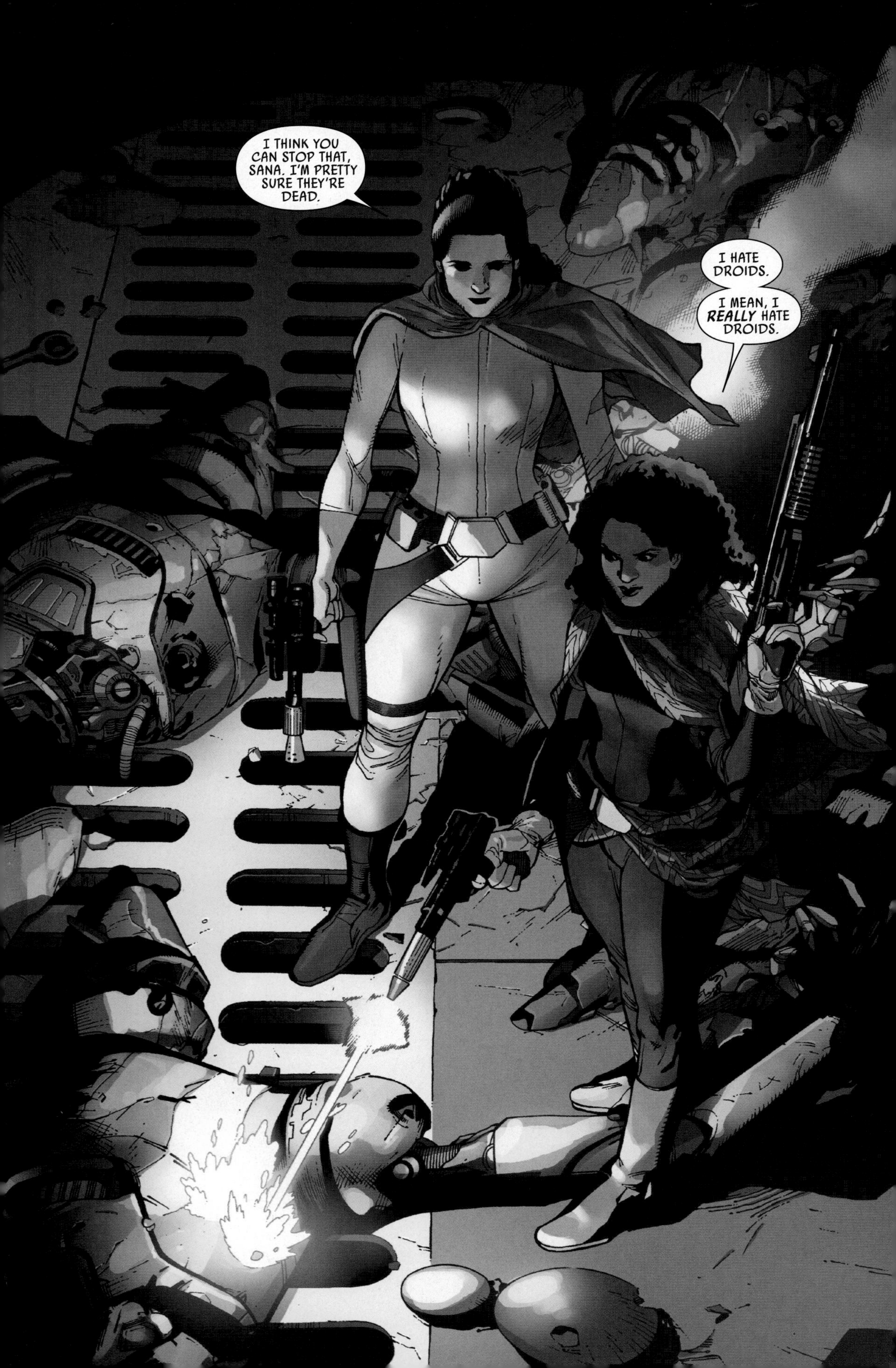
I THINK YOU CAN STOP THAT, SANA. I'M PRETTY SURE THEY'RE DEAD.
I HATE DROIDS.
I MEAN, I *REALLY* HATE DROIDS.

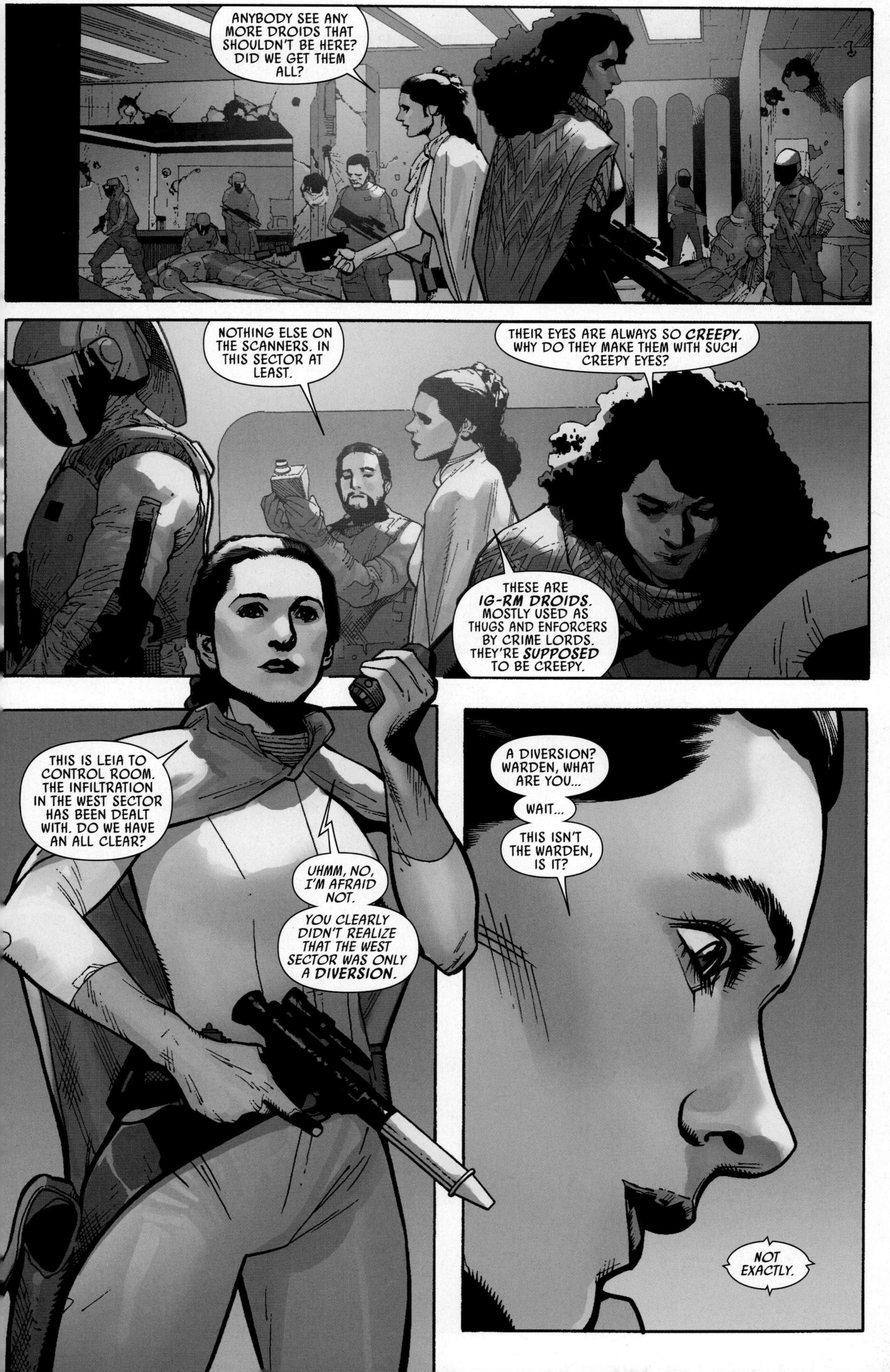

ANYBODY SEE ANY MORE DROIDS THAT SHOULDN'T BE HERE? DID WE GET THEM ALL?
NOTHING ELSE ON THE SCANNERS. IN THIS SECTOR AT LEAST.
THEIR EYES ARE ALWAYS SO CREEPY. WHY DO THEY MAKE THEM WITH SUCH CREEPY EYES?
THESE ARE IG-RM DROIDS. MOSTLY USED AS THUGS AND ENFORCERS BY CRIME LORDS. THEY'RE SUPPOSED TO BE CREEPY.
THIS IS LEIA TO CONTROL ROOM. THE INFILTRATION IN THE WEST SECTOR HAS BEEN DEALT WITH. DO WE HAVE AN ALL CLEAR?
UHMM, NO, I'M AFRAID NOT.
YOU CLEARLY DIDN'T REALIZE THAT THE WEST SECTOR WAS ONLY A DIVERSION.
A DIVERSION? WARDEN, WHAT ARE YOU...
WAIT...
THIS ISN'T THE WARDEN, IS IT?
NOT EXACTLY.

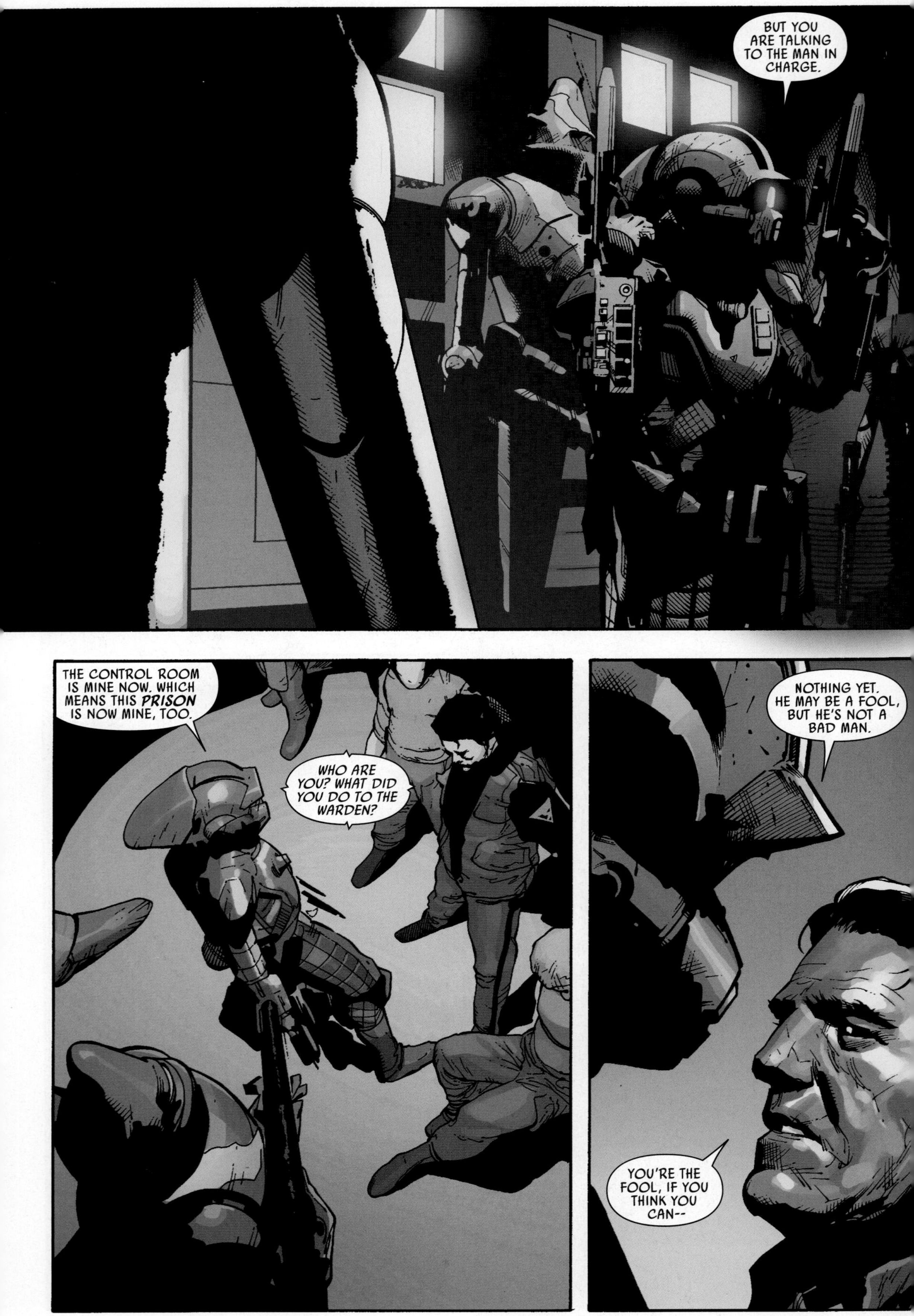
BUT YOU ARE TALKING TO THE MAN IN CHARGE.
THE CONTROL ROOM IS MINE NOW. WHICH MEANS THIS *PRISON* IS NOW MINE, TOO.
WHO ARE YOU? WHAT DID YOU DO TO THE WARDEN?
NOTHING YET. HE MAY BE A FOOL, BUT HE'S NOT A BAD MAN.
YOU'RE THE FOOL, IF YOU THINK YOU CAN--

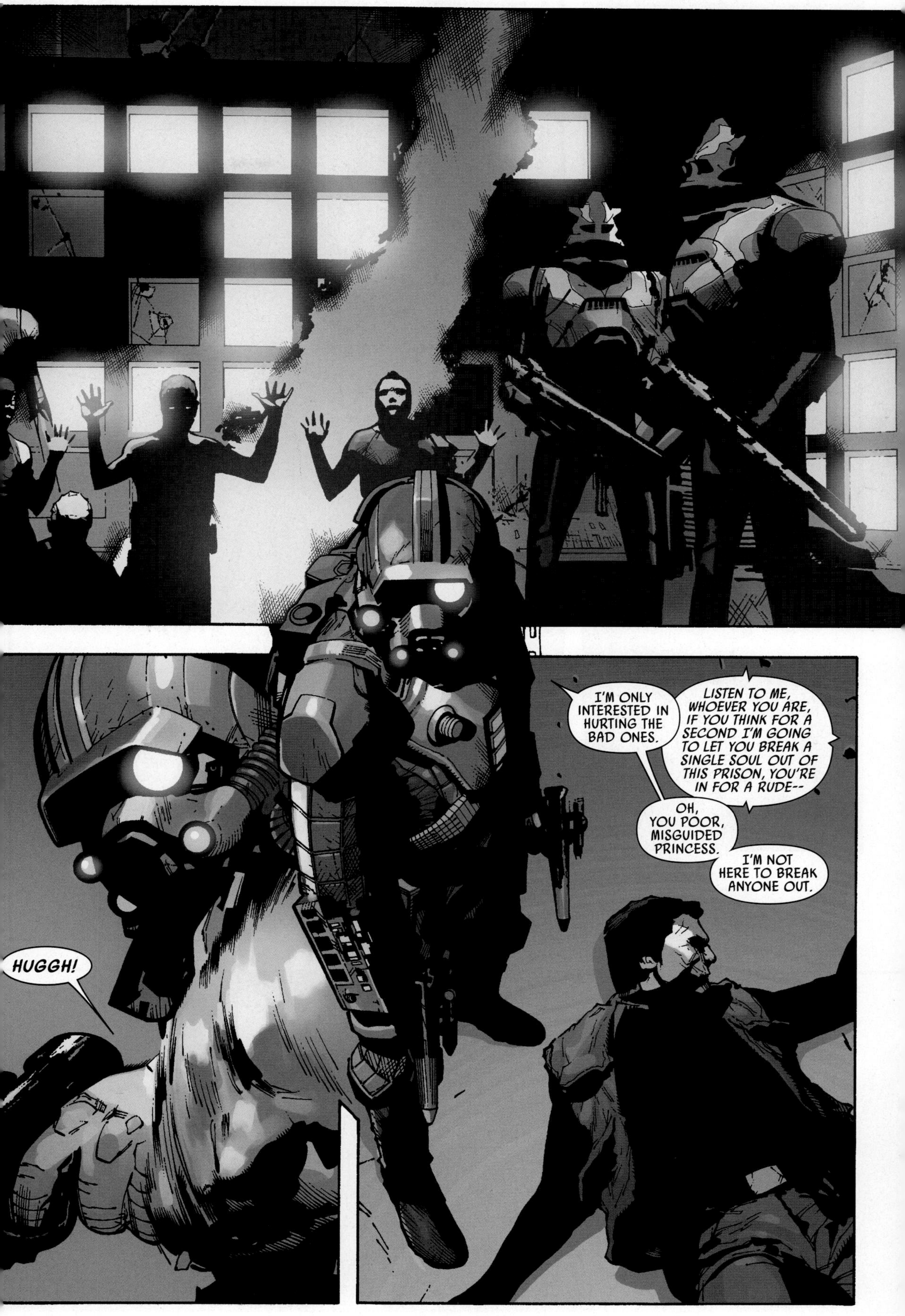
LISTEN TO ME, WHOEVER YOU ARE, IF YOU THINK FOR A SECOND I'M GOING TO LET YOU BREAK A SINGLE SOUL OUT OF THIS PRISON, YOU'RE IN FOR A RUDE--
I'M ONLY INTERESTED IN HURTING THE BAD ONES.
OH, YOU POOR, MISGUIDED PRINCESS.
I'M NOT HERE TO BREAK ANYONE OUT.
HUGGH!

THEY'RE IN POSITION.

TELL ME, PRINCESS... CAN YOU SEE *CELL-BLOCK SEVEN* FROM WHERE YOU ARE?

NO, WHAT ARE YOU...

I'M ACTUALLY HERE TO HELP YOU, LEIA. *YOU'RE* THE ONE WHO NEEDS SAVING HERE, NOT THESE PRISONERS.

THESE PRISONERS ARE BEYOND SALVATION.

OPEN FIRE.

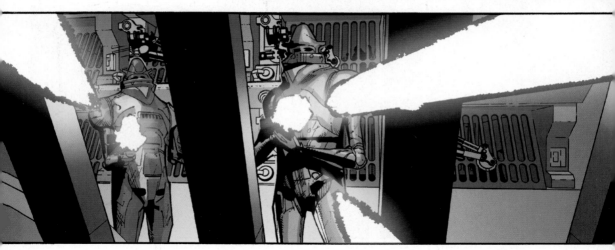

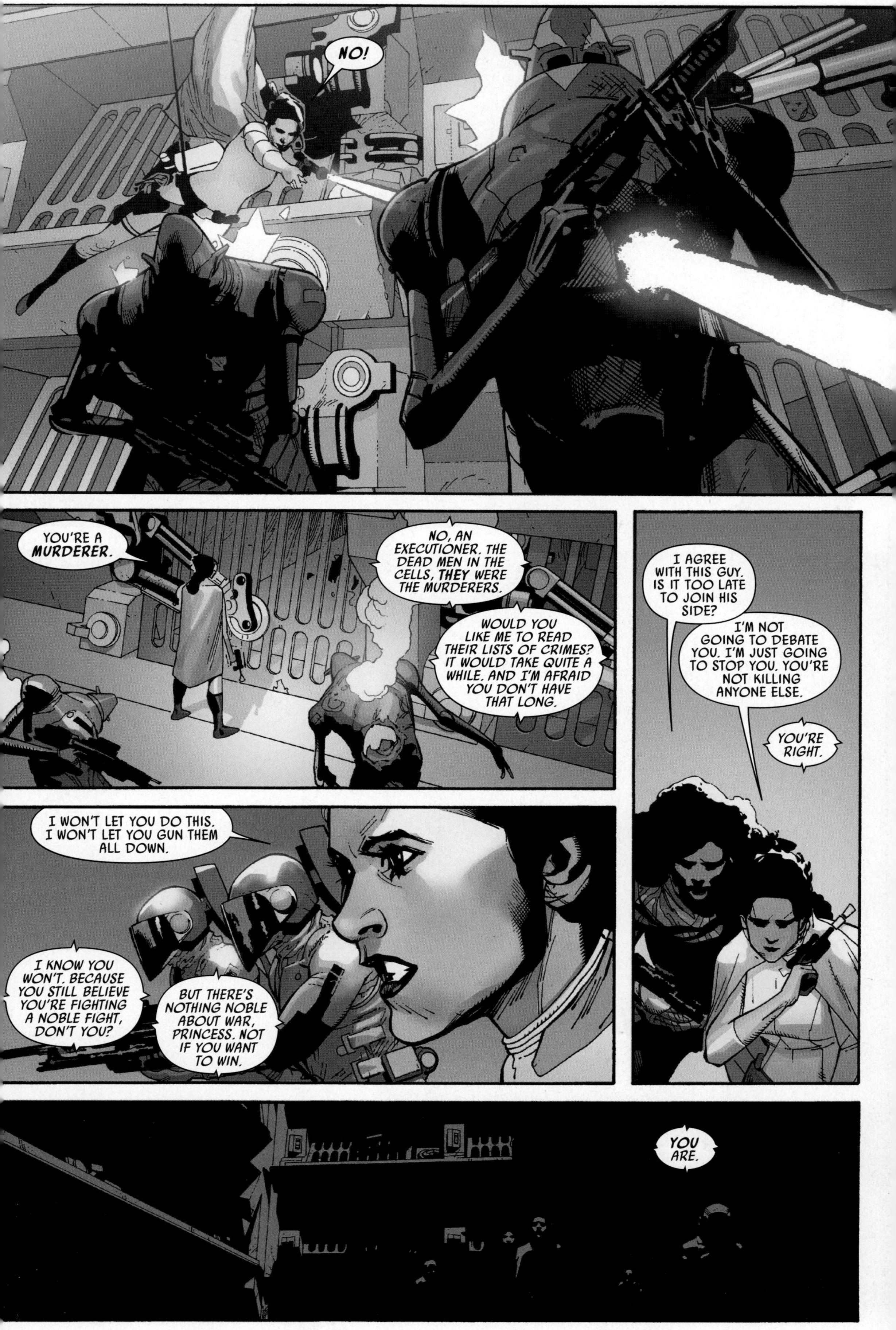
NO!
YOU'RE A MURDERER.
NO, AN EXECUTIONER. THE DEAD MEN IN THE CELLS, THEY WERE THE MURDERERS.
WOULD YOU LIKE ME TO READ THEIR LISTS OF CRIMES? IT WOULD TAKE QUITE A WHILE. AND I'M AFRAID YOU DON'T HAVE THAT LONG.
I WON'T LET YOU DO THIS. I WON'T LET YOU GUN THEM ALL DOWN.
I KNOW YOU WON'T. BECAUSE YOU STILL BELIEVE YOU'RE FIGHTING A NOBLE FIGHT, DON'T YOU?
BUT THERE'S NOTHING NOBLE ABOUT WAR, PRINCESS. NOT IF YOU WANT TO WIN.
I AGREE WITH THIS GUY. IS IT TOO LATE TO JOIN HIS SIDE?
I'M NOT GOING TO DEBATE YOU. I'M JUST GOING TO STOP YOU. YOU'RE NOT KILLING ANYONE ELSE.
YOU'RE RIGHT.
YOU ARE.

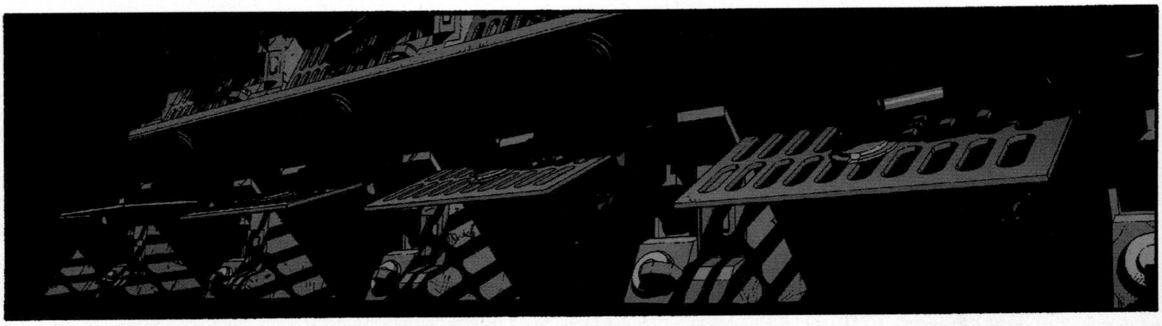

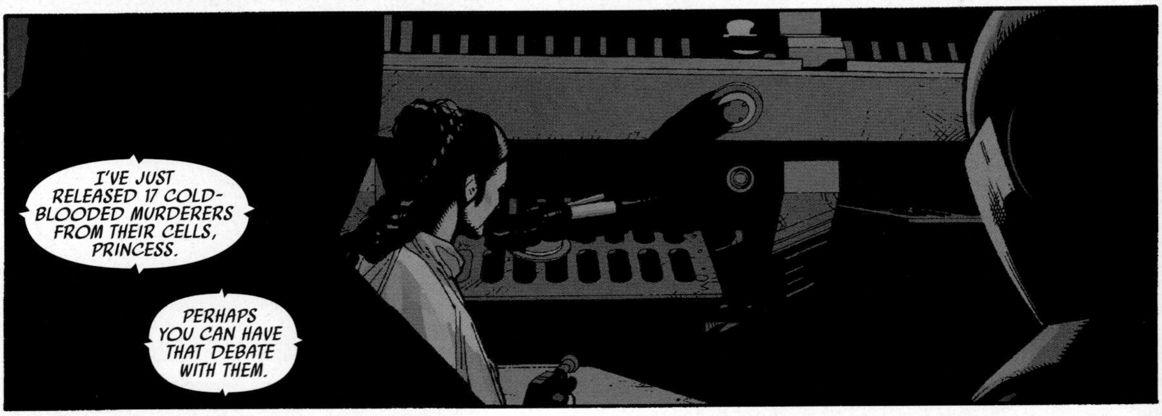
I'VE JUST RELEASED 17 COLD-BLOODED MURDERERS FROM THEIR CELLS, PRINCESS.
PERHAPS YOU CAN HAVE THAT DEBATE WITH THEM.

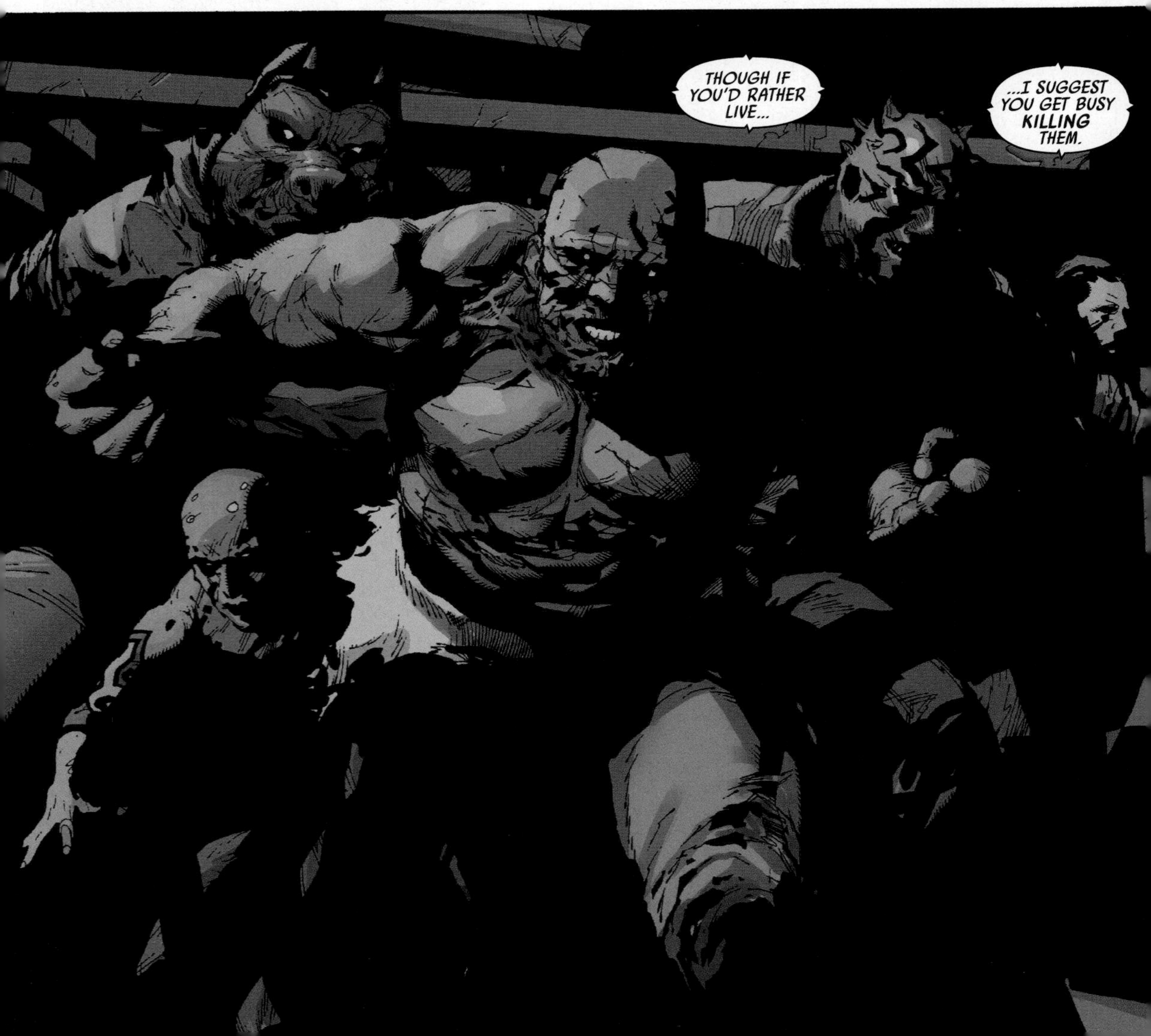
THOUGH IF YOU'D RATHER LIVE...
...I SUGGEST YOU GET BUSY KILLING THEM.

NAR SHADDAA. THE SMUGGLER'S MOON.

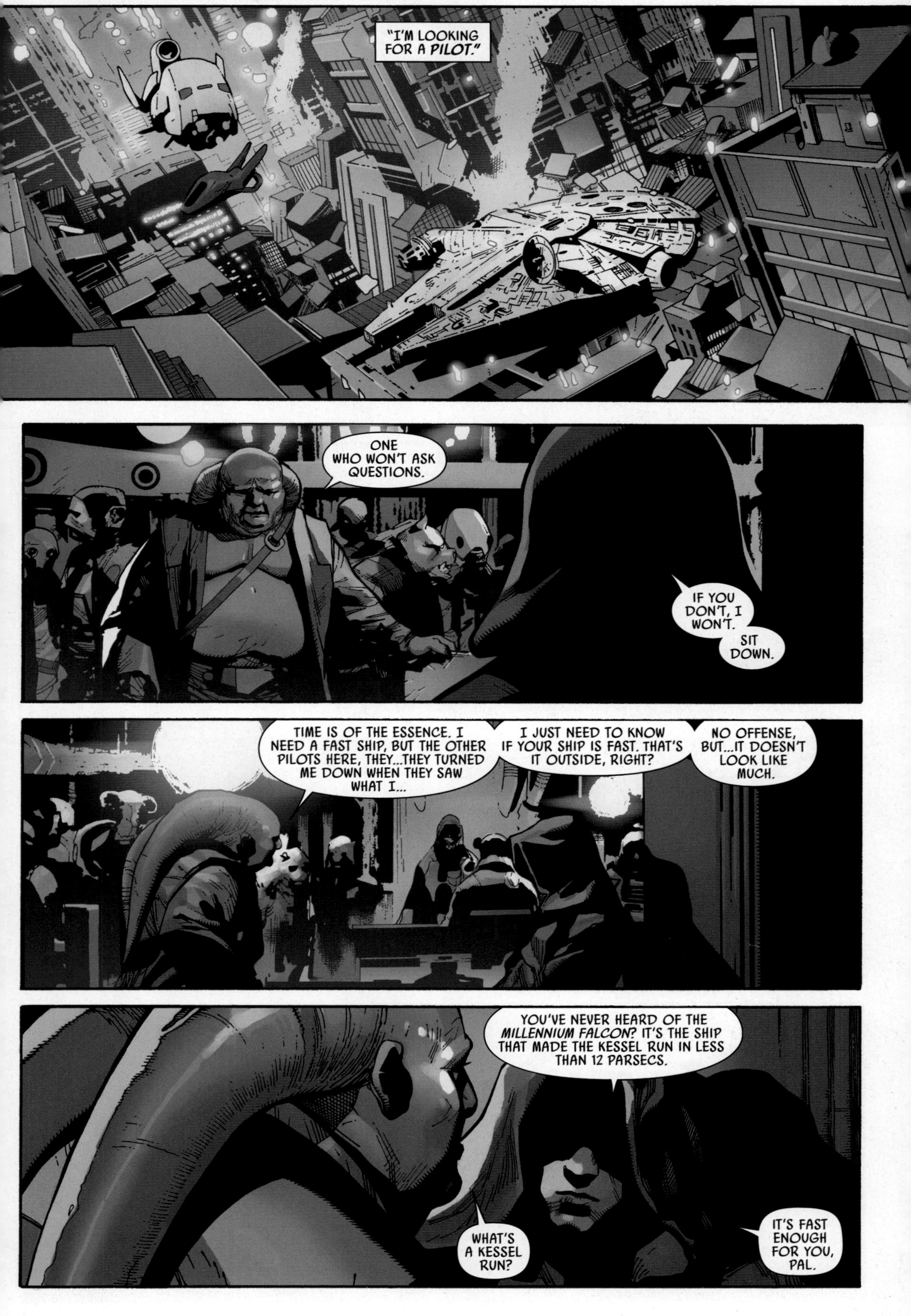
"I'M LOOKING FOR A *PILOT*."
ONE WHO WON'T ASK QUESTIONS.
IF YOU DON'T, I WON'T.
SIT DOWN.
TIME IS OF THE ESSENCE. I NEED A FAST SHIP, BUT THE OTHER PILOTS HERE, THEY...THEY TURNED ME DOWN WHEN THEY SAW WHAT I...
I JUST NEED TO KNOW IF YOUR SHIP IS FAST. THAT'S IT OUTSIDE, RIGHT?
NO OFFENSE, BUT...IT DOESN'T LOOK LIKE MUCH.
YOU'VE NEVER HEARD OF THE *MILLENNIUM FALCON*? IT'S THE SHIP THAT MADE THE KESSEL RUN IN LESS THAN 12 PARSECS.
WHAT'S A KESSEL RUN?
IT'S FAST ENOUGH FOR YOU, PAL.

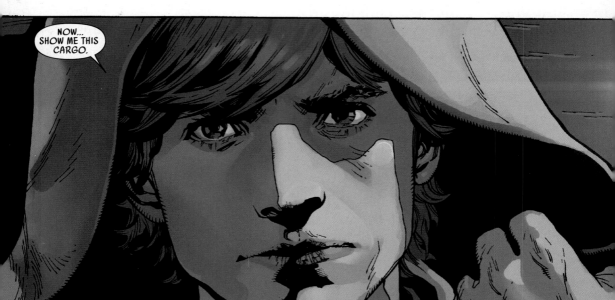

NOW... SHOW ME THIS CARGO.

WELL? HOW'D IT GO?

DID YOU GET 10,000?

FIVE.

FIVE? WE'RE NOT RUNNING A CHARITY HERE, KID. WHAT KIND OF SMUGGLER ARE YOU?

IF YOU WANTED MORE, YOU SHOULD'VE GONE YOURSELF. BUT LET ME GUESS, YOU USED TO CHEAT AT SABACC HERE, TOO.

AT LEAST TELL ME IT'S AN EASY CARGO. BLACK MARKET DROID PARTS? A FEW CRATES OF SPICE MAYBE?

NOT EXACTLY.

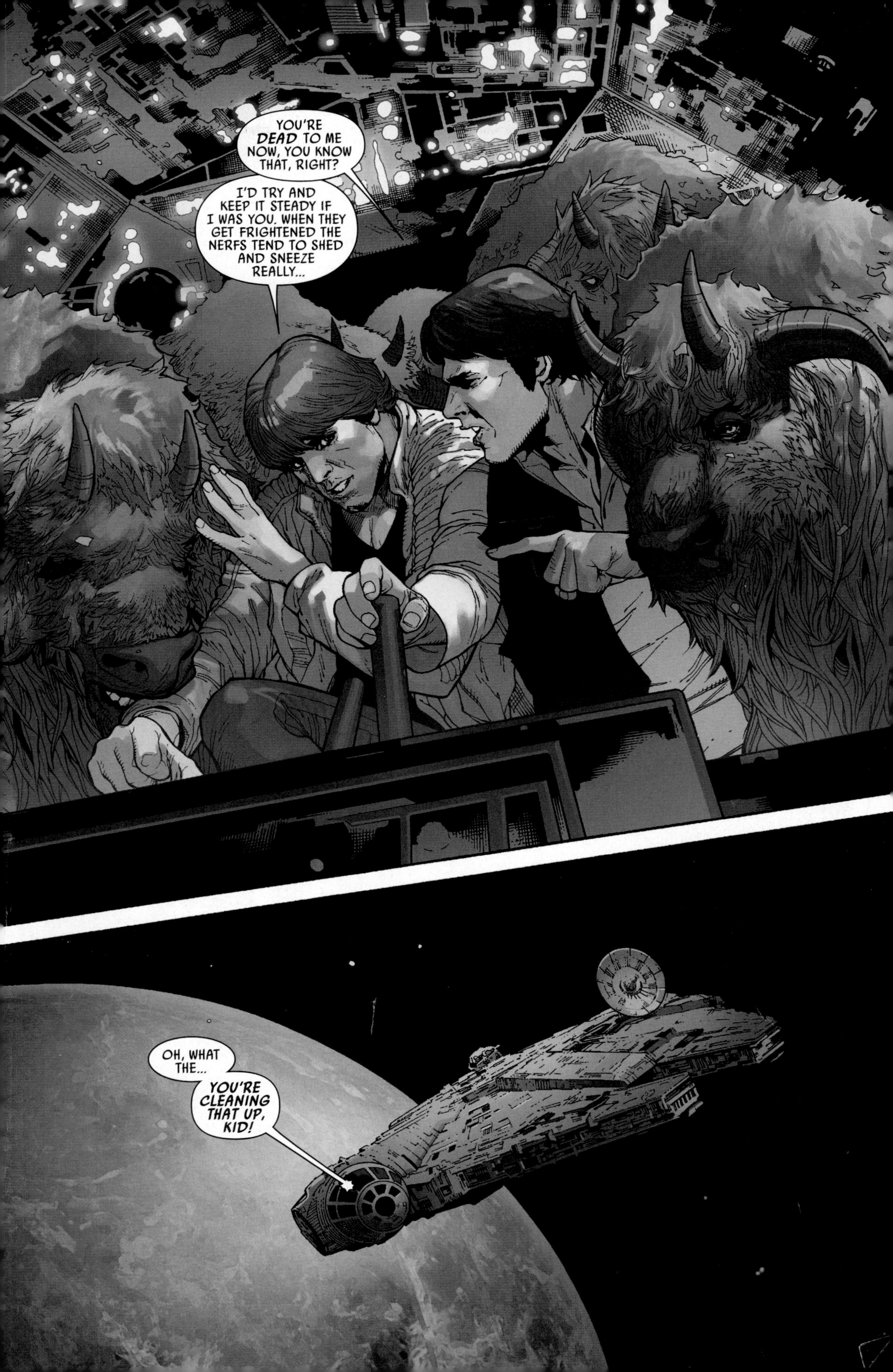
YOU'RE DEAD TO ME NOW, YOU KNOW THAT, RIGHT?
I'D TRY AND KEEP IT STEADY IF I WAS YOU. WHEN THEY GET FRIGHTENED THE NERFS TEND TO SHED AND SNEEZE REALLY...
OH, WHAT THE...
YOU'RE CLEANING THAT UP, KID!

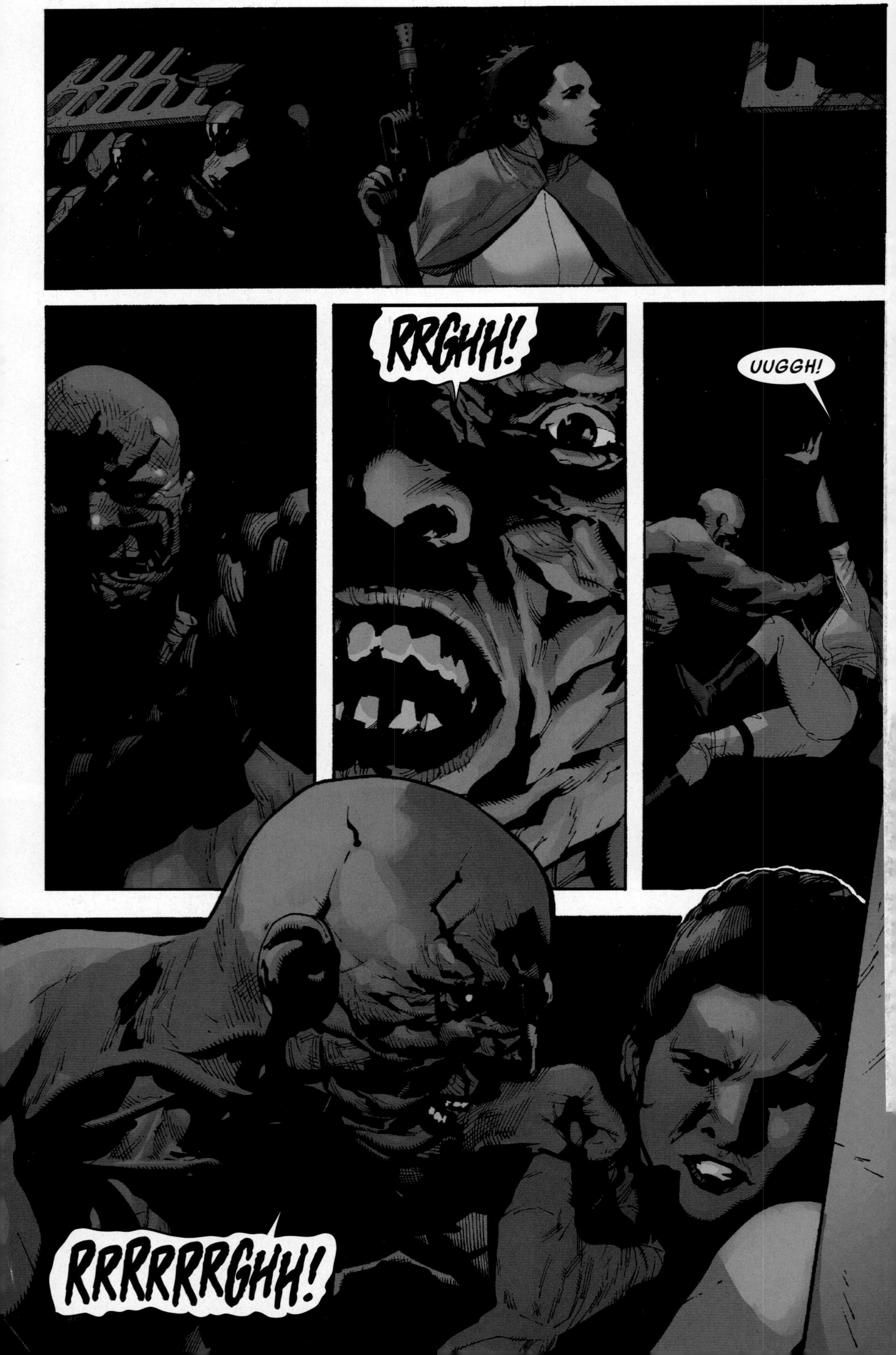
RRGHH!
UUGGH!
RRRRRRGHH!

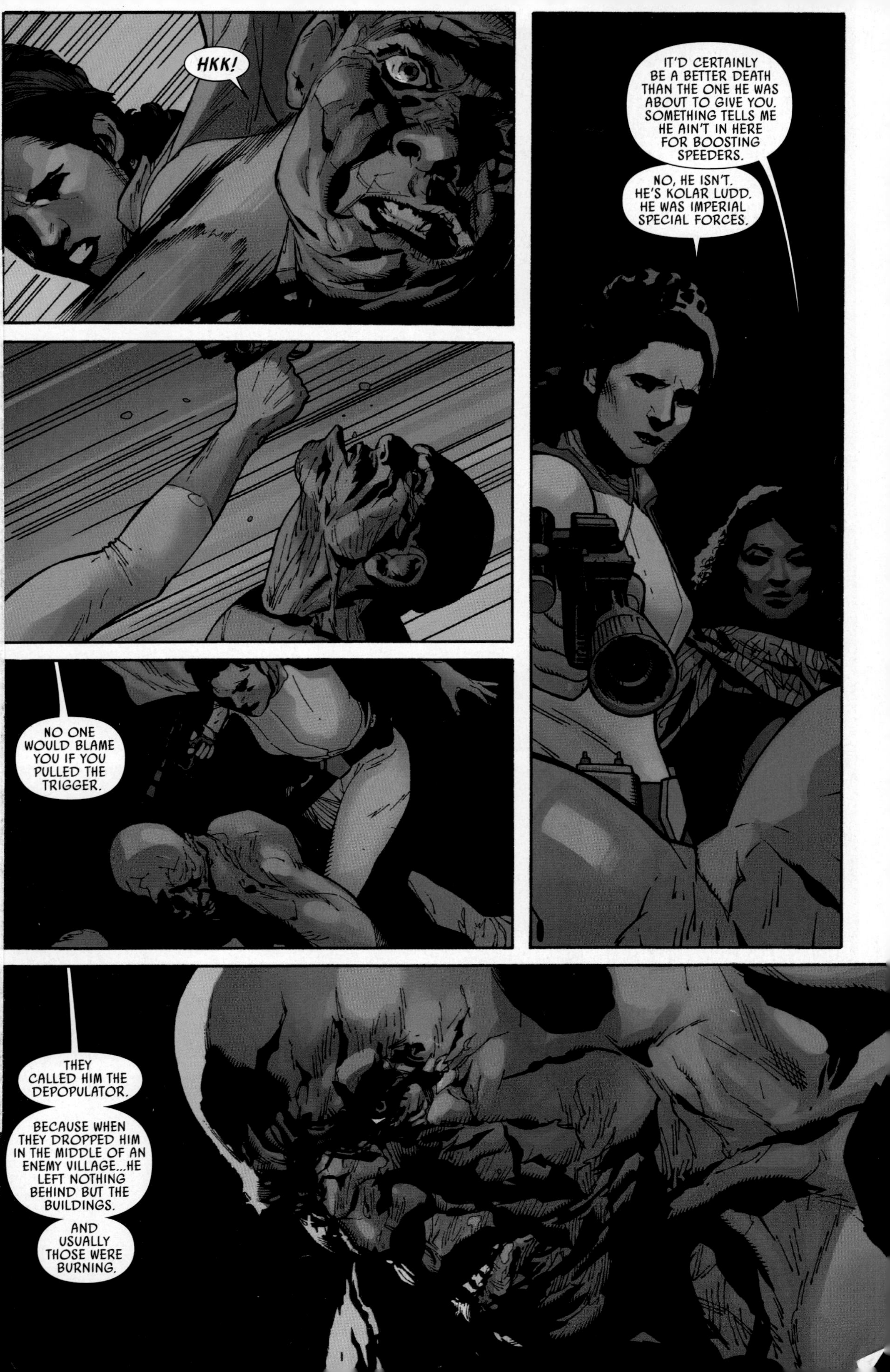
HKK!
IT'D CERTAINLY BE A BETTER DEATH THAN THE ONE HE WAS ABOUT TO GIVE YOU. SOMETHING TELLS ME HE AIN'T IN HERE FOR BOOSTING SPEEDERS.
NO, HE ISN'T. HE'S KOLAR LUDD. HE WAS IMPERIAL SPECIAL FORCES.
NO ONE WOULD BLAME YOU IF YOU PULLED THE TRIGGER.
THEY CALLED HIM THE DEPOPULATOR.
BECAUSE WHEN THEY DROPPED HIM IN THE MIDDLE OF AN ENEMY VILLAGE...HE LEFT NOTHING BEHIND BUT THE BUILDINGS.
AND USUALLY THOSE WERE BURNING.

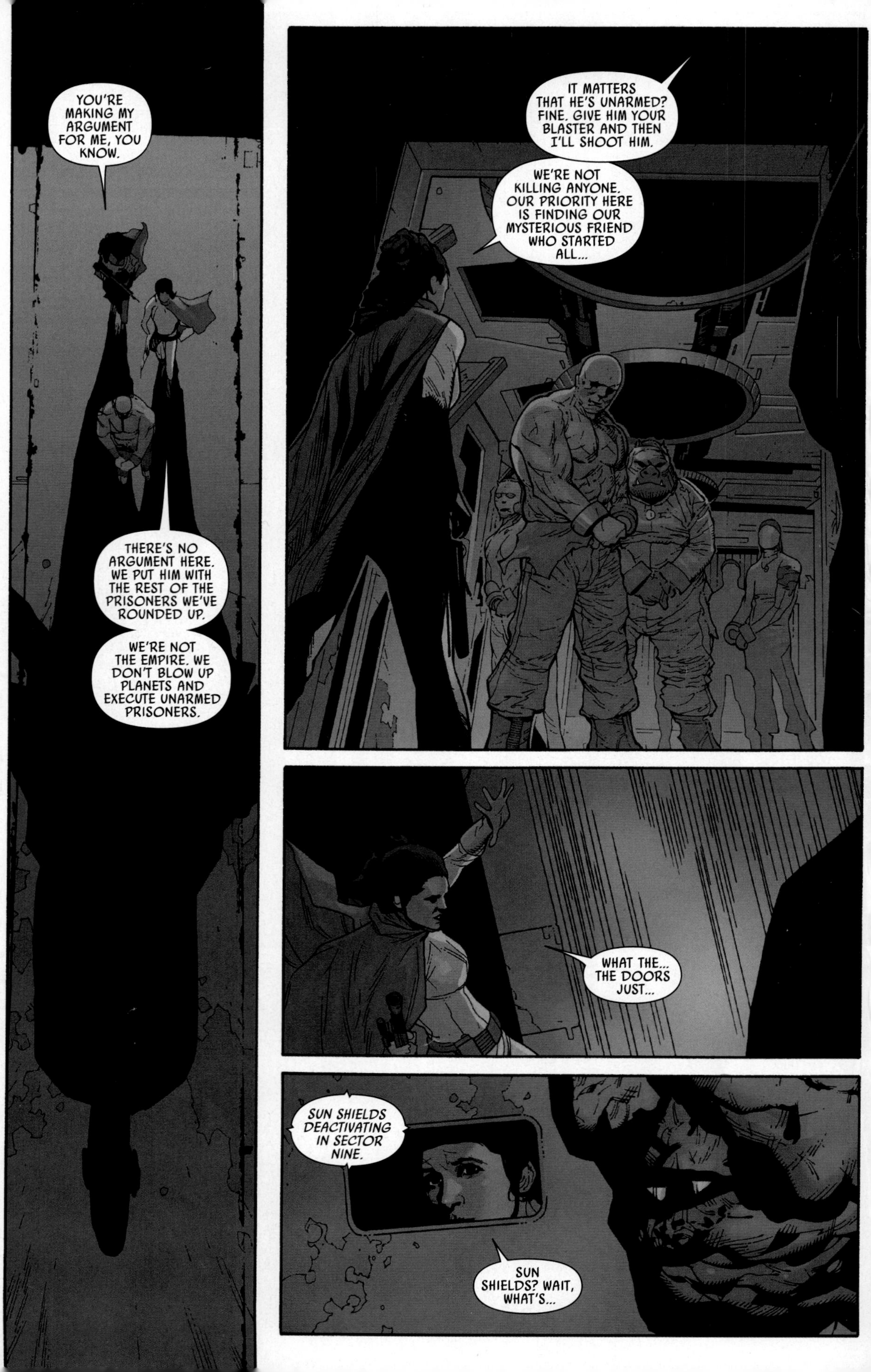
YOU'RE MAKING MY ARGUMENT FOR ME, YOU KNOW.
THERE'S NO ARGUMENT HERE. WE PUT HIM WITH THE REST OF THE PRISONERS WE'VE ROUNDED UP.
WE'RE NOT THE EMPIRE. WE DON'T BLOW UP PLANETS AND EXECUTE UNARMED PRISONERS.
IT MATTERS THAT HE'S UNARMED? FINE. GIVE HIM YOUR BLASTER AND THEN I'LL SHOOT HIM.
WE'RE NOT KILLING ANYONE. OUR PRIORITY HERE IS FINDING OUR MYSTERIOUS FRIEND WHO STARTED ALL...
WHAT THE... THE DOORS JUST...
SUN SHIELDS DEACTIVATING IN SECTOR NINE.
SUN SHIELDS? WAIT, WHAT'S...

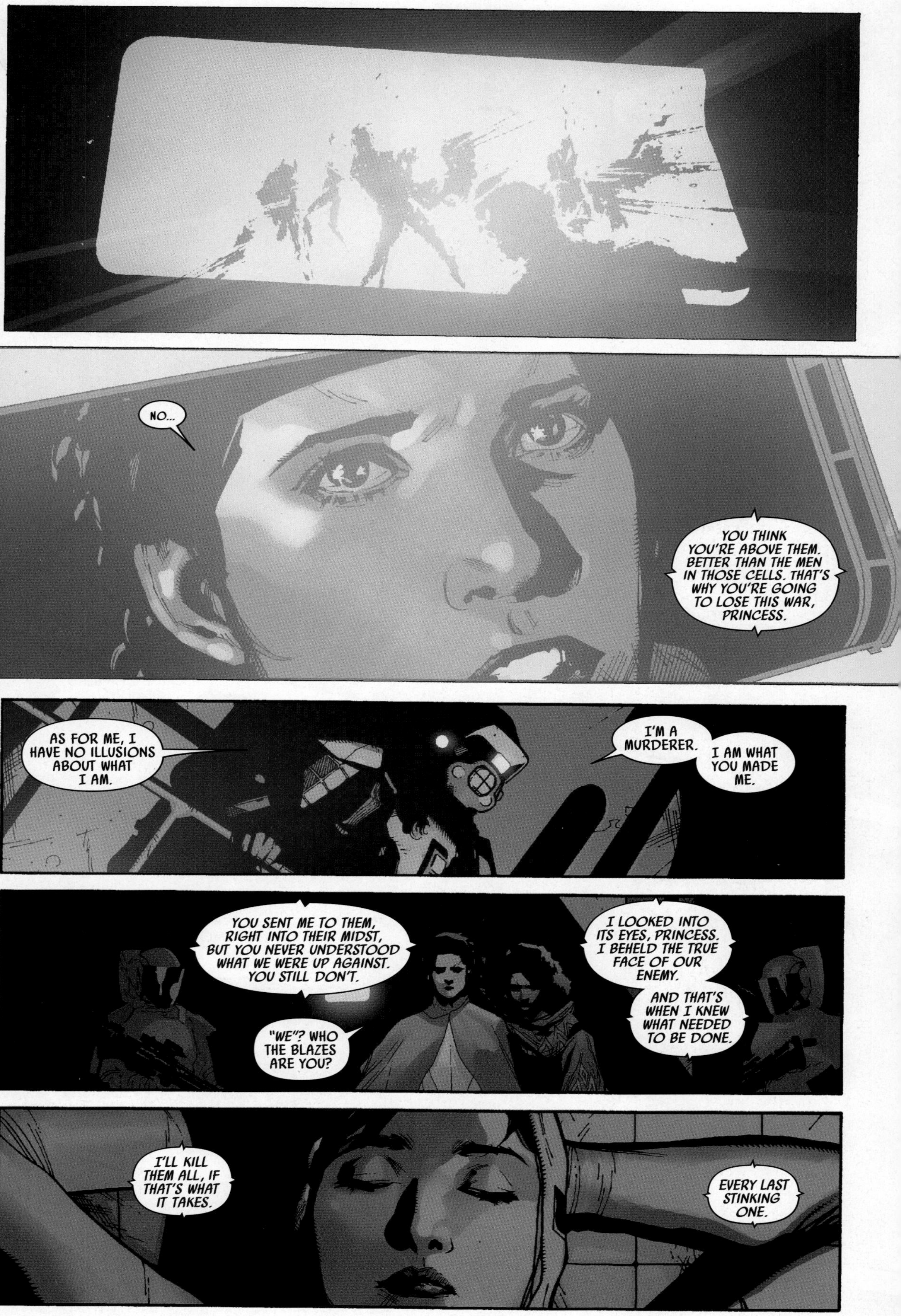
NO...
YOU THINK YOU'RE ABOVE THEM. BETTER THAN THE MEN IN THOSE CELLS. THAT'S WHY YOU'RE GOING TO LOSE THIS WAR, PRINCESS.
AS FOR ME, I HAVE NO ILLUSIONS ABOUT WHAT I AM.
I'M A MURDERER.
I AM WHAT YOU MADE ME.
YOU SENT ME TO THEM, RIGHT INTO THEIR MIDST, BUT YOU NEVER UNDERSTOOD WHAT WE WERE UP AGAINST. YOU STILL DON'T.
"WE"? WHO THE BLAZES ARE YOU?
I LOOKED INTO ITS EYES, PRINCESS. I BEHELD THE TRUE FACE OF OUR ENEMY.
AND THAT'S WHEN I KNEW WHAT NEEDED TO BE DONE.
I'LL KILL THEM ALL, IF THAT'S WHAT IT TAKES.
EVERY LAST STINKING ONE.

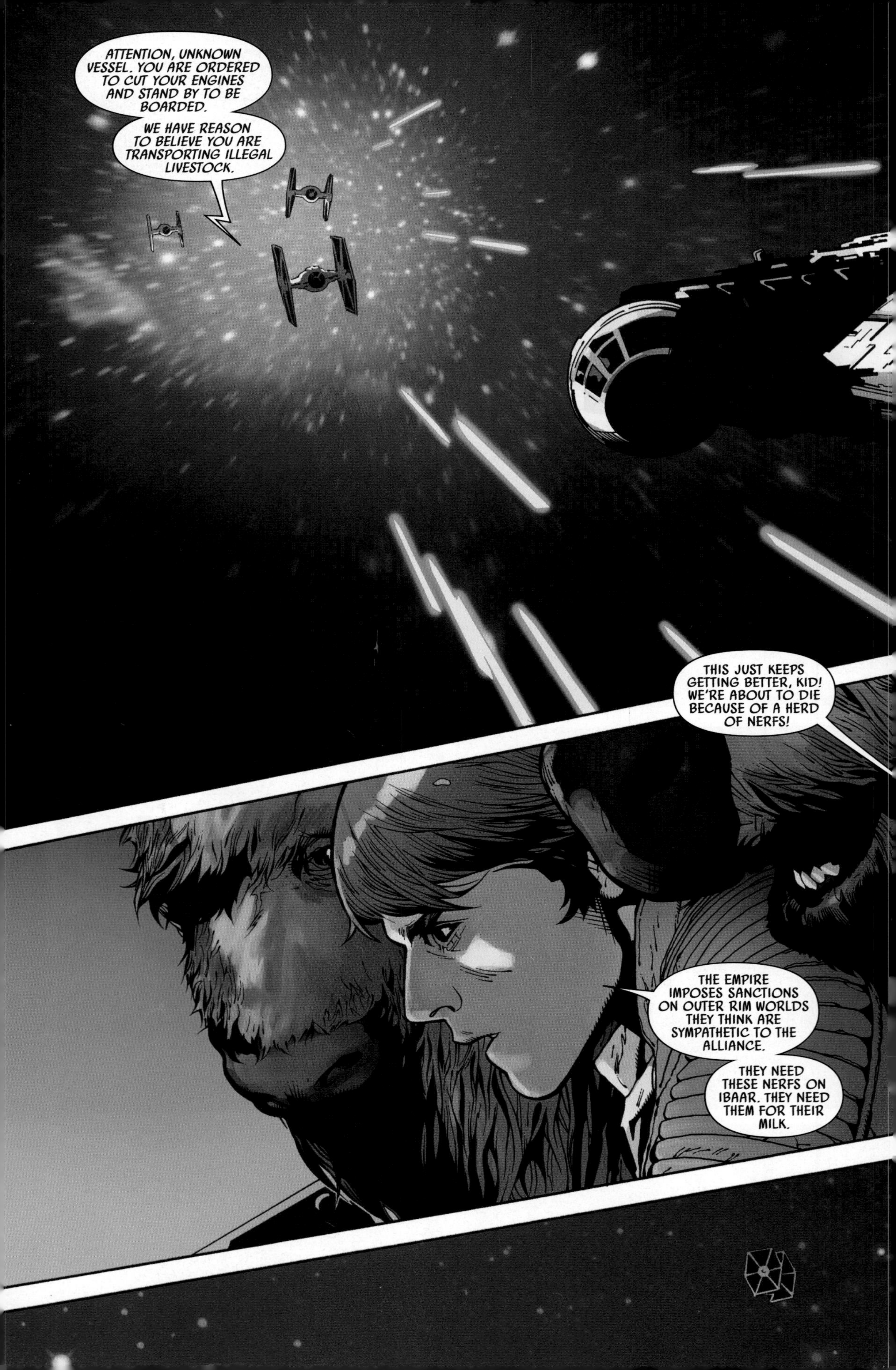
ATTENTION, UNKNOWN VESSEL. YOU ARE ORDERED TO CUT YOUR ENGINES AND STAND BY TO BE BOARDED.
WE HAVE REASON TO BELIEVE YOU ARE TRANSPORTING ILLEGAL LIVESTOCK.
THIS JUST KEEPS GETTING BETTER, KID! WE'RE ABOUT TO DIE BECAUSE OF A HERD OF NERFS!
THE EMPIRE IMPOSES SANCTIONS ON OUTER RIM WORLDS THEY THINK ARE SYMPATHETIC TO THE ALLIANCE.
THEY NEED THESE NERFS ON IBAAR. THEY NEED THEM FOR THEIR MILK.

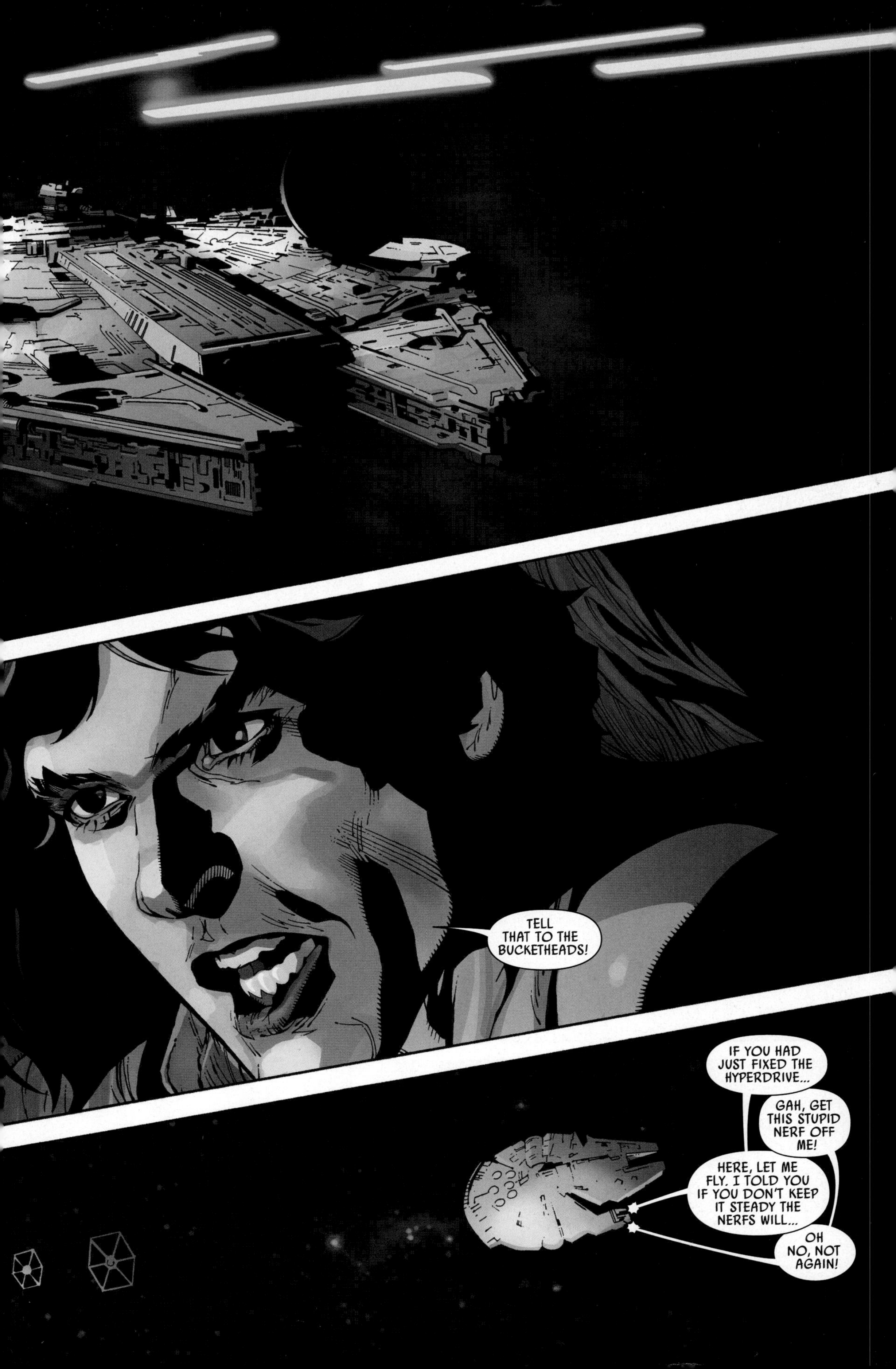
TELL THAT TO THE BUCKETHEADS!
IF YOU HAD JUST FIXED THE HYPERDRIVE...
GAH, GET THIS STUPID NERF OFF ME!
HERE, LET ME FLY. I TOLD YOU IF YOU DON'T KEEP IT STEADY THE NERFS WILL...
OH NO, NOT AGAIN!

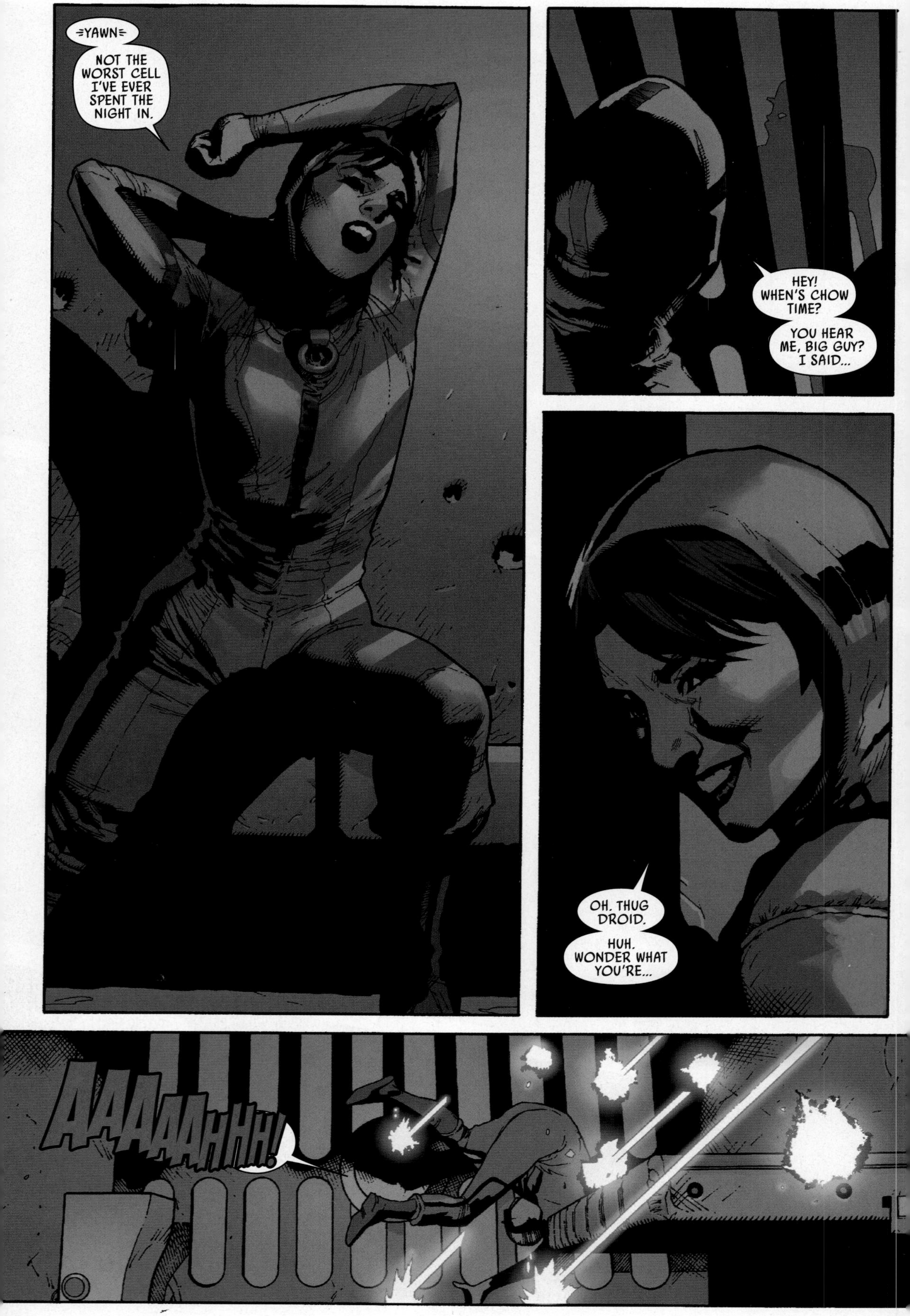
=YAWN=
NOT THE WORST CELL I'VE EVER SPENT THE NIGHT IN.
HEY! WHEN'S CHOW TIME?
YOU HEAR ME, BIG GUY? I SAID...
OH. THUG DROID.
HUH. WONDER WHAT YOU'RE...
AAAAAAHHH!

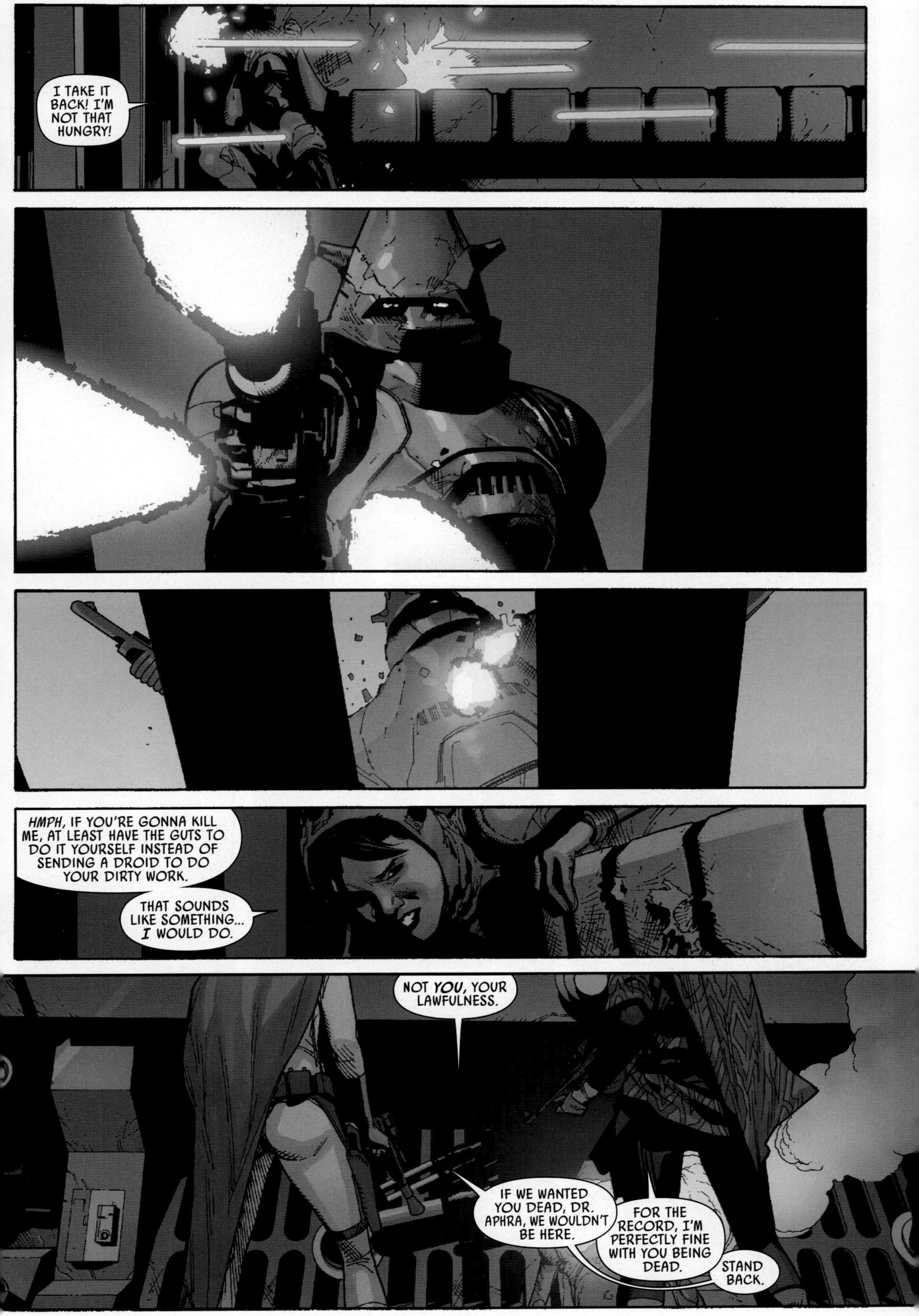

I TAKE IT BACK! I'M NOT THAT HUNGRY!
HMPH, IF YOU'RE GONNA KILL ME, AT LEAST HAVE THE GUTS TO DO IT YOURSELF INSTEAD OF SENDING A DROID TO DO YOUR DIRTY WORK.
THAT SOUNDS LIKE SOMETHING... *I* WOULD DO.
NOT *YOU*, YOUR LAWFULNESS.
IF WE WANTED YOU DEAD, DR. APHRA, WE WOULDN'T BE HERE.
FOR THE RECORD, I'M PERFECTLY FINE WITH YOU BEING DEAD.
STAND BACK.

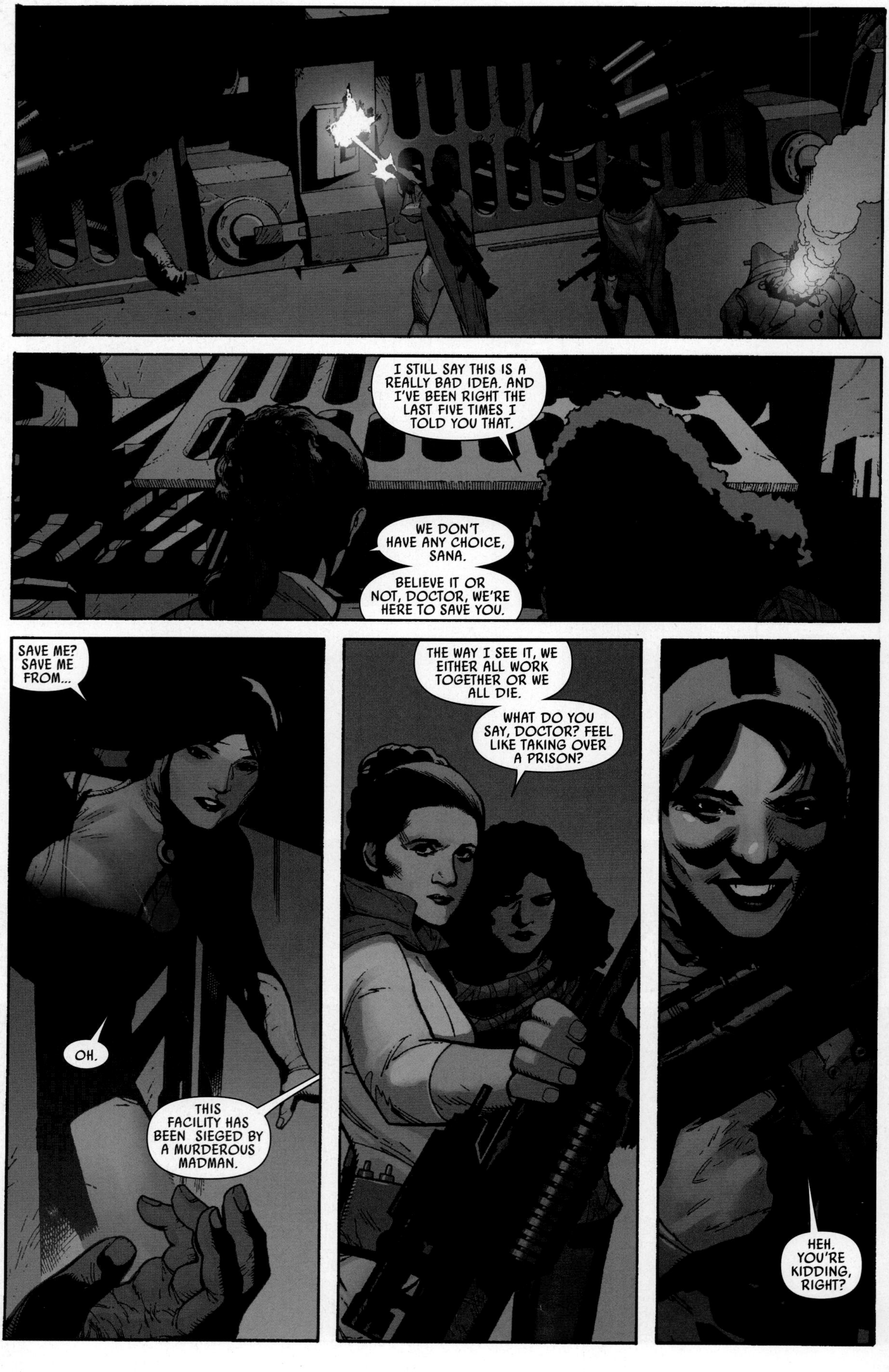
I STILL SAY THIS IS A REALLY BAD IDEA. AND I'VE BEEN RIGHT THE LAST FIVE TIMES I TOLD YOU THAT.
WE DON'T HAVE ANY CHOICE, SANA.
BELIEVE IT OR NOT, DOCTOR, WE'RE HERE TO SAVE YOU.
SAVE ME? SAVE ME FROM...
OH.
THIS FACILITY HAS BEEN SIEGED BY A MURDEROUS MADMAN.
THE WAY I SEE IT, WE EITHER ALL WORK TOGETHER OR WE ALL DIE.
WHAT DO YOU SAY, DOCTOR? FEEL LIKE TAKING OVER A PRISON?
HEH. YOU'RE KIDDING, RIGHT?

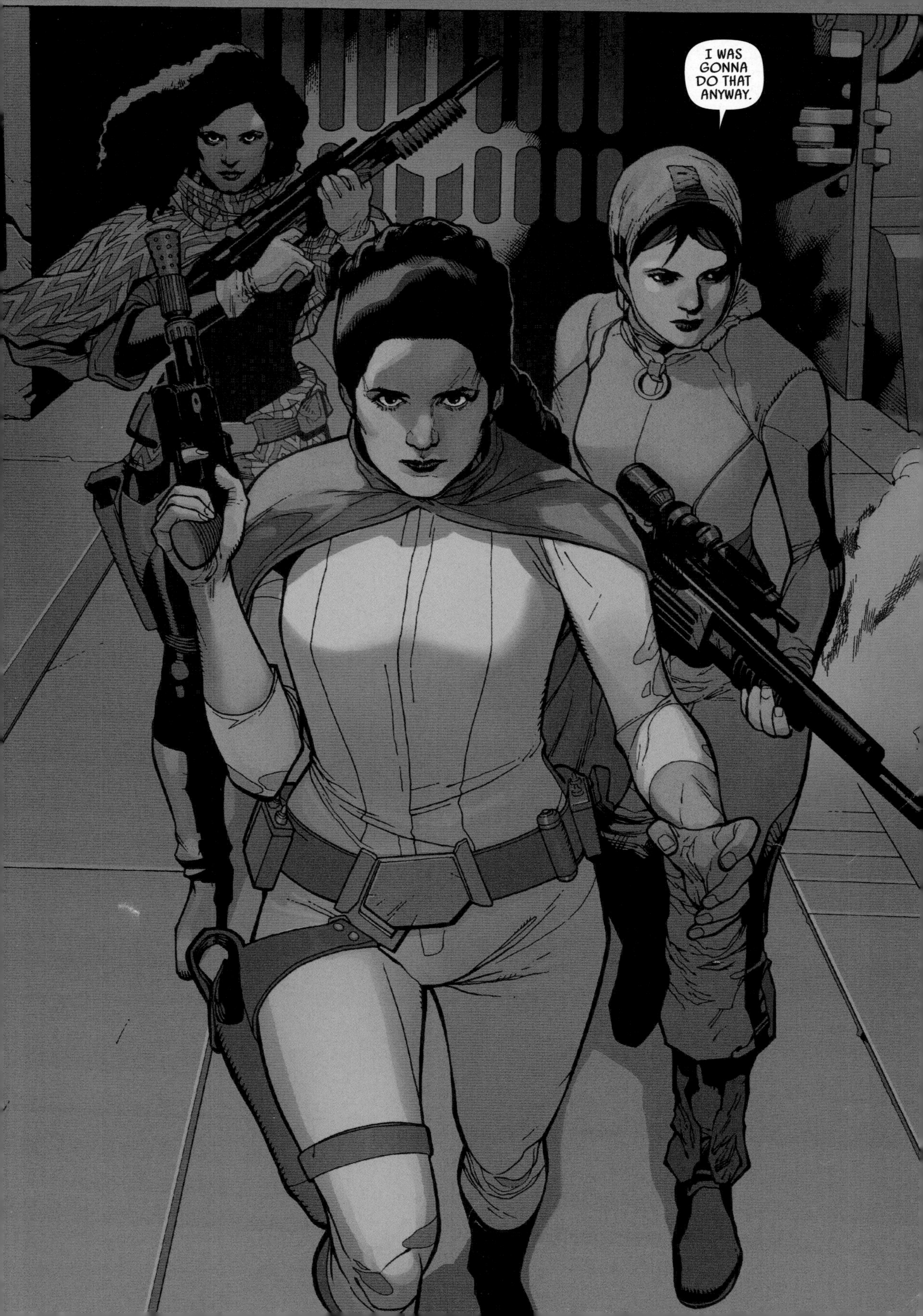
I WAS GONNA DO THAT ANYWAY.

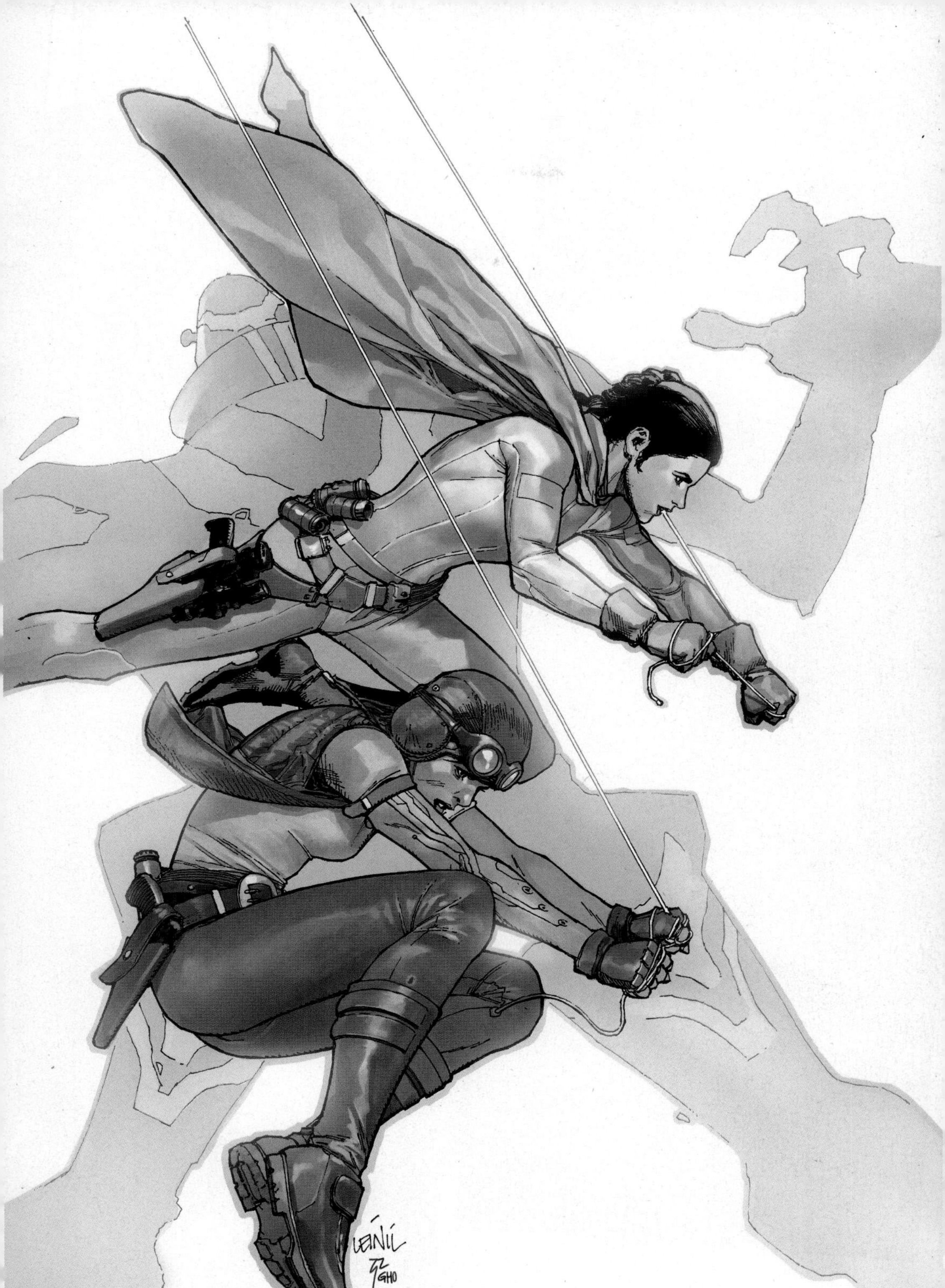

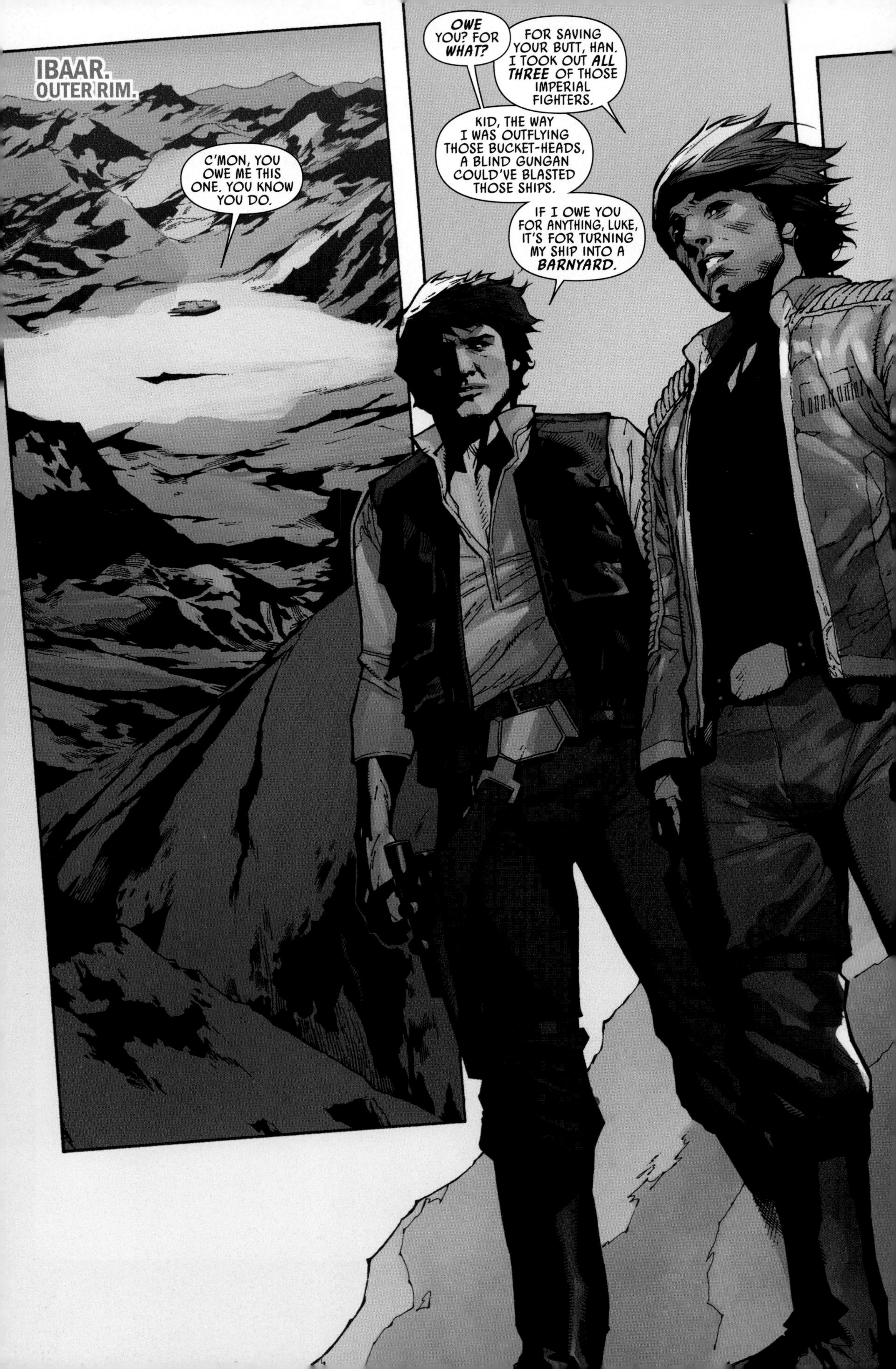
IBAAR.
OUTER RIM.
C'MON, YOU OWE ME THIS ONE. YOU KNOW YOU DO.
OWE YOU? FOR WHAT?
FOR SAVING YOUR BUTT, HAN. I TOOK OUT ALL THREE OF THOSE IMPERIAL FIGHTERS.
KID, THE WAY I WAS OUTFLYING THOSE BUCKET-HEADS, A BLIND GUNGAN COULD'VE BLASTED THOSE SHIPS.
IF I OWE YOU FOR ANYTHING, LUKE, IT'S FOR TURNING MY SHIP INTO A BARNYARD.

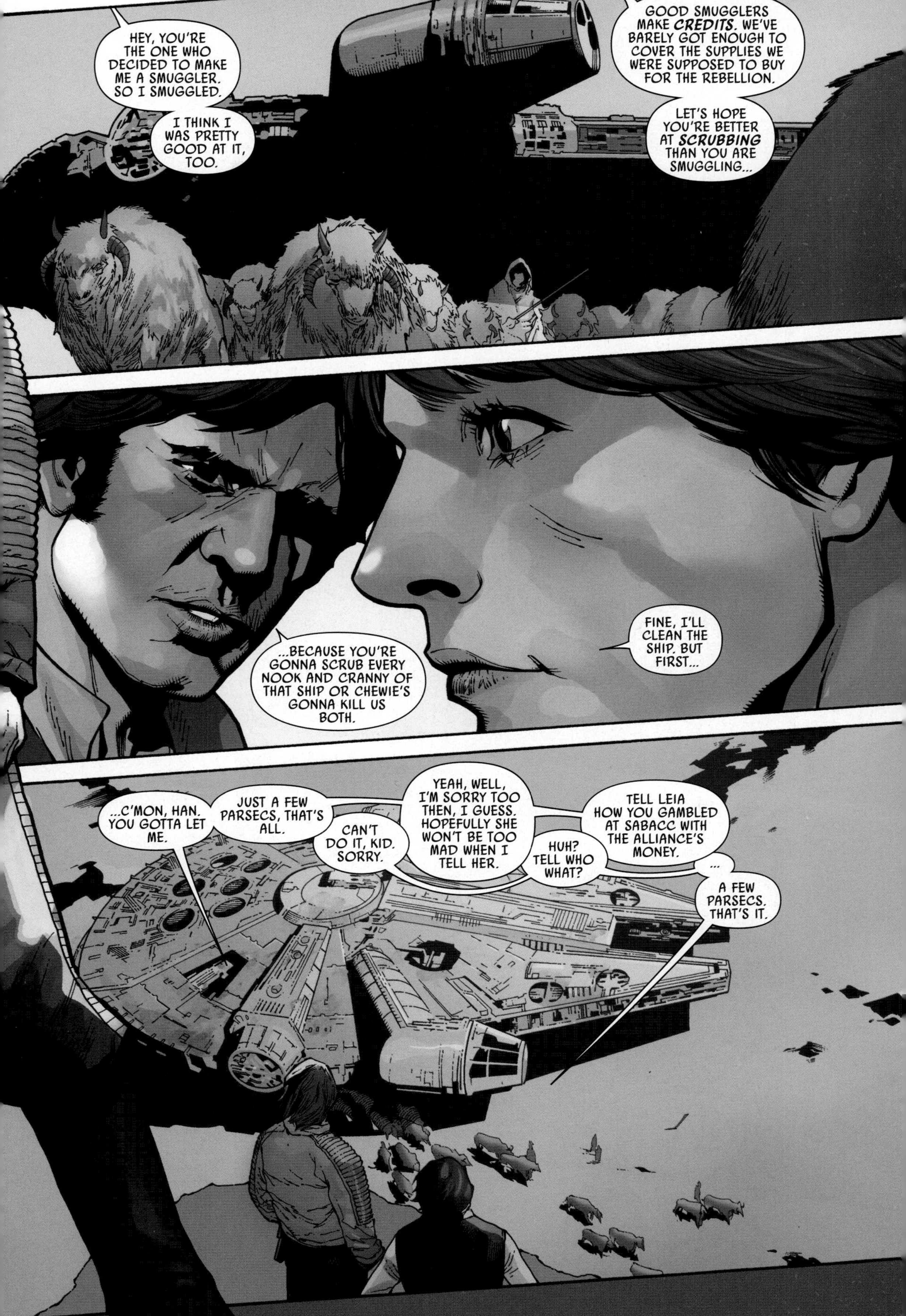
HEY, YOU'RE THE ONE WHO DECIDED TO MAKE ME A SMUGGLER. SO I SMUGGLED.
I THINK I WAS PRETTY GOOD AT IT, TOO.
GOOD SMUGGLERS MAKE *CREDITS.* WE'VE BARELY GOT ENOUGH TO COVER THE SUPPLIES WE WERE SUPPOSED TO BUY FOR THE REBELLION.
LET'S HOPE YOU'RE BETTER AT *SCRUBBING* THAN YOU ARE SMUGGLING...
...BECAUSE YOU'RE GONNA SCRUB EVERY NOOK AND CRANNY OF THAT SHIP OR CHEWIE'S GONNA KILL US BOTH.
FINE, I'LL CLEAN THE SHIP. BUT FIRST...
...C'MON, HAN. YOU GOTTA LET ME.
JUST A FEW PARSECS, THAT'S ALL.
CAN'T DO IT, KID. SORRY.
YEAH, WELL, I'M SORRY TOO THEN, I GUESS. HOPEFULLY SHE WON'T BE TOO MAD WHEN I TELL HER.
HUH? TELL WHO WHAT?
TELL LEIA HOW YOU GAMBLED AT SABACC WITH THE ALLIANCE'S MONEY.
...
A FEW PARSECS. THAT'S IT.

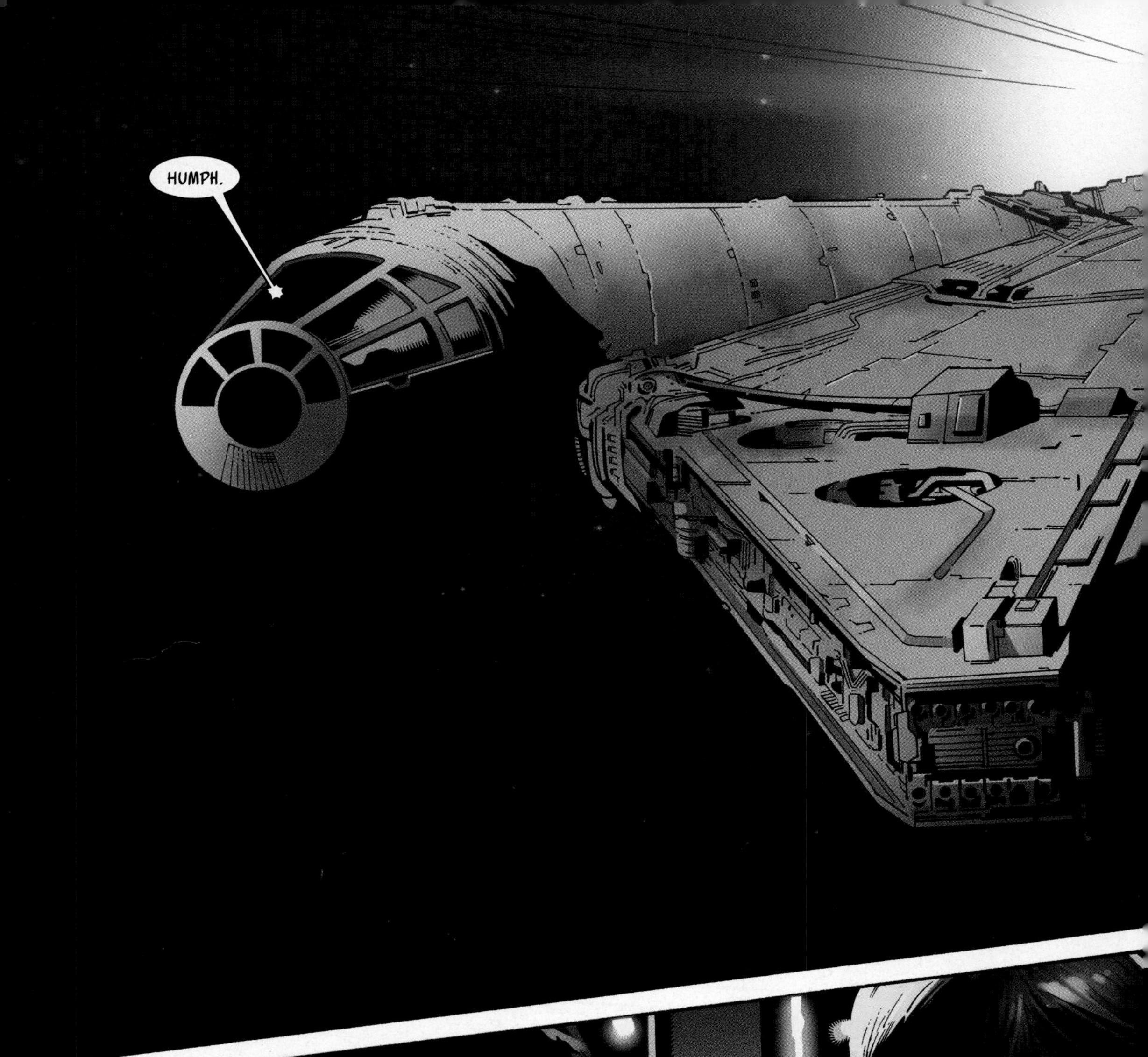
HUMPH.

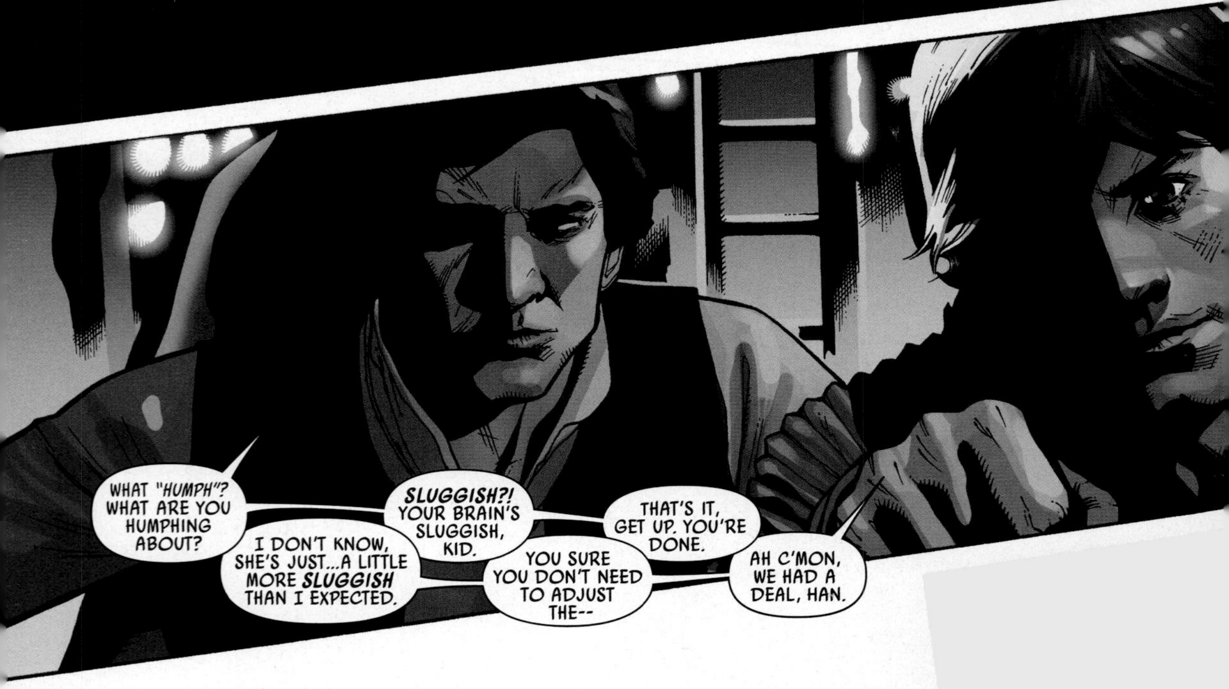
WHAT "HUMPH"? WHAT ARE YOU HUMPHING ABOUT?
I DON'T KNOW, SHE'S JUST...A LITTLE MORE SLUGGISH THAN I EXPECTED.
SLUGGISH?! YOUR BRAIN'S SLUGGISH, KID.
YOU SURE YOU DON'T NEED TO ADJUST THE--
THAT'S IT, GET UP. YOU'RE DONE.
AH C'MON, WE HAD A DEAL, HAN.

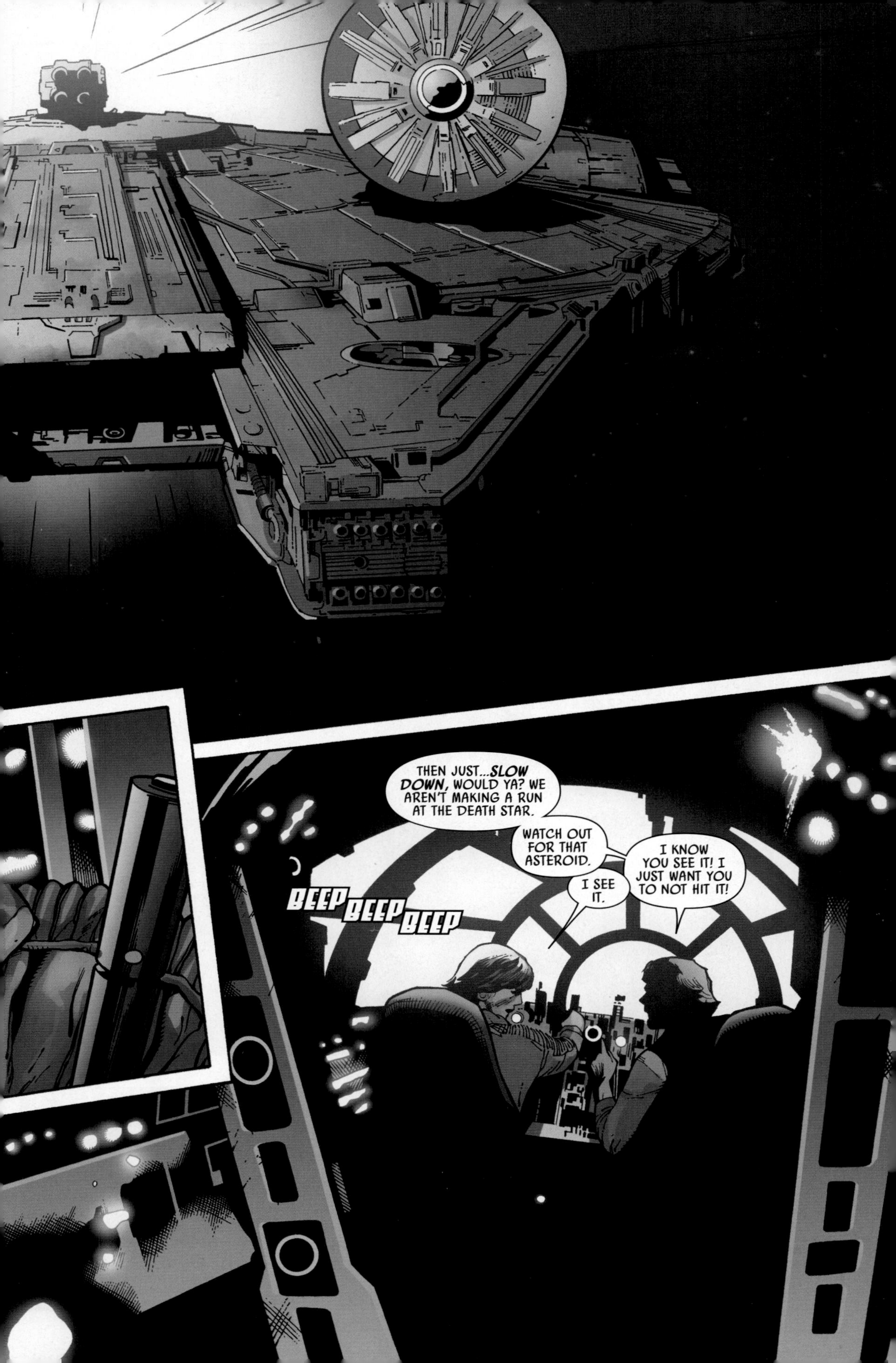
THEN JUST...**SLOW DOWN,** WOULD YA? WE AREN'T MAKING A RUN AT THE DEATH STAR.
WATCH OUT FOR THAT ASTEROID.
I KNOW YOU SEE IT! I JUST WANT YOU TO NOT HIT IT!
I SEE IT.
BEEP BEEP BEEP

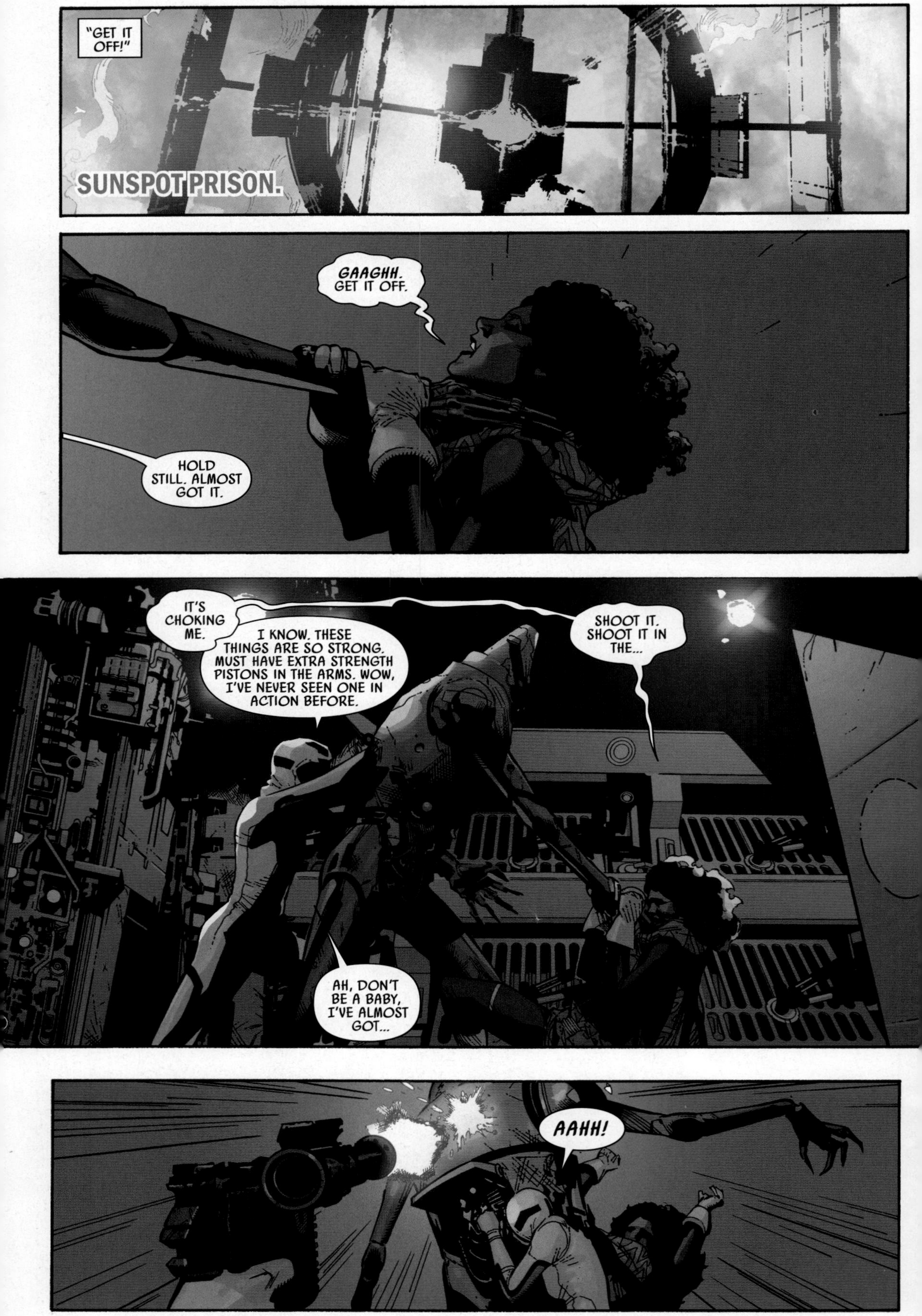
"GET IT OFF!"
SUNSPOT PRISON.
GAAGHH. GET IT OFF.
HOLD STILL. ALMOST GOT IT.
IT'S CHOKING ME.
I KNOW. THESE THINGS ARE SO STRONG. MUST HAVE EXTRA STRENGTH PISTONS IN THE ARMS. WOW, I'VE NEVER SEEN ONE IN ACTION BEFORE.
SHOOT IT. SHOOT IT IN THE...
AH, DON'T BE A BABY, I'VE ALMOST GOT...
AAHH!

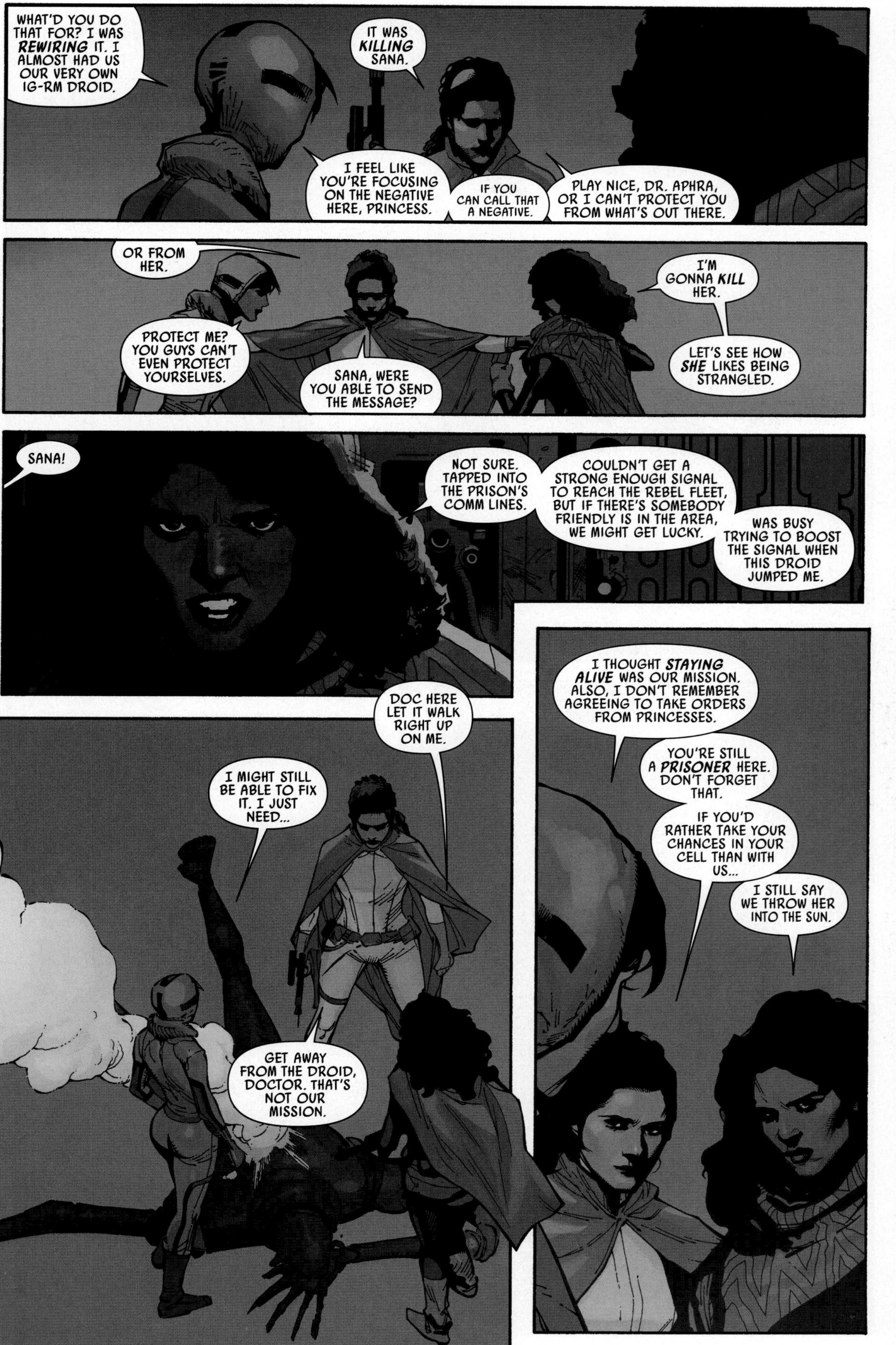
WHAT'D YOU DO THAT FOR? I WAS REWIRING IT. I ALMOST HAD US OUR VERY OWN IG-RM DROID.
IT WAS KILLING SANA.
I FEEL LIKE YOU'RE FOCUSING ON THE NEGATIVE HERE, PRINCESS.
IF YOU CAN CALL THAT A NEGATIVE.
PLAY NICE, DR. APHRA, OR I CAN'T PROTECT YOU FROM WHAT'S OUT THERE.
OR FROM HER.
PROTECT ME? YOU GUYS CAN'T EVEN PROTECT YOURSELVES.
SANA, WERE YOU ABLE TO SEND THE MESSAGE?
I'M GONNA KILL HER.
LET'S SEE HOW SHE LIKES BEING STRANGLED.
SANA!
NOT SURE. TAPPED INTO THE PRISON'S COMM LINES.
COULDN'T GET A STRONG ENOUGH SIGNAL TO REACH THE REBEL FLEET, BUT IF THERE'S SOMEBODY FRIENDLY IS IN THE AREA, WE MIGHT GET LUCKY.
WAS BUSY TRYING TO BOOST THE SIGNAL WHEN THIS DROID JUMPED ME.
DOC HERE LET IT WALK RIGHT UP ON ME.
I MIGHT STILL BE ABLE TO FIX IT. I JUST NEED...
GET AWAY FROM THE DROID, DOCTOR. THAT'S NOT OUR MISSION.
I THOUGHT STAYING ALIVE WAS OUR MISSION. ALSO, I DON'T REMEMBER AGREEING TO TAKE ORDERS FROM PRINCESSES.
YOU'RE STILL A PRISONER HERE. DON'T FORGET THAT.
IF YOU'D RATHER TAKE YOUR CHANCES IN YOUR CELL THAN WITH US...
I STILL SAY WE THROW HER INTO THE SUN.

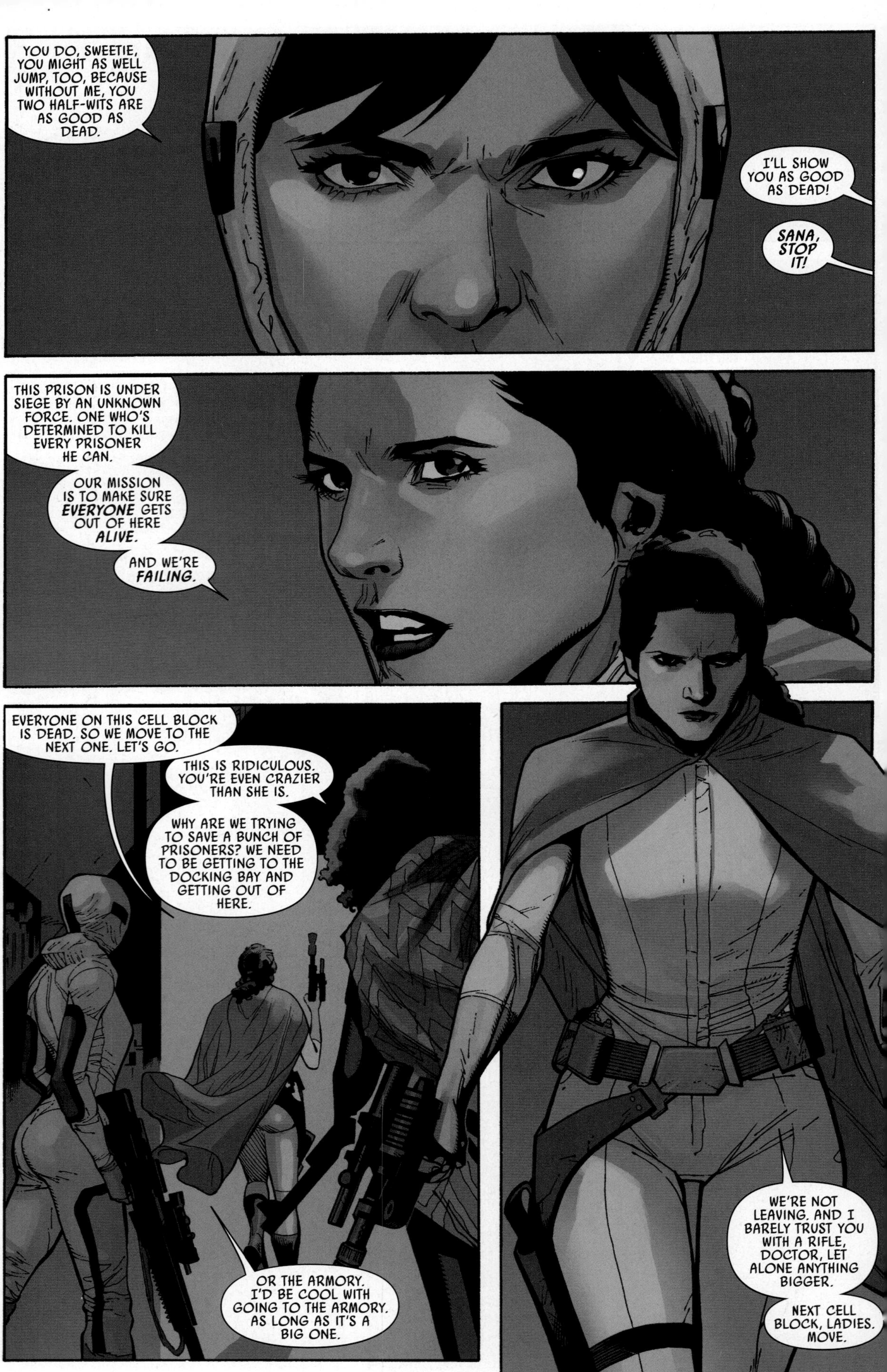
YOU DO, SWEETIE, YOU MIGHT AS WELL JUMP, TOO, BECAUSE WITHOUT ME, YOU TWO HALF-WITS ARE AS GOOD AS DEAD.
I'LL SHOW YOU AS GOOD AS DEAD!
SANA, STOP IT!
THIS PRISON IS UNDER SIEGE BY AN UNKNOWN FORCE. ONE WHO'S DETERMINED TO KILL EVERY PRISONER HE CAN.
OUR MISSION IS TO MAKE SURE EVERYONE GETS OUT OF HERE ALIVE.
AND WE'RE FAILING.
EVERYONE ON THIS CELL BLOCK IS DEAD. SO WE MOVE TO THE NEXT ONE. LET'S GO.
THIS IS RIDICULOUS. YOU'RE EVEN CRAZIER THAN SHE IS.
WHY ARE WE TRYING TO SAVE A BUNCH OF PRISONERS? WE NEED TO BE GETTING TO THE DOCKING BAY AND GETTING OUT OF HERE.
OR THE ARMORY. I'D BE COOL WITH GOING TO THE ARMORY. AS LONG AS IT'S A BIG ONE.
WE'RE NOT LEAVING. AND I BARELY TRUST YOU WITH A RIFLE, DOCTOR, LET ALONE ANYTHING BIGGER.
NEXT CELL BLOCK, LADIES. MOVE.

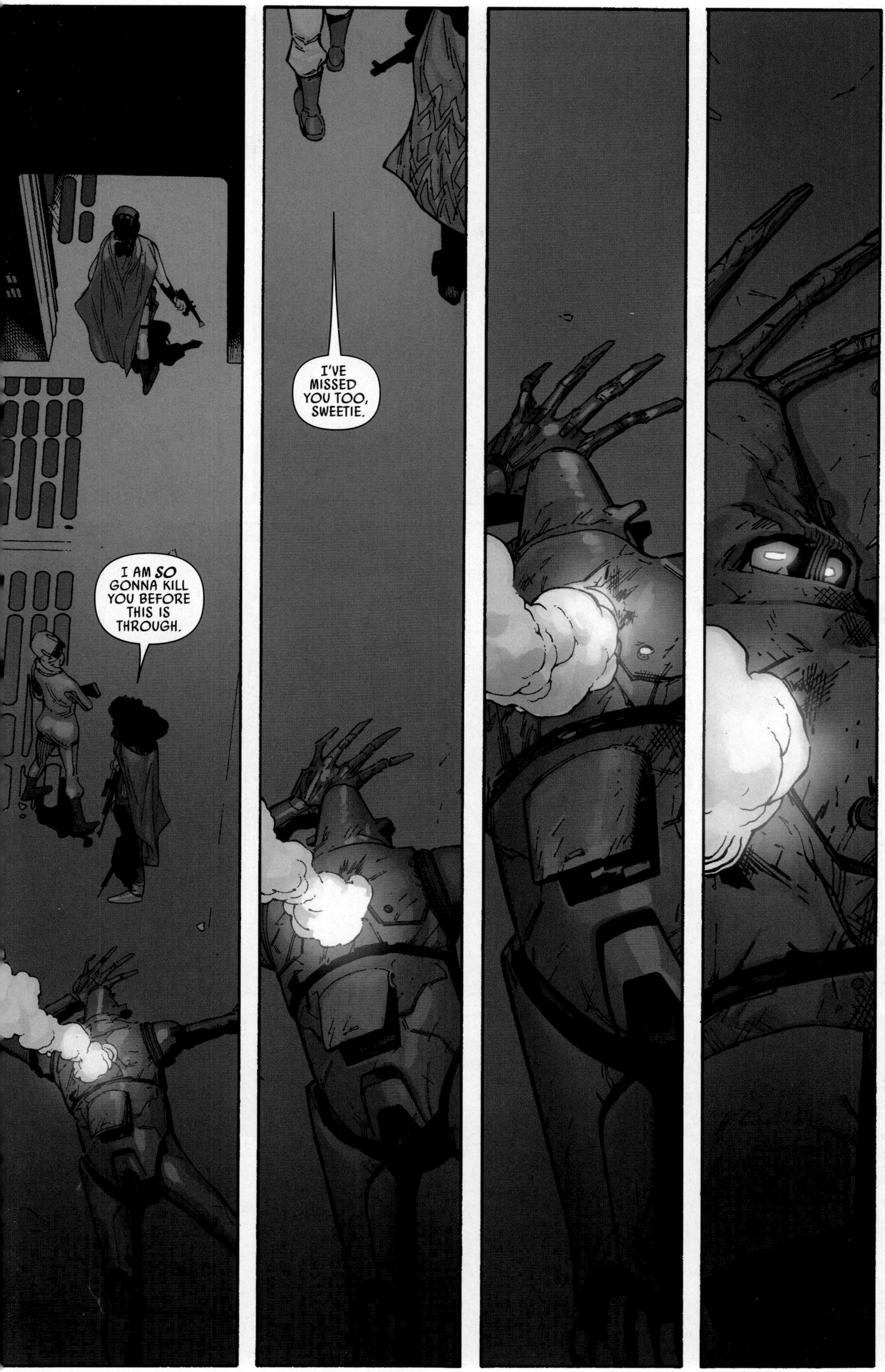
I AM SO GONNA KILL YOU BEFORE THIS IS THROUGH.
I'VE MISSED YOU TOO, SWEETIE.

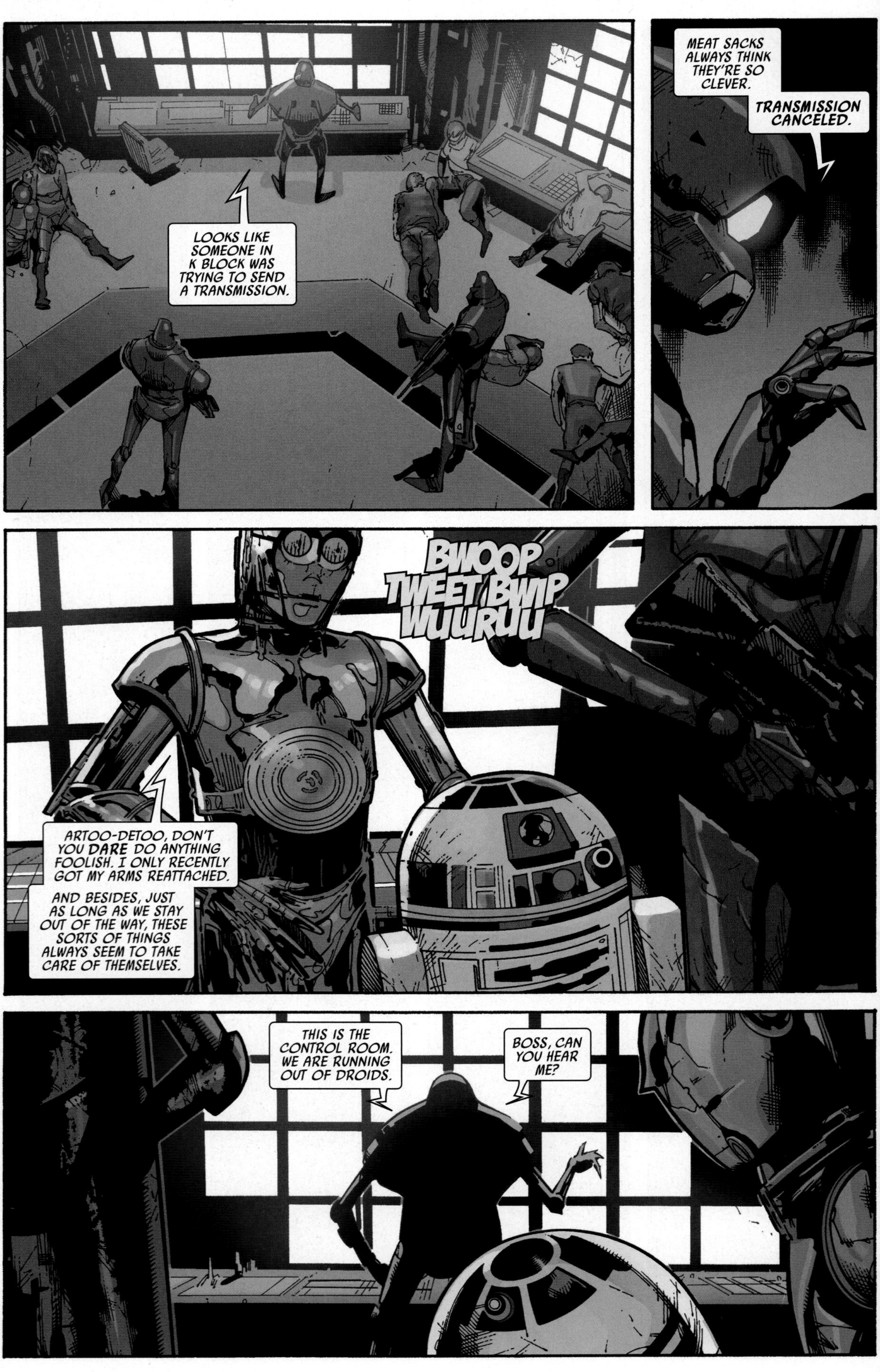
LOOKS LIKE SOMEONE IN K BLOCK WAS TRYING TO SEND A TRANSMISSION.
MEAT SACKS ALWAYS THINK THEY'RE SO CLEVER.
TRANSMISSION CANCELED.
BWOOP TWEET BWIP WUURUU
ARTOO-DETOO, DON'T YOU DARE DO ANYTHING FOOLISH. I ONLY RECENTLY GOT MY ARMS REATTACHED.
AND BESIDES, JUST AS LONG AS WE STAY OUT OF THE WAY, THESE SORTS OF THINGS ALWAYS SEEM TO TAKE CARE OF THEMSELVES.
THIS IS THE CONTROL ROOM. WE ARE RUNNING OUT OF DROIDS.
BOSS, CAN YOU HEAR ME?

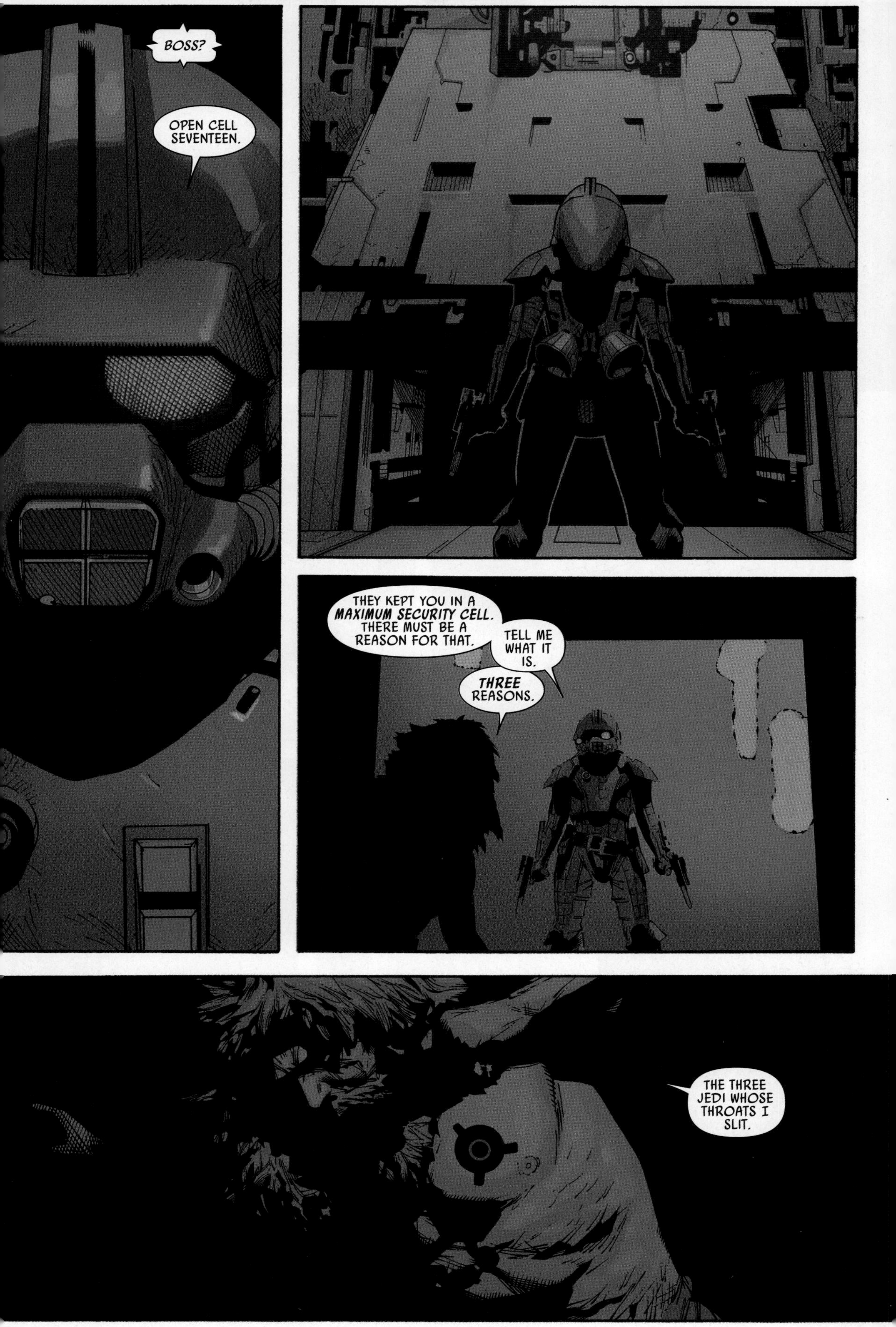
BOSS?
OPEN CELL SEVENTEEN.
THEY KEPT YOU IN A *MAXIMUM SECURITY CELL*. THERE MUST BE A REASON FOR THAT.
TELL ME WHAT IT IS.
THREE REASONS.
THE THREE JEDI WHOSE THROATS I SLIT.

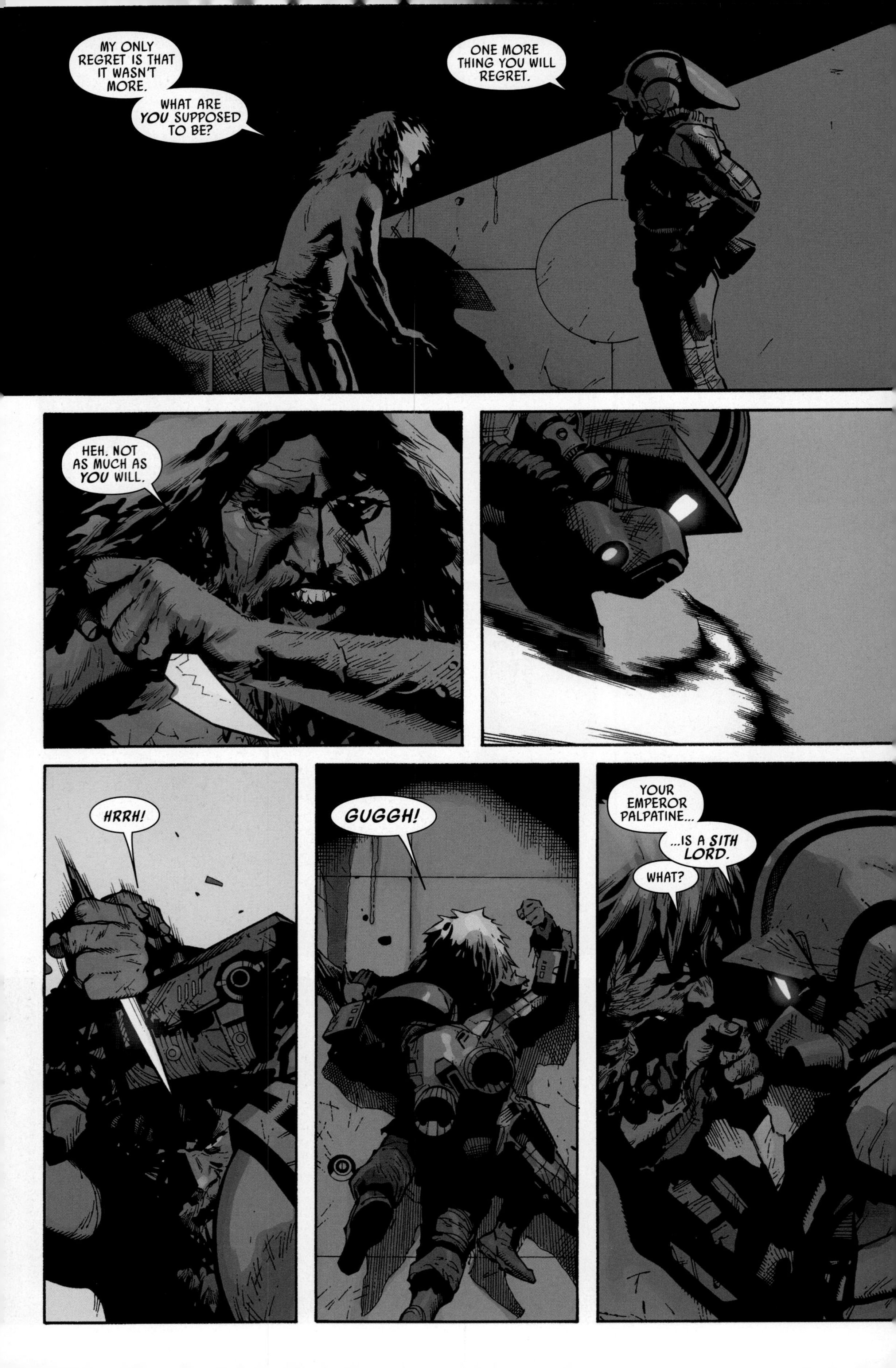
MY ONLY REGRET IS THAT IT WASN'T MORE.
WHAT ARE YOU SUPPOSED TO BE?
ONE MORE THING YOU WILL REGRET.
HEH. NOT AS MUCH AS YOU WILL.
HRRH!
GUGGH!
YOUR EMPEROR PALPATINE...
...IS A SITH LORD.
WHAT?

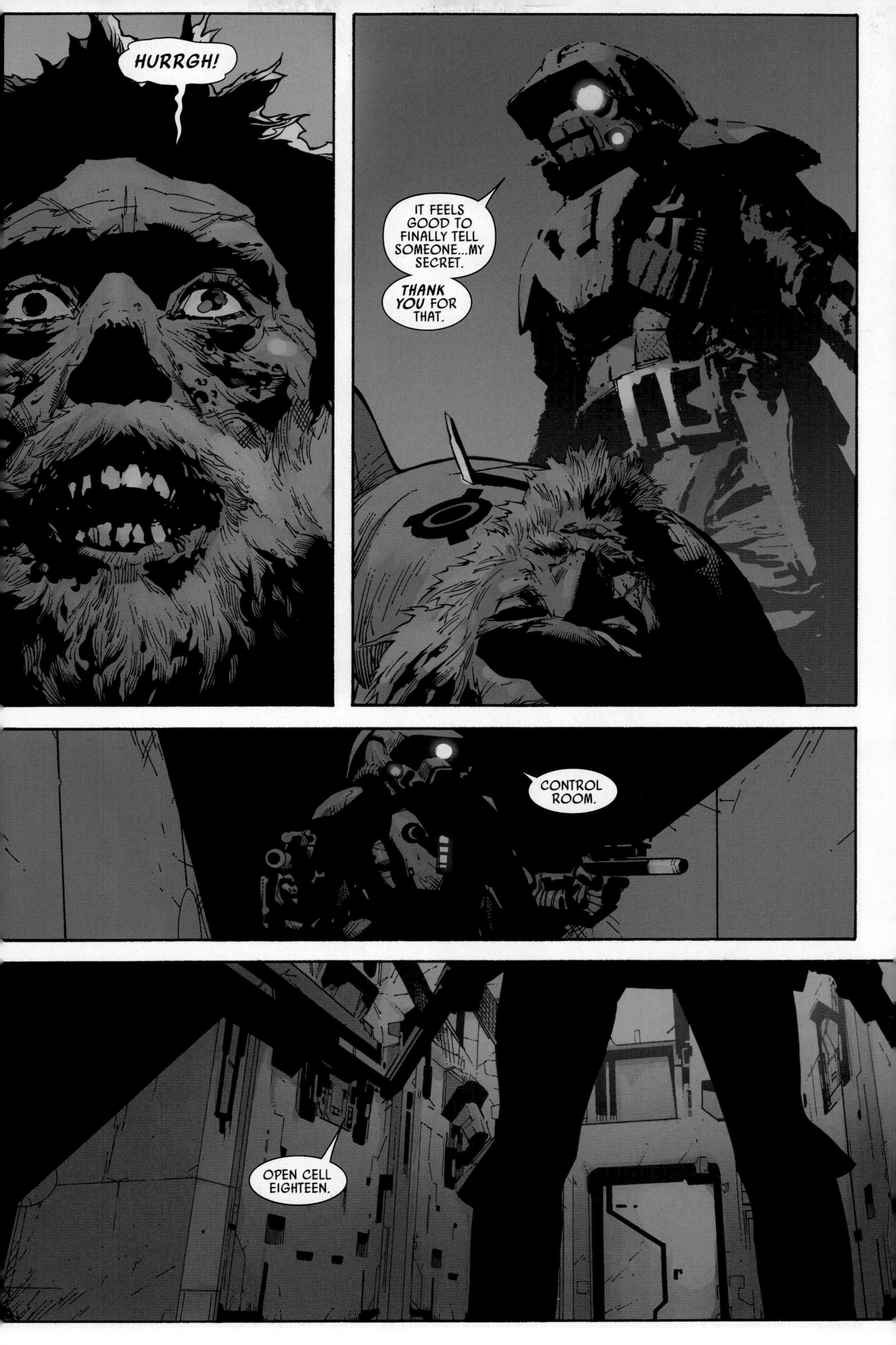
HURRGH!
IT FEELS GOOD TO FINALLY TELL SOMEONE...MY SECRET.
THANK YOU FOR THAT.
CONTROL ROOM.
OPEN CELL EIGHTEEN.

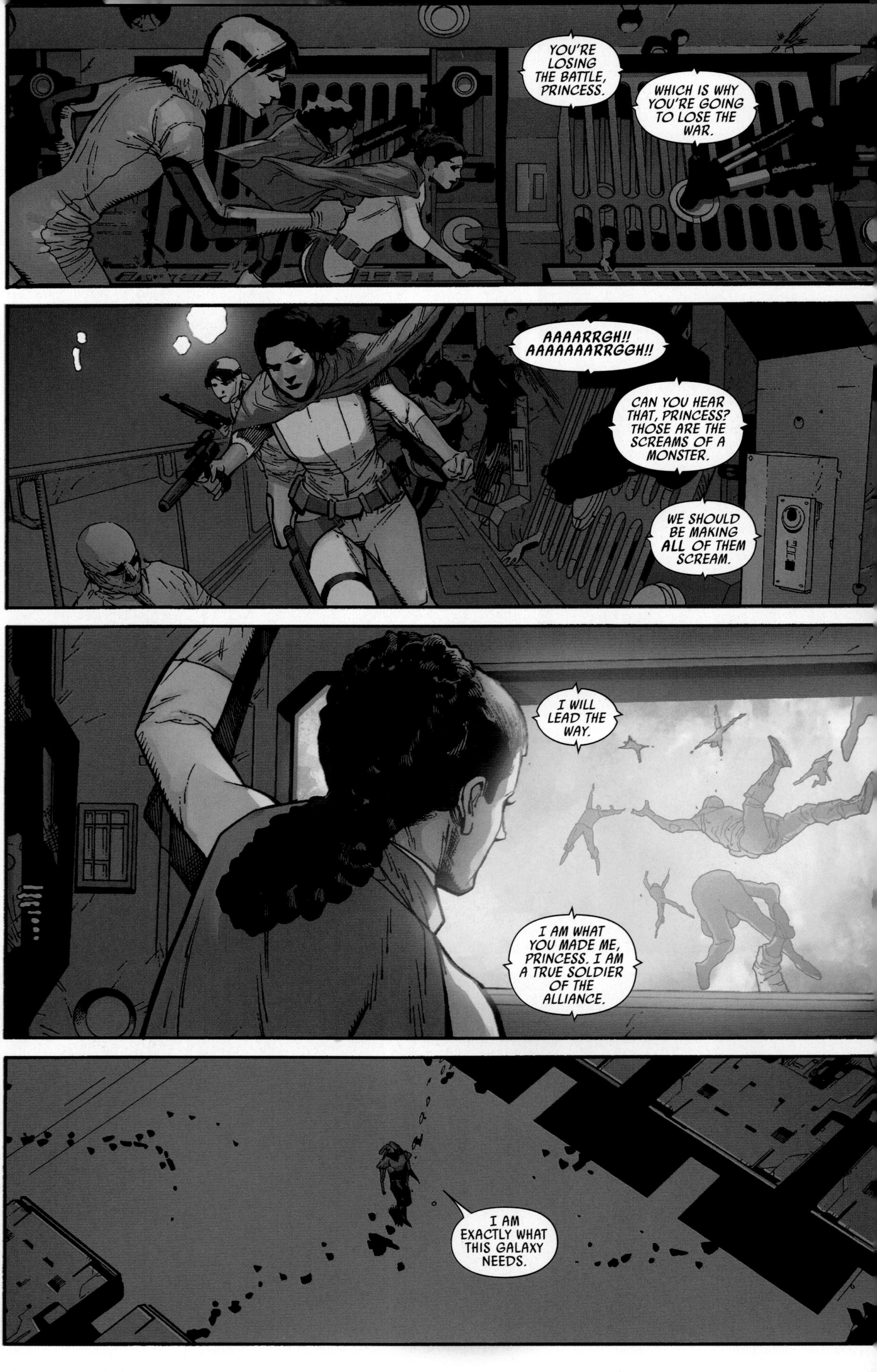
YOU'RE LOSING THE BATTLE, PRINCESS.
WHICH IS WHY YOU'RE GOING TO LOSE THE WAR.
AAAAARRGH!! AAAAAAAARRGGH!!
CAN YOU HEAR THAT, PRINCESS? THOSE ARE THE SCREAMS OF A MONSTER.
WE SHOULD BE MAKING ALL OF THEM SCREAM.
I WILL LEAD THE WAY.
I AM WHAT YOU MADE ME, PRINCESS. I AM A TRUE SOLDIER OF THE ALLIANCE.
I AM EXACTLY WHAT THIS GALAXY NEEDS.

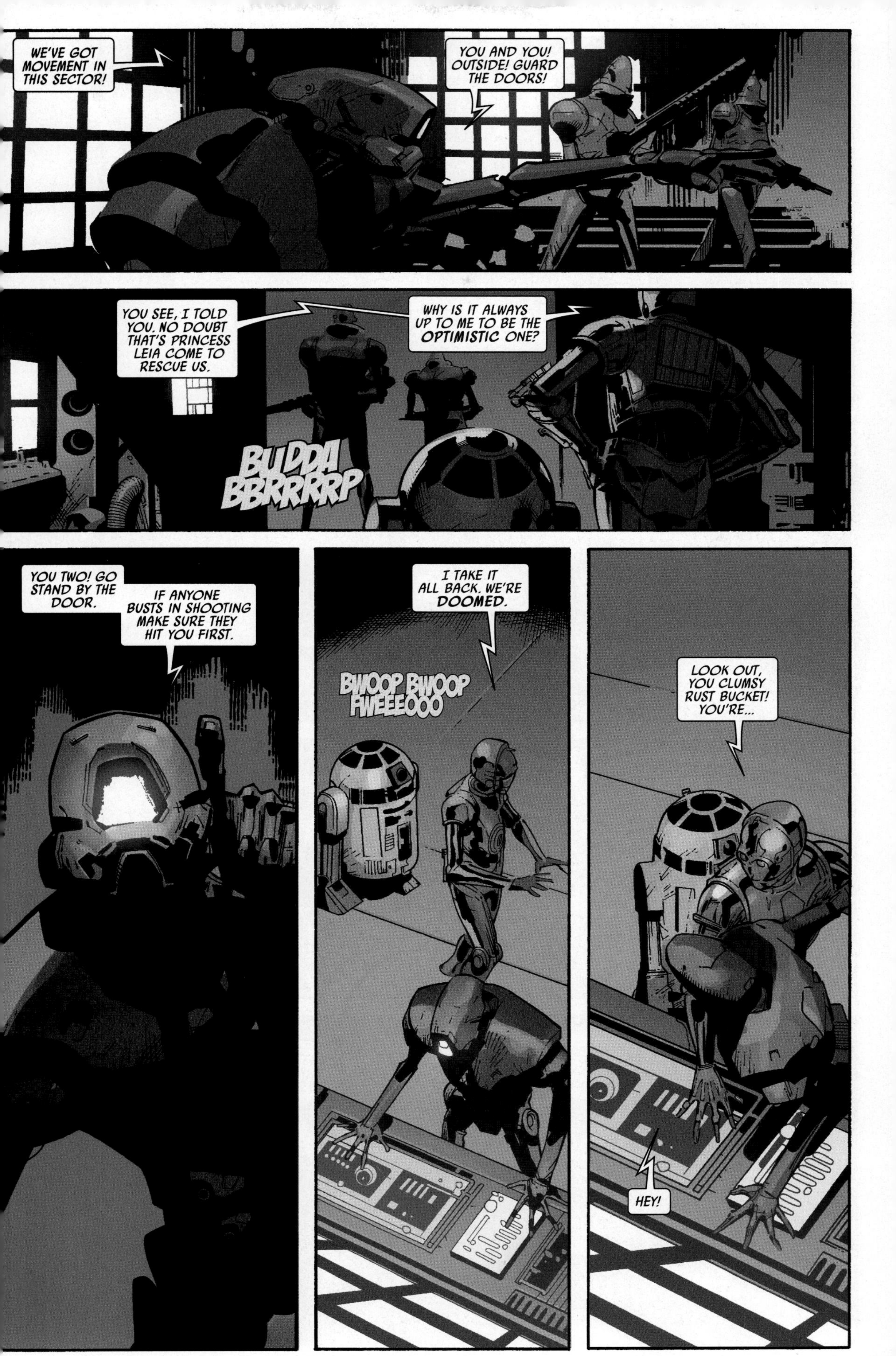
WE'VE GOT MOVEMENT IN THIS SECTOR!
YOU AND YOU! OUTSIDE! GUARD THE DOORS!
YOU SEE, I TOLD YOU. NO DOUBT THAT'S PRINCESS LEIA COME TO RESCUE US.
WHY IS IT ALWAYS UP TO ME TO BE THE OPTIMISTIC ONE?
BUDDA BBRRRRP
YOU TWO! GO STAND BY THE DOOR.
IF ANYONE BUSTS IN SHOOTING MAKE SURE THEY HIT YOU FIRST.
I TAKE IT ALL BACK. WE'RE DOOMED.
BWOOP BWOOP FWEEEOOO
LOOK OUT, YOU CLUMSY RUST BUCKET! YOU'RE...
HEY!

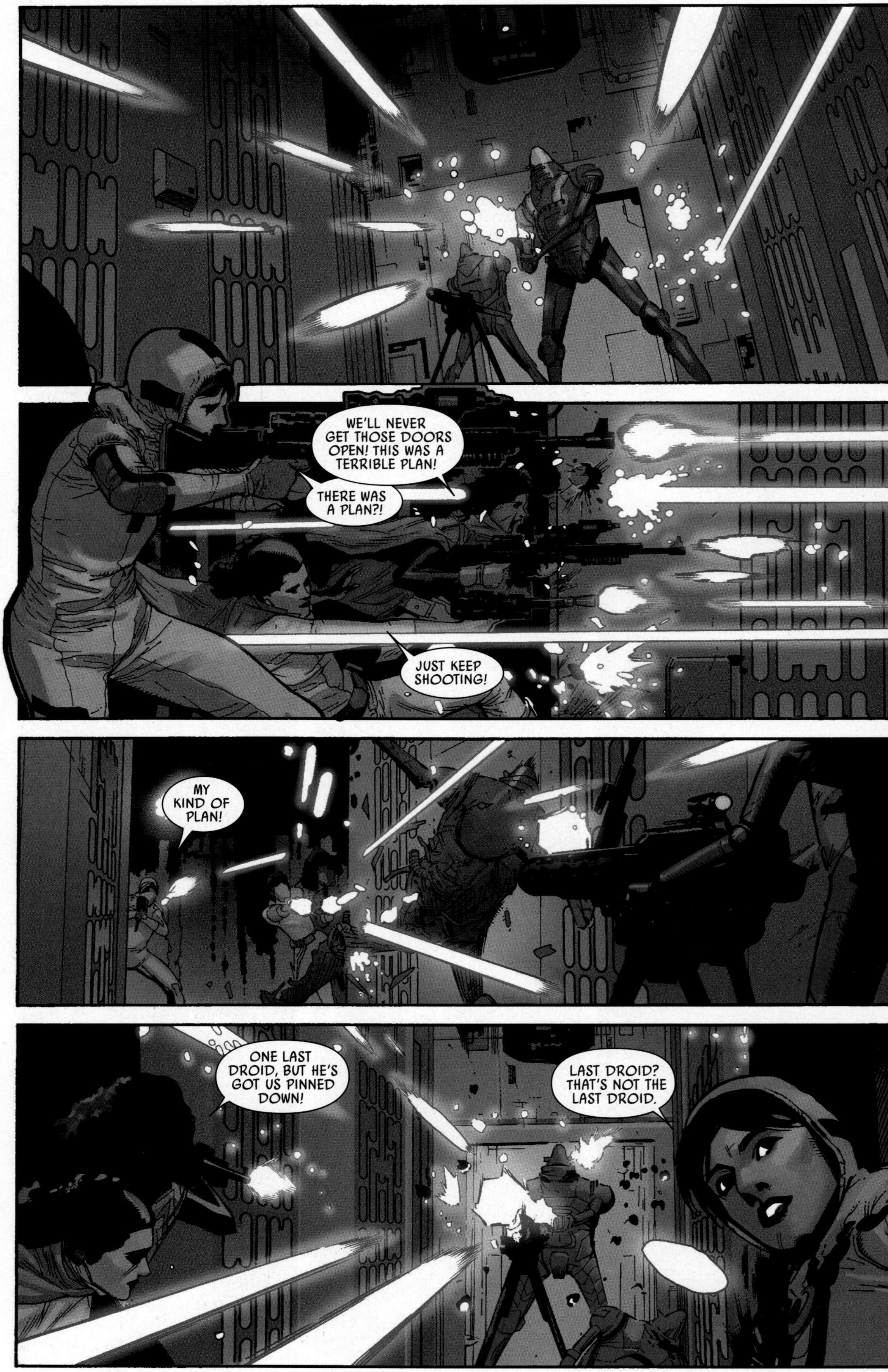
WE'LL NEVER GET THOSE DOORS OPEN! THIS WAS A TERRIBLE PLAN!
THERE WAS A PLAN?!
JUST KEEP SHOOTING!
MY KIND OF PLAN!
ONE LAST DROID, BUT HE'S GOT US PINNED DOWN!
LAST DROID? THAT'S NOT THE LAST DROID.

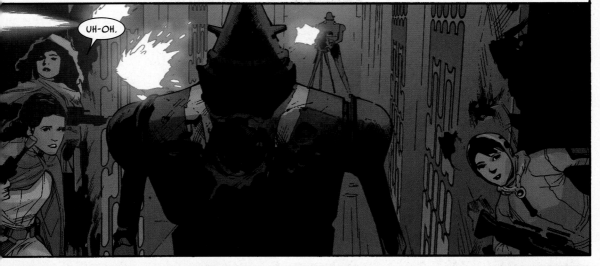

UH-OH.

SEE? TOLD YOU I WAS REWIRING IT.

WWWRRRZZT

WWWRRRZZT
VZZZZK

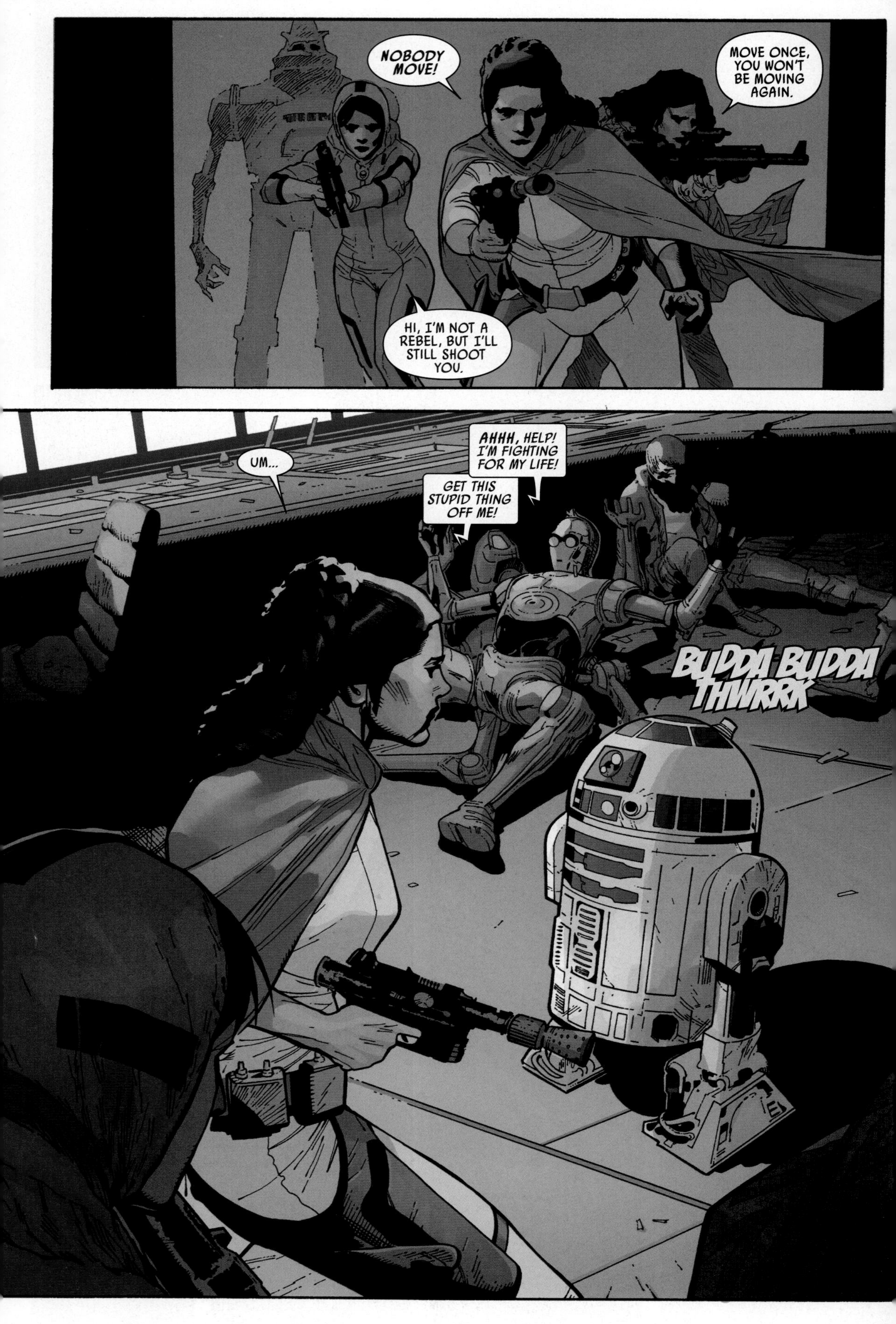
NOBODY MOVE!
MOVE ONCE, YOU WON'T BE MOVING AGAIN.
HI, I'M NOT A REBEL, BUT I'LL STILL SHOOT YOU.
UM...
AHHH, HELP! I'M FIGHTING FOR MY LIFE!
GET THIS STUPID THING OFF ME!
BUDDA BUDDA THWRRK

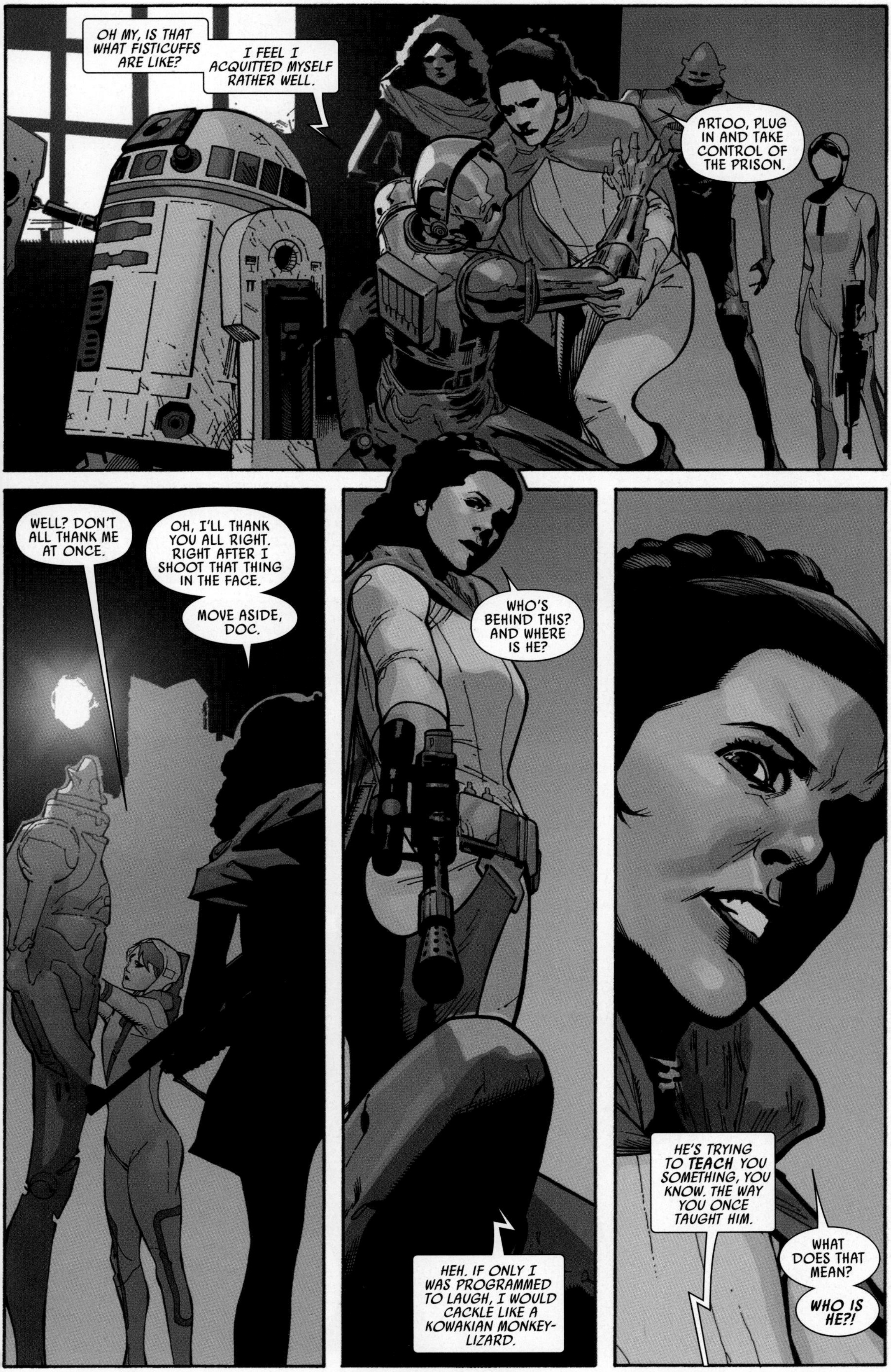
OH MY, IS THAT WHAT FISTICUFFS ARE LIKE?
I FEEL I ACQUITTED MYSELF RATHER WELL.
ARTOO, PLUG IN AND TAKE CONTROL OF THE PRISON.
WELL? DON'T ALL THANK ME AT ONCE.
OH, I'LL THANK YOU ALL RIGHT. RIGHT AFTER I SHOOT THAT THING IN THE FACE.
MOVE ASIDE, DOC.
WHO'S BEHIND THIS? AND WHERE IS HE?
HEH. IF ONLY I WAS PROGRAMMED TO LAUGH, I WOULD CACKLE LIKE A KOWAKIAN MONKEY-LIZARD.
HE'S TRYING TO TEACH YOU SOMETHING, YOU KNOW. THE WAY YOU ONCE TAUGHT HIM.
WHAT DOES THAT MEAN?
WHO IS HE?!

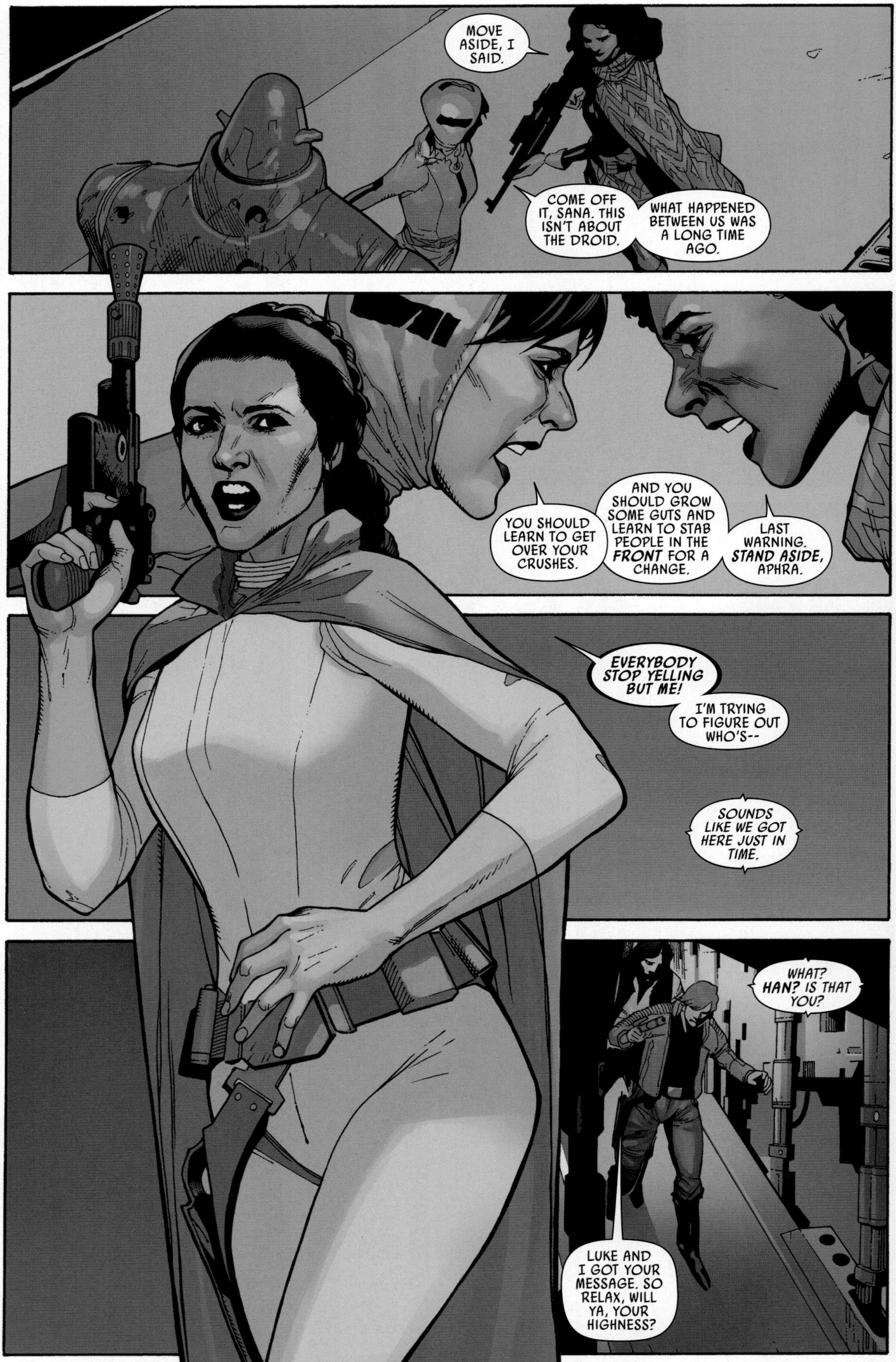
MOVE ASIDE, I SAID.
COME OFF IT, SANA. THIS ISN'T ABOUT THE DROID.
WHAT HAPPENED BETWEEN US WAS A LONG TIME AGO.
YOU SHOULD LEARN TO GET OVER YOUR CRUSHES.
AND YOU SHOULD GROW SOME GUTS AND LEARN TO STAB PEOPLE IN THE **FRONT** FOR A CHANGE.
LAST WARNING. ***STAND ASIDE,*** APHRA.
EVERYBODY STOP YELLING BUT ME!
I'M TRYING TO FIGURE OUT WHO'S--
SOUNDS LIKE WE GOT HERE JUST IN TIME.
*WHAT? **HAN?** IS THAT YOU?*
LUKE AND I GOT YOUR MESSAGE. SO RELAX, WILL YA, YOUR HIGHNESS?

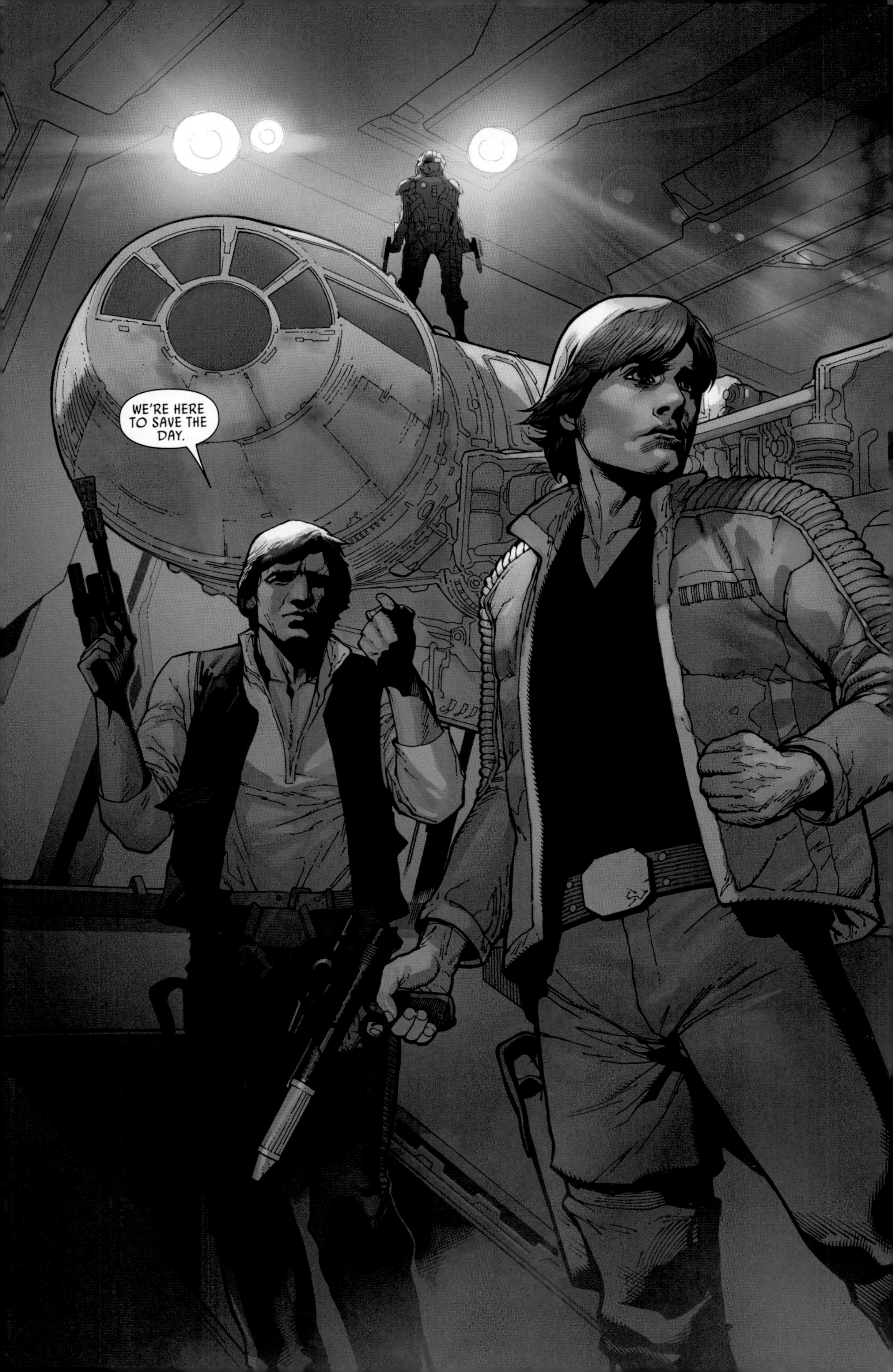
WE'RE HERE TO SAVE THE DAY.

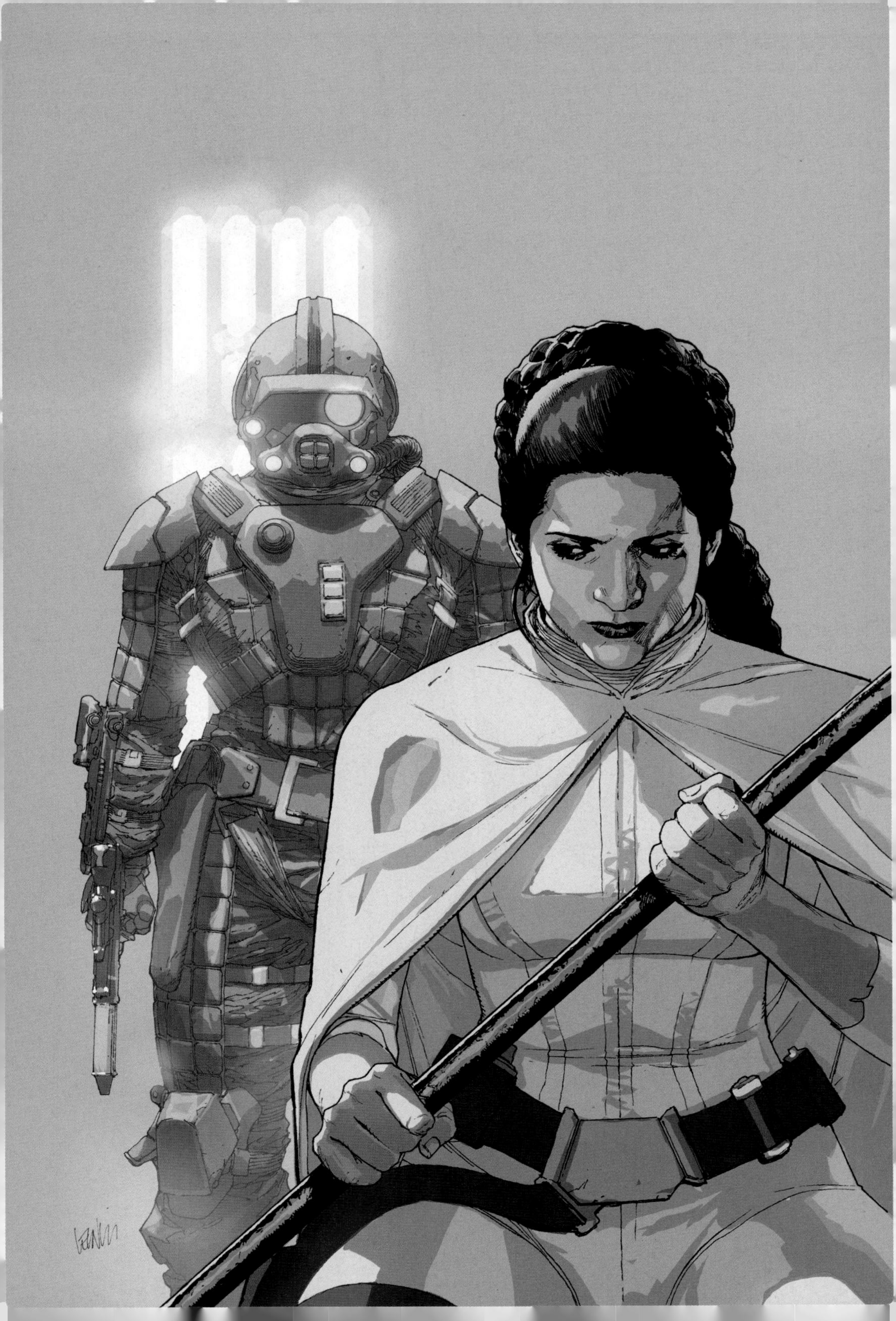

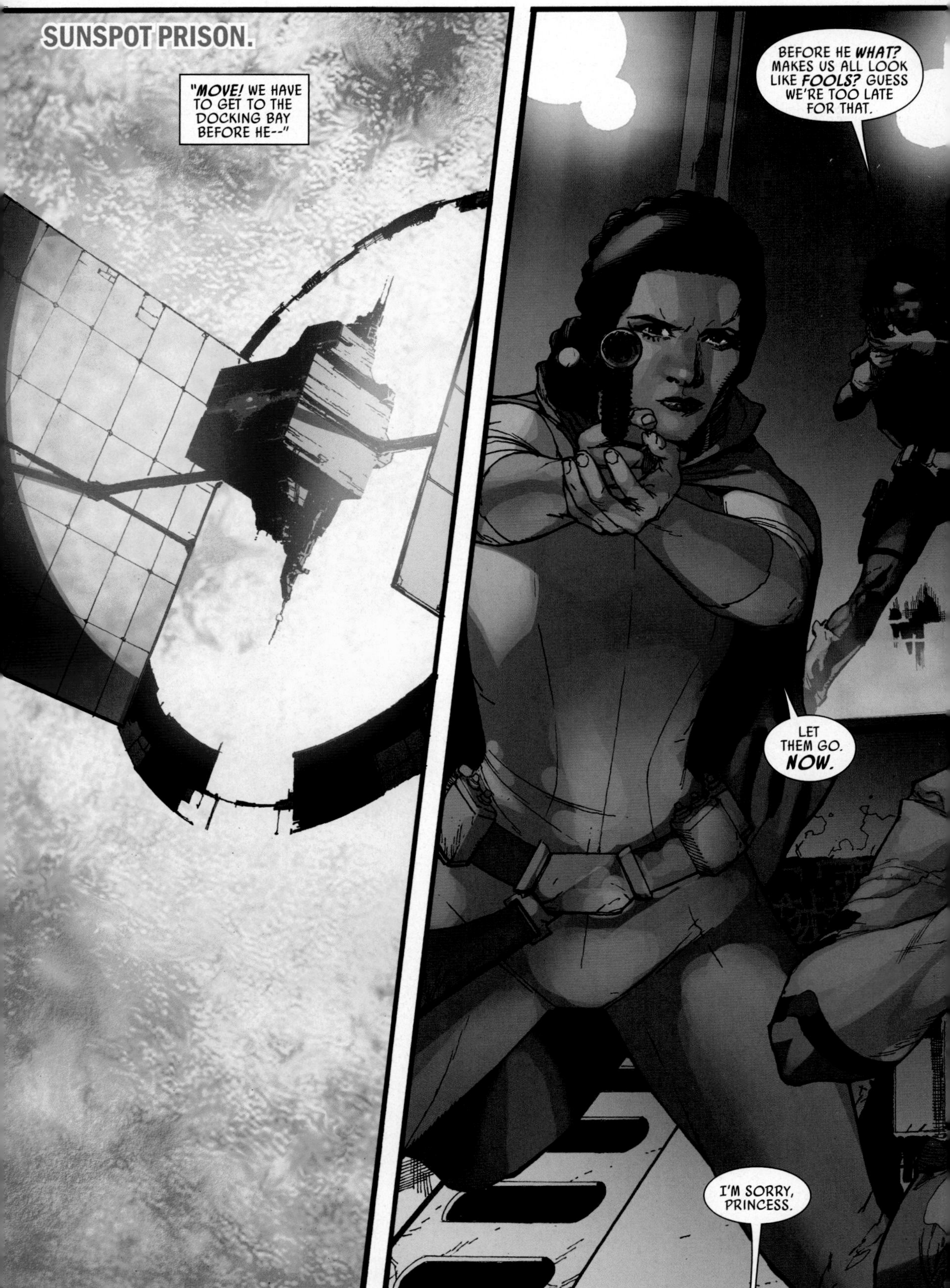
SUNSPOT PRISON.
"MOVE! WE HAVE TO GET TO THE DOCKING BAY BEFORE HE--"
BEFORE HE WHAT? MAKES US ALL LOOK LIKE FOOLS? GUESS WE'RE TOO LATE FOR THAT.
LET THEM GO. NOW.
I'M SORRY, PRINCESS.

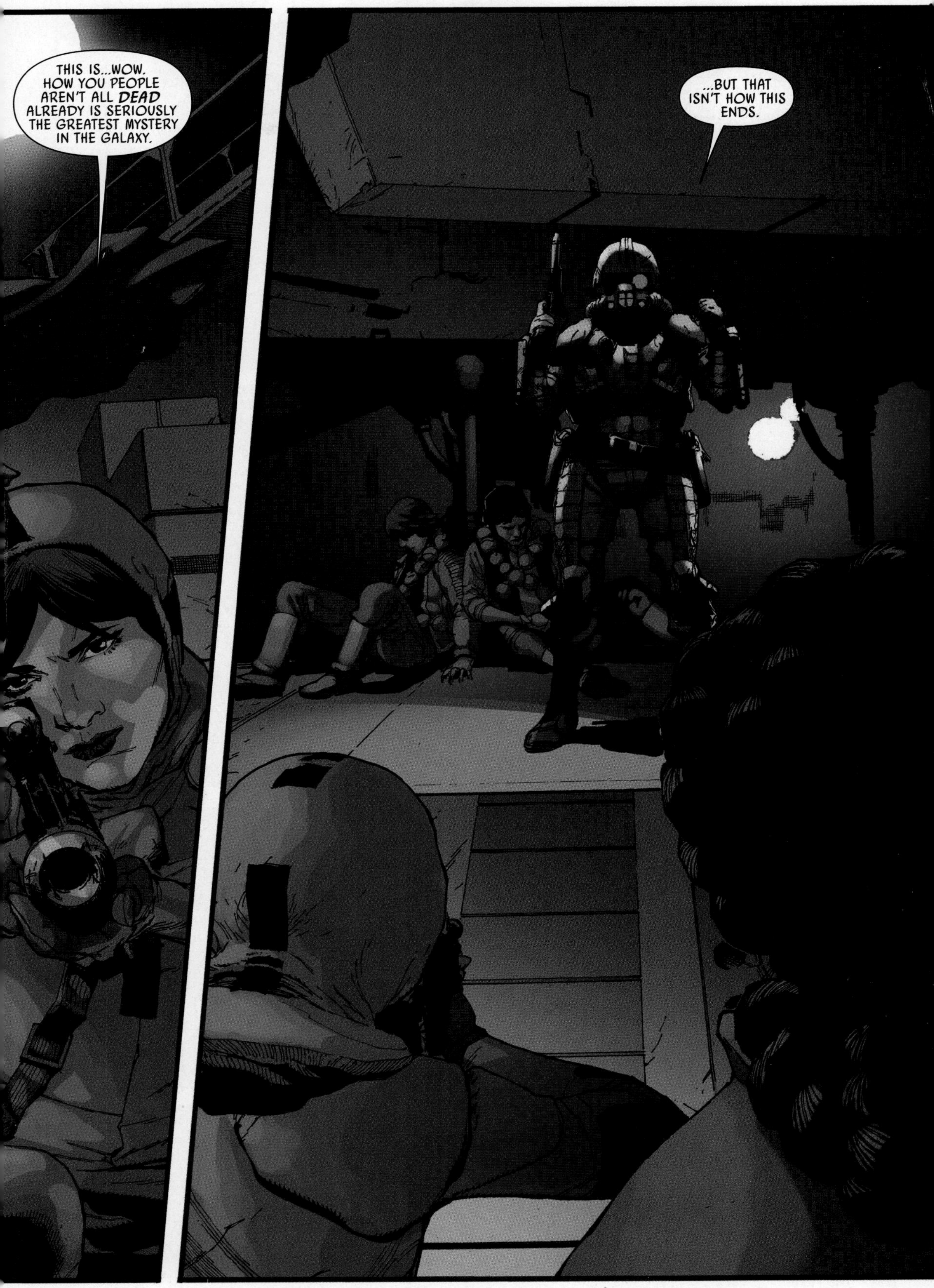
THIS IS...WOW. HOW YOU PEOPLE AREN'T ALL DEAD ALREADY IS SERIOUSLY THE GREATEST MYSTERY IN THE GALAXY.
...BUT THAT ISN'T HOW THIS ENDS.

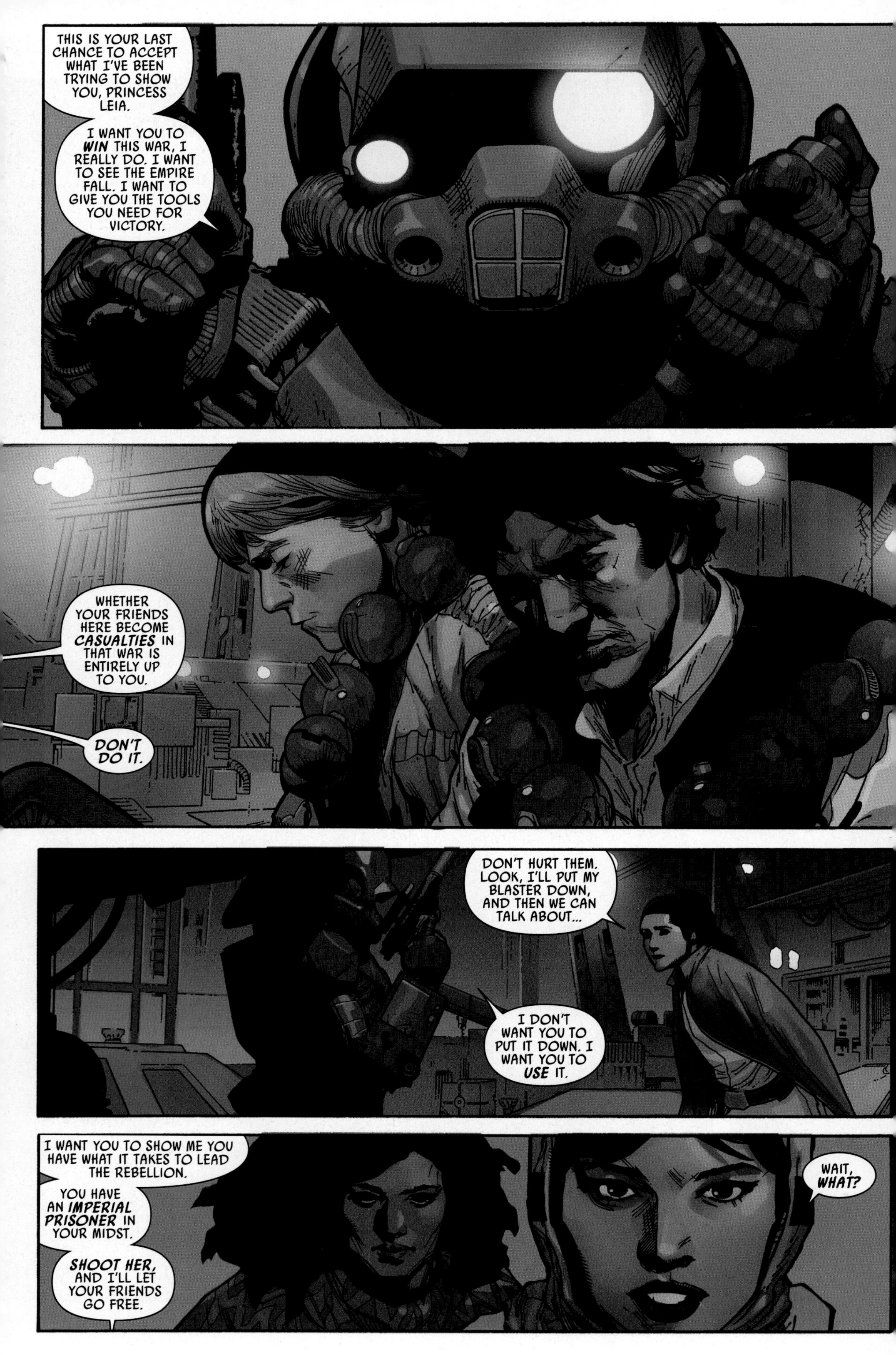
THIS IS YOUR LAST CHANCE TO ACCEPT WHAT I'VE BEEN TRYING TO SHOW YOU, PRINCESS LEIA.
I WANT YOU TO WIN THIS WAR, I REALLY DO. I WANT TO SEE THE EMPIRE FALL. I WANT TO GIVE YOU THE TOOLS YOU NEED FOR VICTORY.
WHETHER YOUR FRIENDS HERE BECOME CASUALTIES IN THAT WAR IS ENTIRELY UP TO YOU.
DON'T DO IT.
DON'T HURT THEM. LOOK, I'LL PUT MY BLASTER DOWN, AND THEN WE CAN TALK ABOUT...
I DON'T WANT YOU TO PUT IT DOWN. I WANT YOU TO USE IT.
I WANT YOU TO SHOW ME YOU HAVE WHAT IT TAKES TO LEAD THE REBELLION.
YOU HAVE AN IMPERIAL PRISONER IN YOUR MIDST.
SHOOT HER, AND I'LL LET YOUR FRIENDS GO FREE.
WAIT, WHAT?

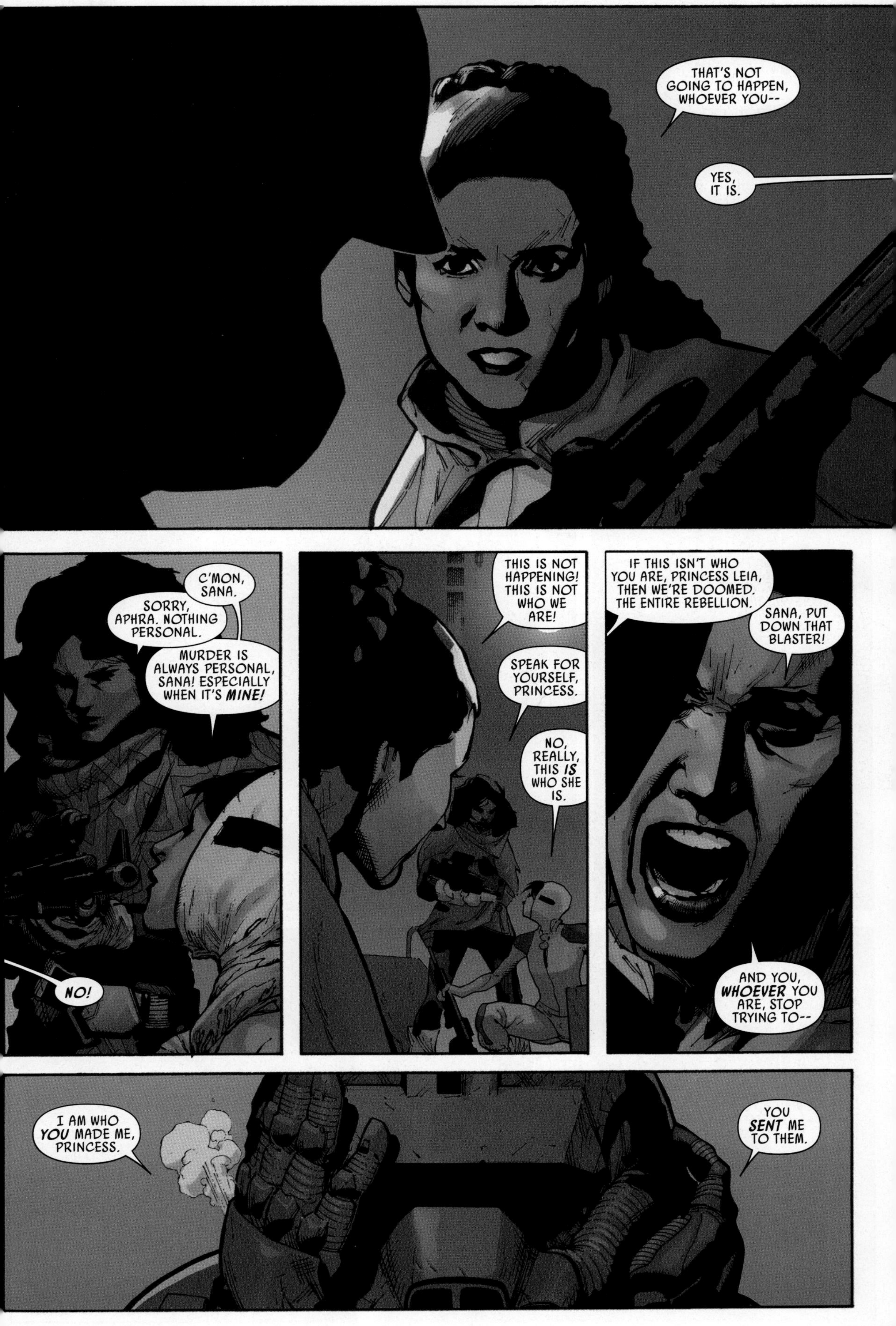
THAT'S NOT GOING TO HAPPEN, WHOEVER YOU--
YES, IT IS.
C'MON, SANA.
SORRY, APHRA. NOTHING PERSONAL.
MURDER IS ALWAYS PERSONAL, SANA! ESPECIALLY WHEN IT'S MINE!
NO!
THIS IS NOT HAPPENING! THIS IS NOT WHO WE ARE!
SPEAK FOR YOURSELF, PRINCESS.
NO, REALLY, THIS IS WHO SHE IS.
IF THIS ISN'T WHO YOU ARE, PRINCESS LEIA, THEN WE'RE DOOMED. THE ENTIRE REBELLION.
SANA, PUT DOWN THAT BLASTER!
AND YOU, WHOEVER YOU ARE, STOP TRYING TO--
I AM WHO YOU MADE ME, PRINCESS.
YOU SENT ME TO THEM.

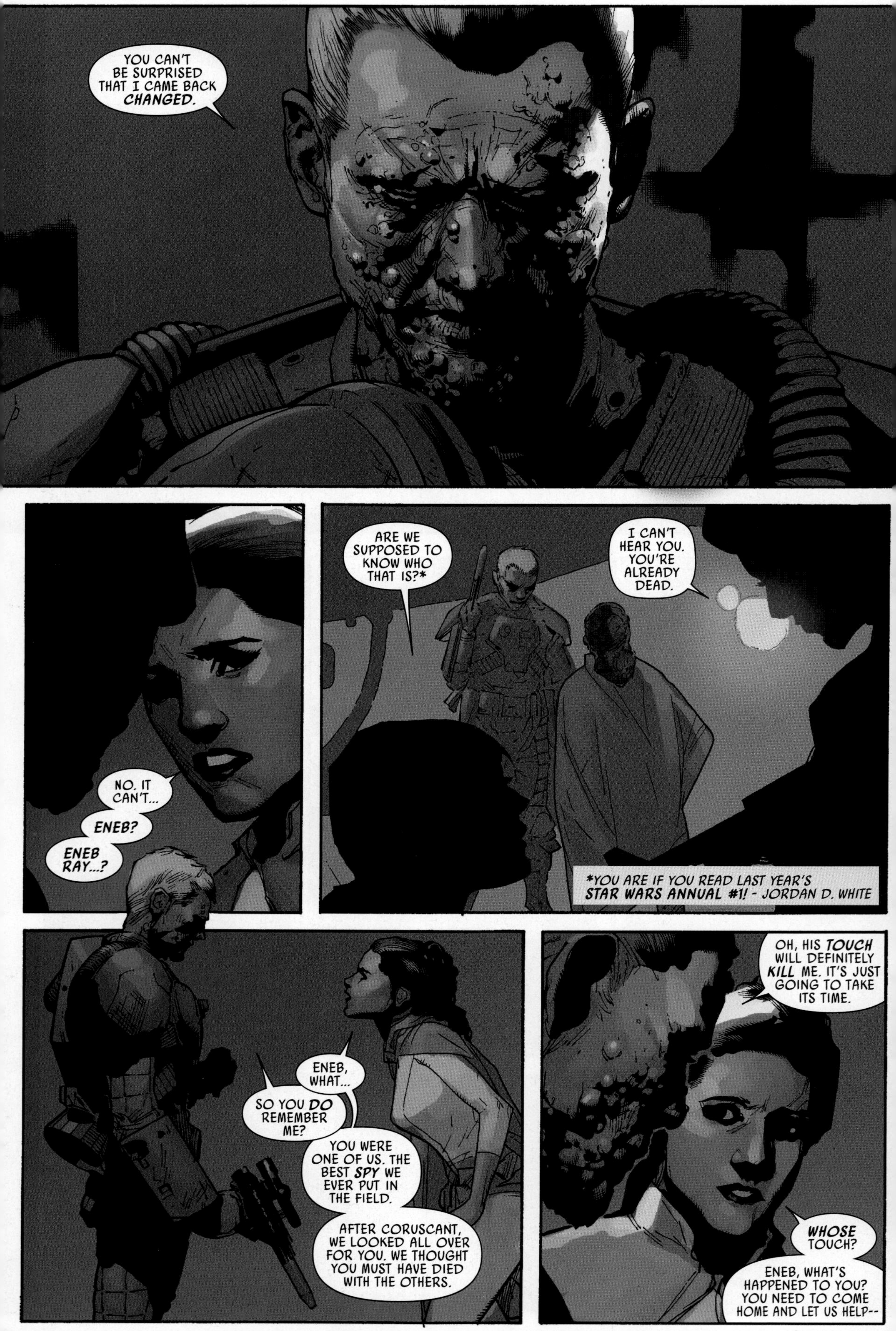

YOU CAN'T BE SURPRISED THAT I CAME BACK *CHANGED.*
NO. IT CAN'T...
ENEB?
ENEB RAY...?
ARE WE SUPPOSED TO KNOW WHO THAT IS?*
I CAN'T HEAR YOU. YOU'RE ALREADY DEAD.
*YOU ARE IF YOU READ LAST YEAR'S **STAR WARS ANNUAL #1!** - JORDAN D. WHITE
ENEB, WHAT...
SO YOU *DO* REMEMBER ME?
YOU WERE ONE OF US. THE BEST *SPY* WE EVER PUT IN THE FIELD.
AFTER CORUSCANT, WE LOOKED ALL OVER FOR YOU. WE THOUGHT YOU MUST HAVE DIED WITH THE OTHERS.
OH, HIS *TOUCH* WILL DEFINITELY *KILL* ME. IT'S JUST GOING TO TAKE ITS TIME.
WHOSE TOUCH?
ENEB, WHAT'S HAPPENED TO YOU? YOU NEED TO COME HOME AND LET US HELP--

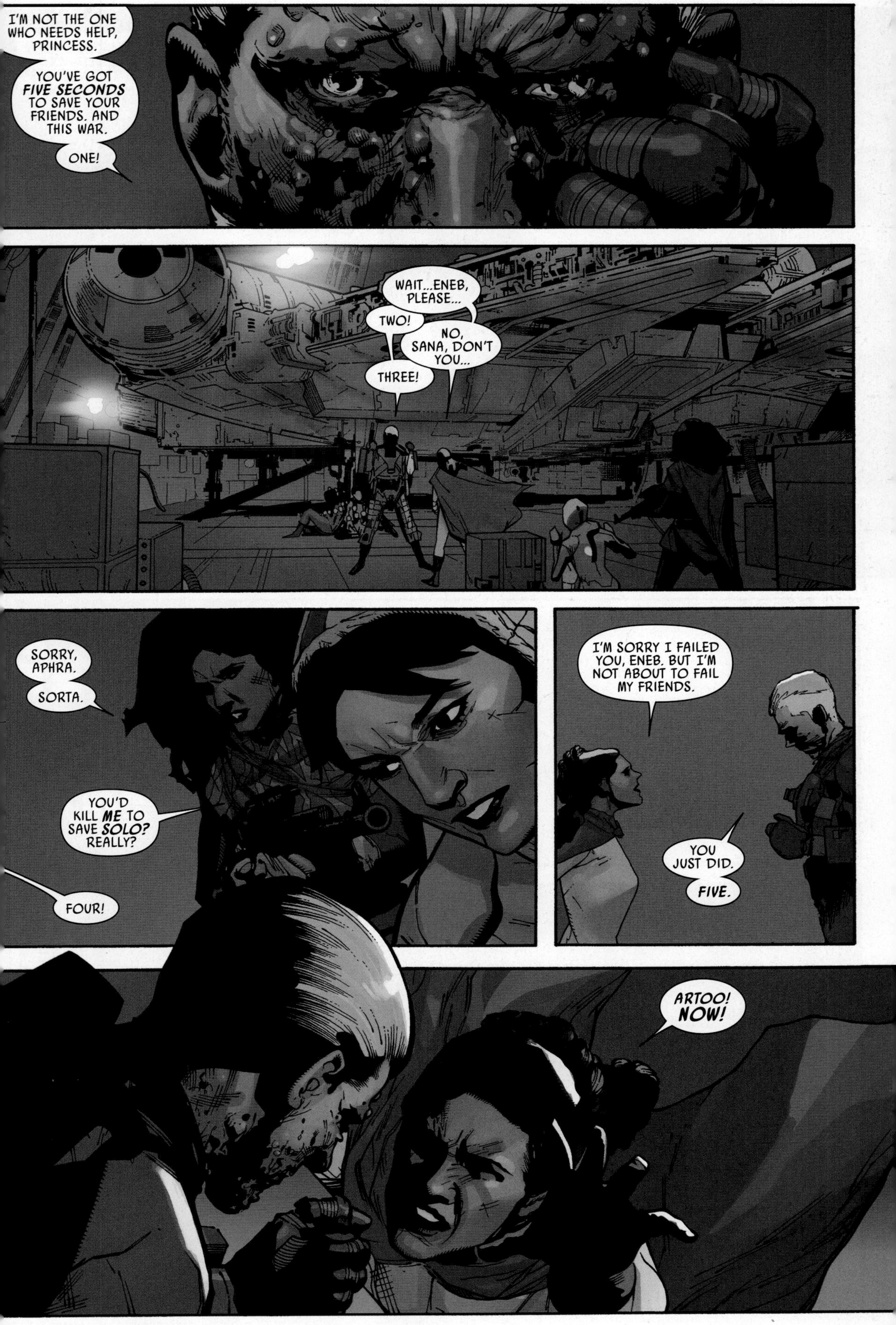
I'M NOT THE ONE WHO NEEDS HELP, PRINCESS.
YOU'VE GOT FIVE SECONDS TO SAVE YOUR FRIENDS. AND THIS WAR.
ONE!
WAIT...ENEB, PLEASE...
TWO!
NO, SANA, DON'T YOU...
THREE!
SORRY, APHRA.
SORTA.
YOU'D KILL ME TO SAVE SOLO? REALLY?
FOUR!
I'M SORRY I FAILED YOU, ENEB. BUT I'M NOT ABOUT TO FAIL MY FRIENDS.
YOU JUST DID.
FIVE.
ARTOO! NOW!

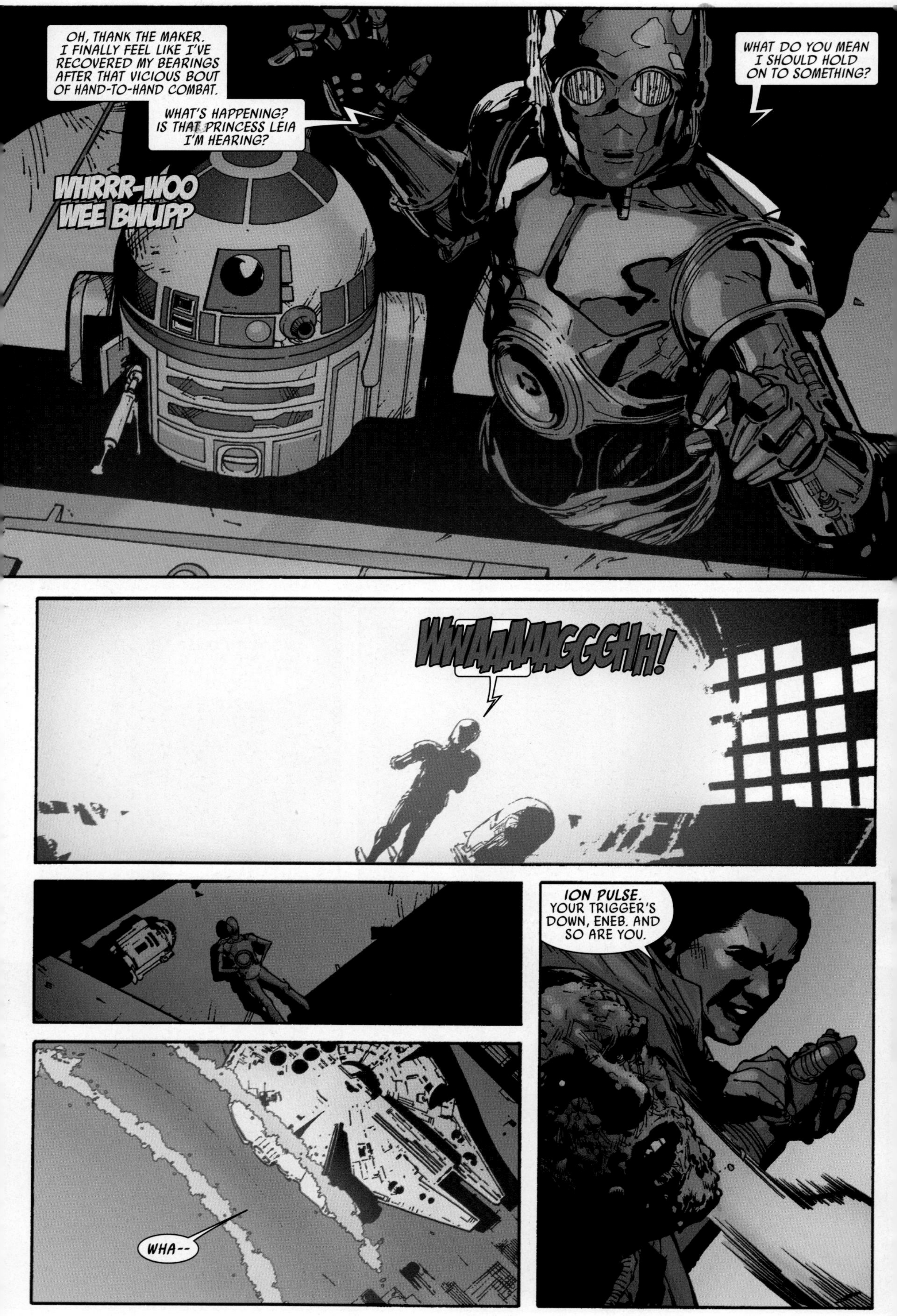
OH, THANK THE MAKER. I FINALLY FEEL LIKE I'VE RECOVERED MY BEARINGS AFTER THAT VICIOUS BOUT OF HAND-TO-HAND COMBAT.
WHAT'S HAPPENING? IS THAT PRINCESS LEIA I'M HEARING?
WHRRR-WOO WEE BWUPP
WHAT DO YOU MEAN I SHOULD HOLD ON TO SOMETHING?
WWAAAAAGGGHH!
ION PULSE. YOUR TRIGGER'S DOWN, ENEB. AND SO ARE YOU.
WHA--

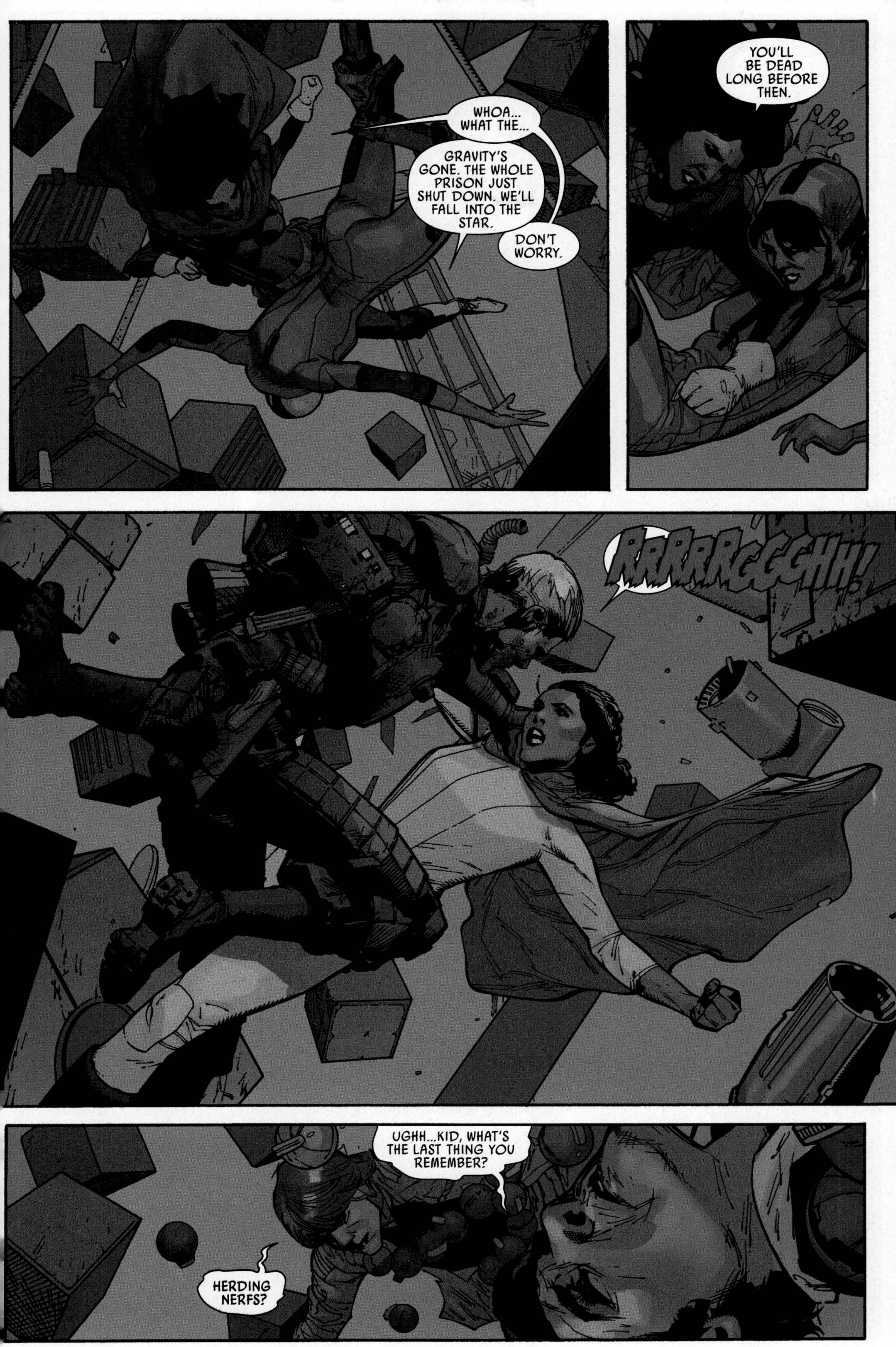
WHOA... WHAT THE...
GRAVITY'S GONE. THE WHOLE PRISON JUST SHUT DOWN. WE'LL FALL INTO THE STAR.
DON'T WORRY.
YOU'LL BE DEAD LONG BEFORE THEN.
RRRRRGGGHH!
UGHH...KID, WHAT'S THE LAST THING YOU REMEMBER?
HERDING NERFS?

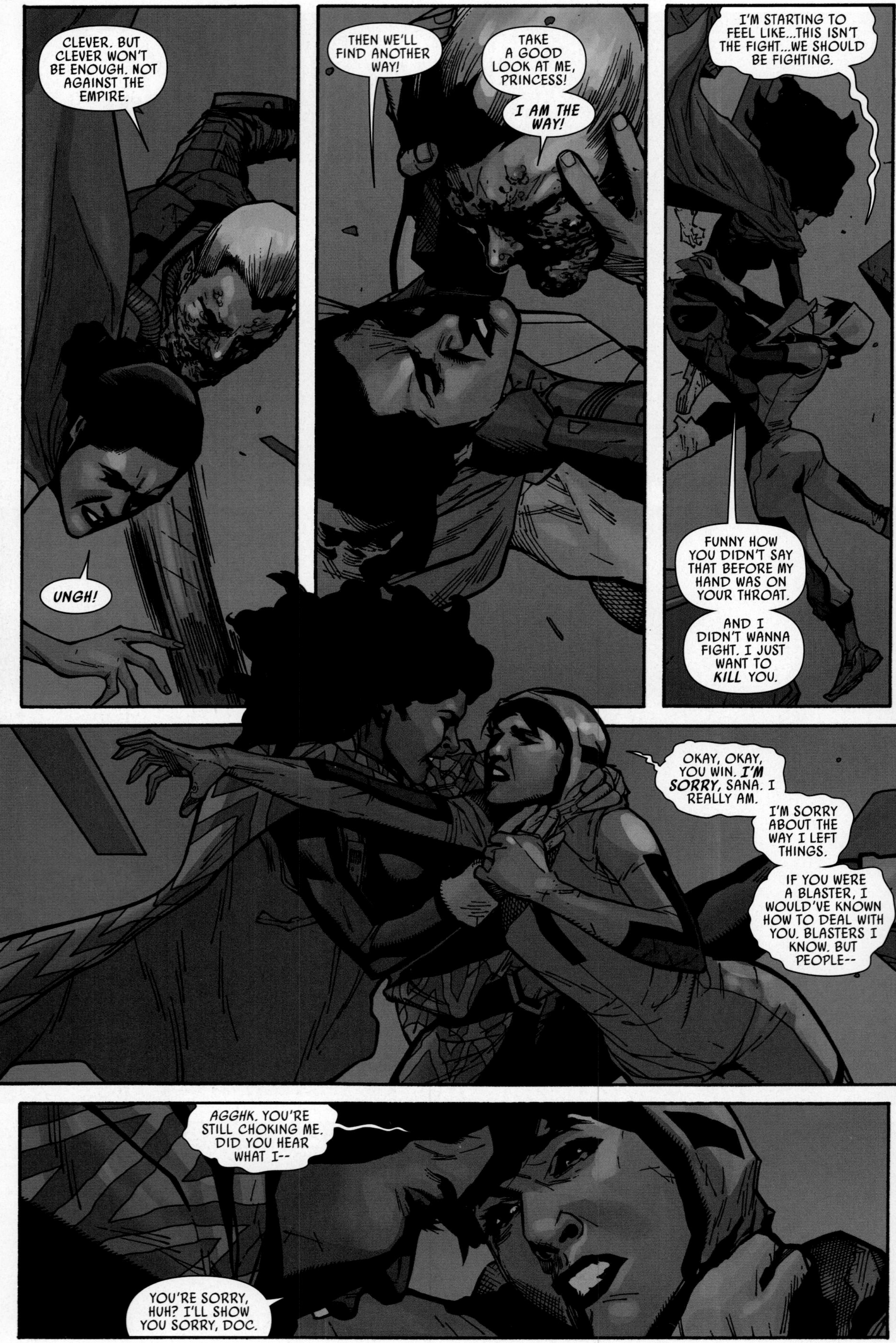
CLEVER. BUT CLEVER WON'T BE ENOUGH. NOT AGAINST THE EMPIRE.
UNGH!
THEN WE'LL FIND ANOTHER WAY!
TAKE A GOOD LOOK AT ME, PRINCESS!
I AM THE WAY!
I'M STARTING TO FEEL LIKE...THIS ISN'T THE FIGHT...WE SHOULD BE FIGHTING.
FUNNY HOW YOU DIDN'T SAY THAT BEFORE MY HAND WAS ON YOUR THROAT.
AND I DIDN'T WANNA FIGHT. I JUST WANT TO KILL YOU.
OKAY, OKAY, YOU WIN. I'M SORRY, SANA. I REALLY AM.
I'M SORRY ABOUT THE WAY I LEFT THINGS.
IF YOU WERE A BLASTER, I WOULD'VE KNOWN HOW TO DEAL WITH YOU. BLASTERS I KNOW. BUT PEOPLE--
AGGHK. YOU'RE STILL CHOKING ME. DID YOU HEAR WHAT I--
YOU'RE SORRY, HUH? I'LL SHOW YOU SORRY, DOC.

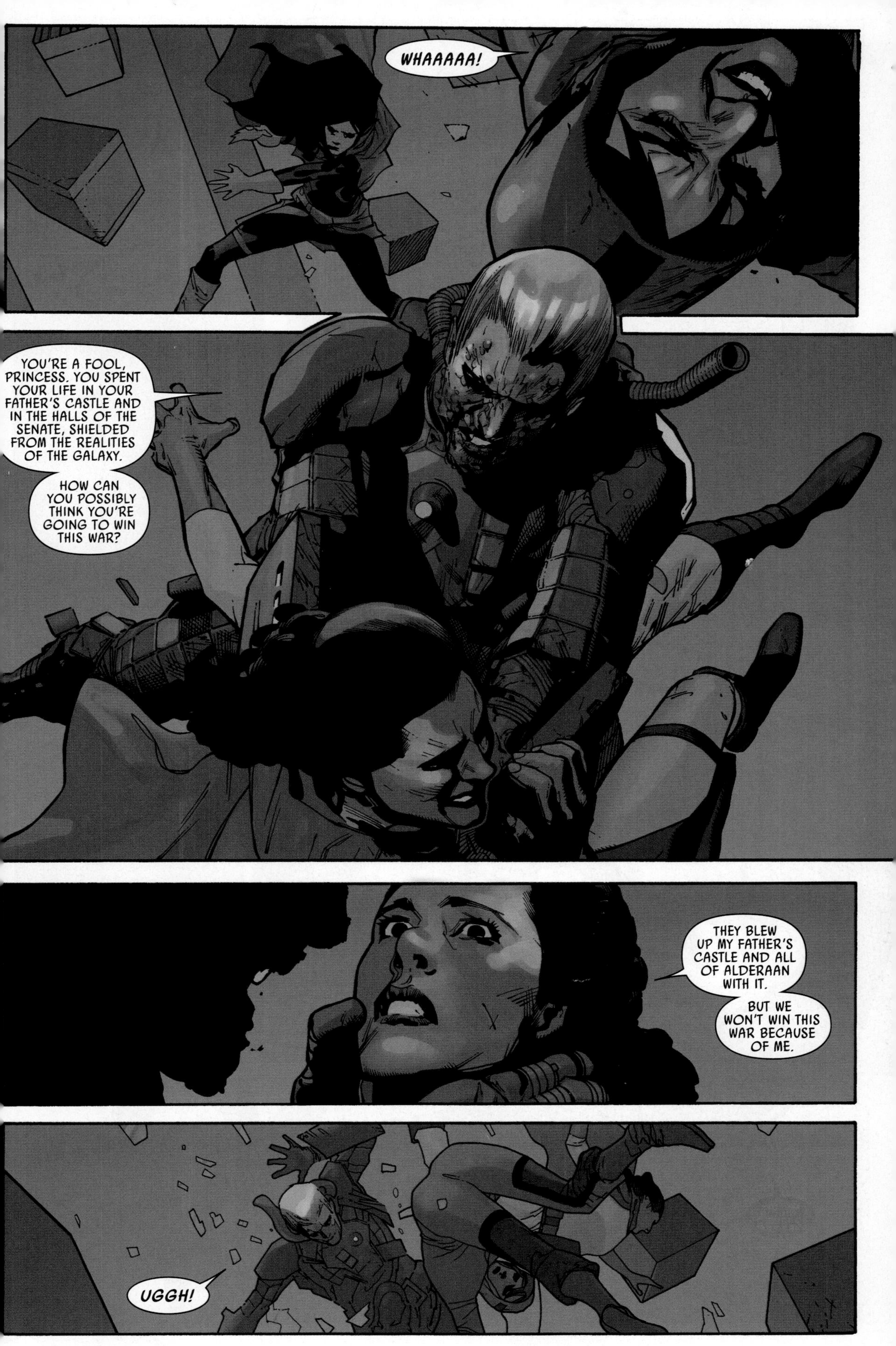
WHAAAAA!
YOU'RE A FOOL, PRINCESS. YOU SPENT YOUR LIFE IN YOUR FATHER'S CASTLE AND IN THE HALLS OF THE SENATE, SHIELDED FROM THE REALITIES OF THE GALAXY.
HOW CAN YOU POSSIBLY THINK YOU'RE GOING TO WIN THIS WAR?
THEY BLEW UP MY FATHER'S CASTLE AND ALL OF ALDERAAN WITH IT.
BUT WE WON'T WIN THIS WAR BECAUSE OF ME.
UGGH!

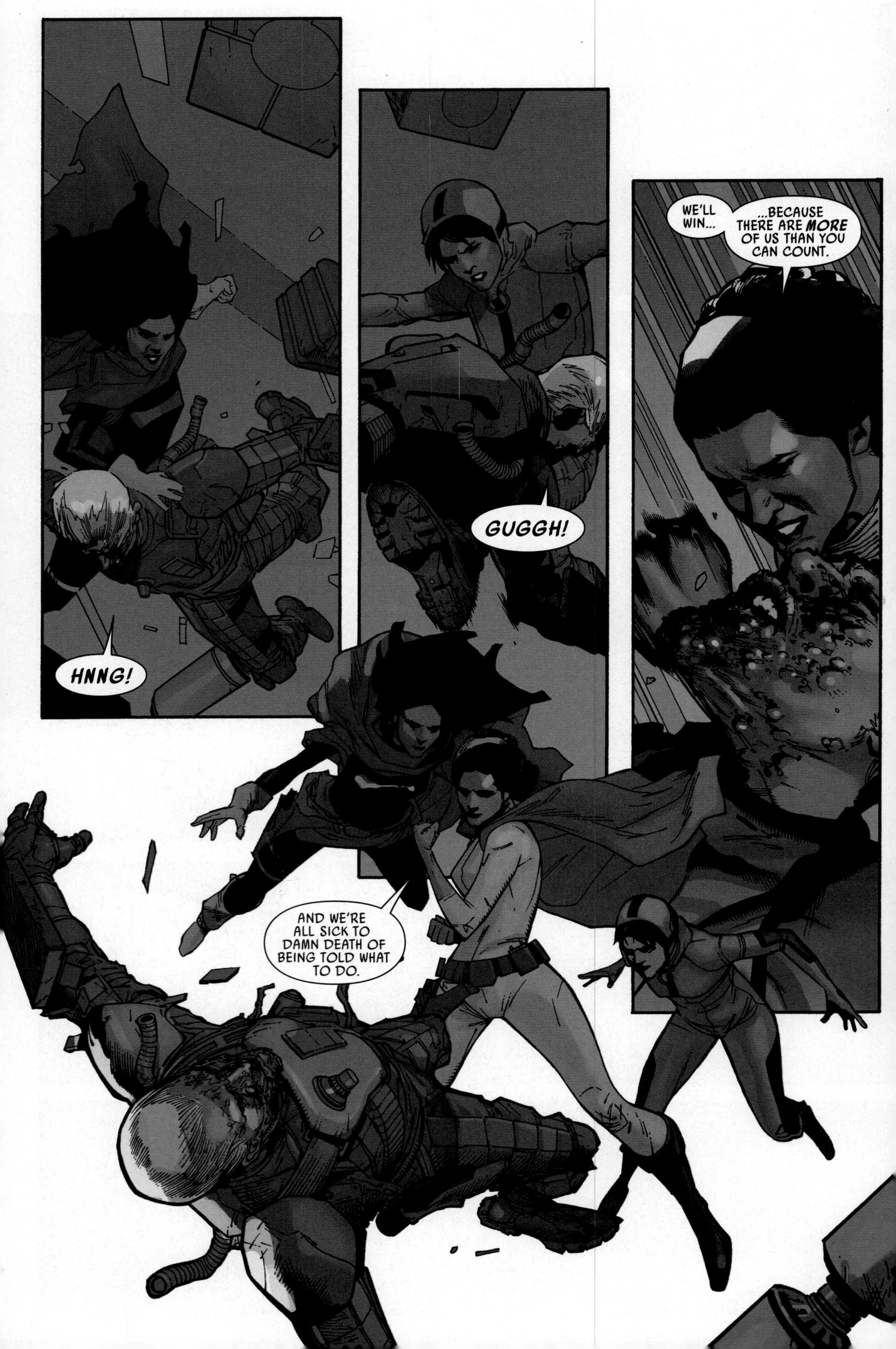
HNNG!
GUGGH!
WE'LL WIN...
...BECAUSE THERE ARE MORE OF US THAN YOU CAN COUNT.
AND WE'RE ALL SICK TO DAMN DEATH OF BEING TOLD WHAT TO DO.

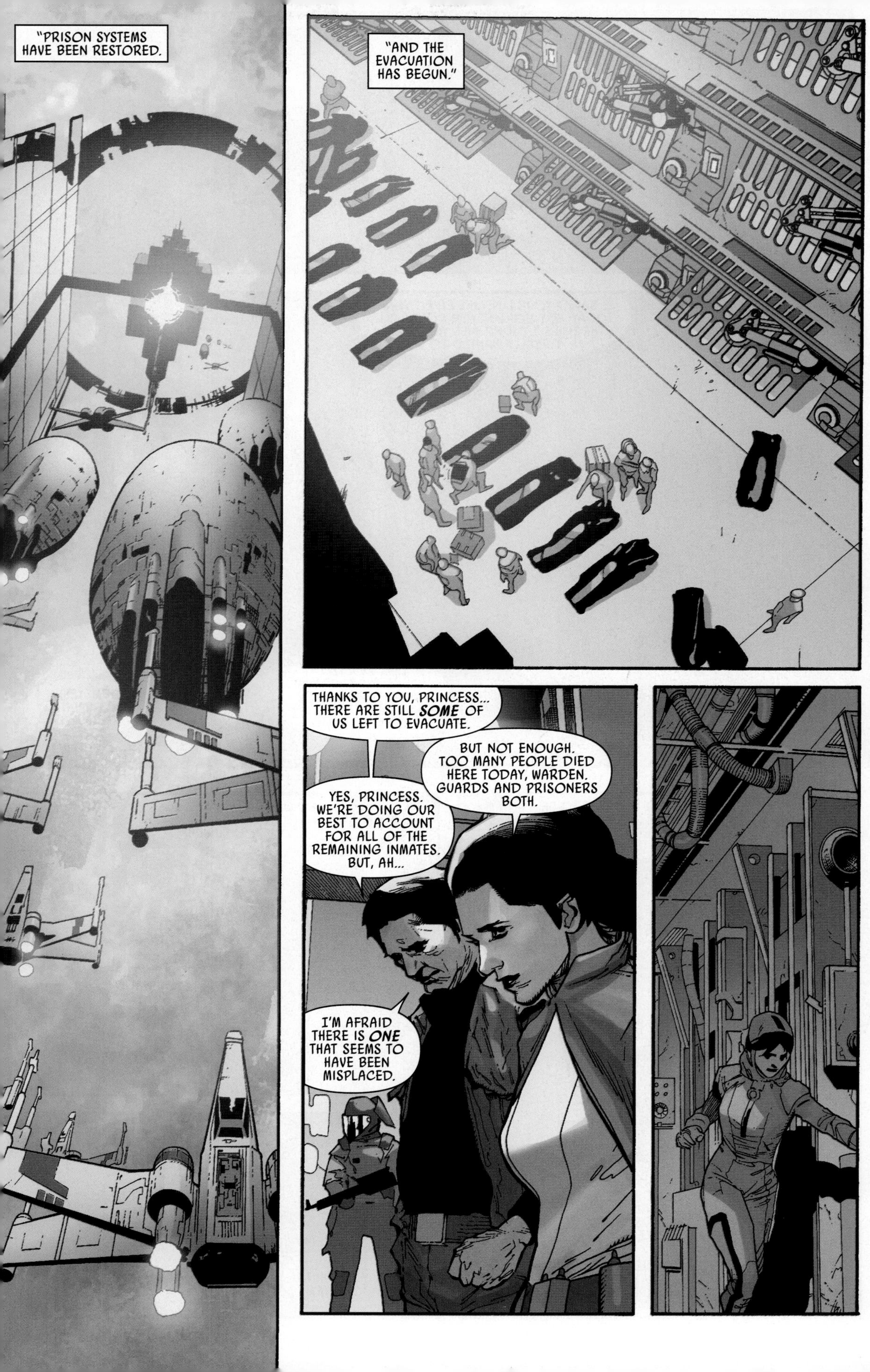
"PRISON SYSTEMS HAVE BEEN RESTORED.
"AND THE EVACUATION HAS BEGUN."
THANKS TO YOU, PRINCESS... THERE ARE STILL SOME OF US LEFT TO EVACUATE.
BUT NOT ENOUGH. TOO MANY PEOPLE DIED HERE TODAY, WARDEN. GUARDS AND PRISONERS BOTH.
YES, PRINCESS. WE'RE DOING OUR BEST TO ACCOUNT FOR ALL OF THE REMAINING INMATES. BUT, AH...
I'M AFRAID THERE IS ONE THAT SEEMS TO HAVE BEEN MISPLACED.

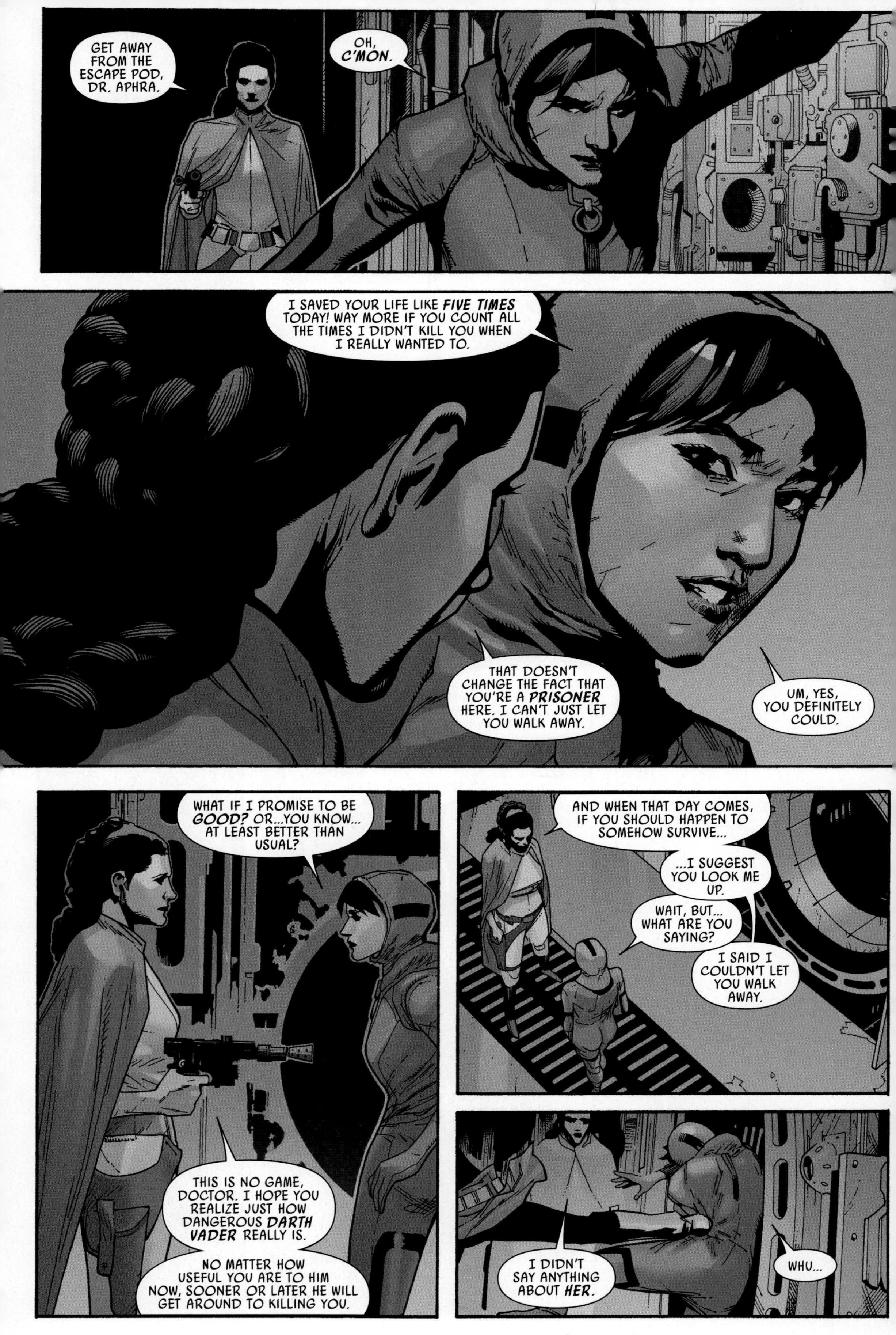
GET AWAY FROM THE ESCAPE POD, DR. APHRA.
OH, *C'MON.*
I SAVED YOUR LIFE LIKE *FIVE TIMES* TODAY! WAY MORE IF YOU COUNT ALL THE TIMES I DIDN'T KILL YOU WHEN I REALLY WANTED TO.
THAT DOESN'T CHANGE THE FACT THAT YOU'RE A *PRISONER* HERE. I CAN'T JUST LET YOU WALK AWAY.
UM, YES, YOU DEFINITELY COULD.
WHAT IF I PROMISE TO BE *GOOD?* OR...YOU KNOW... AT LEAST BETTER THAN USUAL?
THIS IS NO GAME, DOCTOR. I HOPE YOU REALIZE JUST HOW DANGEROUS *DARTH VADER* REALLY IS.
NO MATTER HOW USEFUL YOU ARE TO HIM NOW, SOONER OR LATER HE WILL GET AROUND TO KILLING YOU.
AND WHEN THAT DAY COMES, IF YOU SHOULD HAPPEN TO SOMEHOW SURVIVE...
...I SUGGEST YOU LOOK ME UP.
WAIT, BUT... WHAT ARE YOU SAYING?
I SAID I COULDN'T LET YOU WALK AWAY.
I DIDN'T SAY ANYTHING ABOUT *HER.*
WHU...

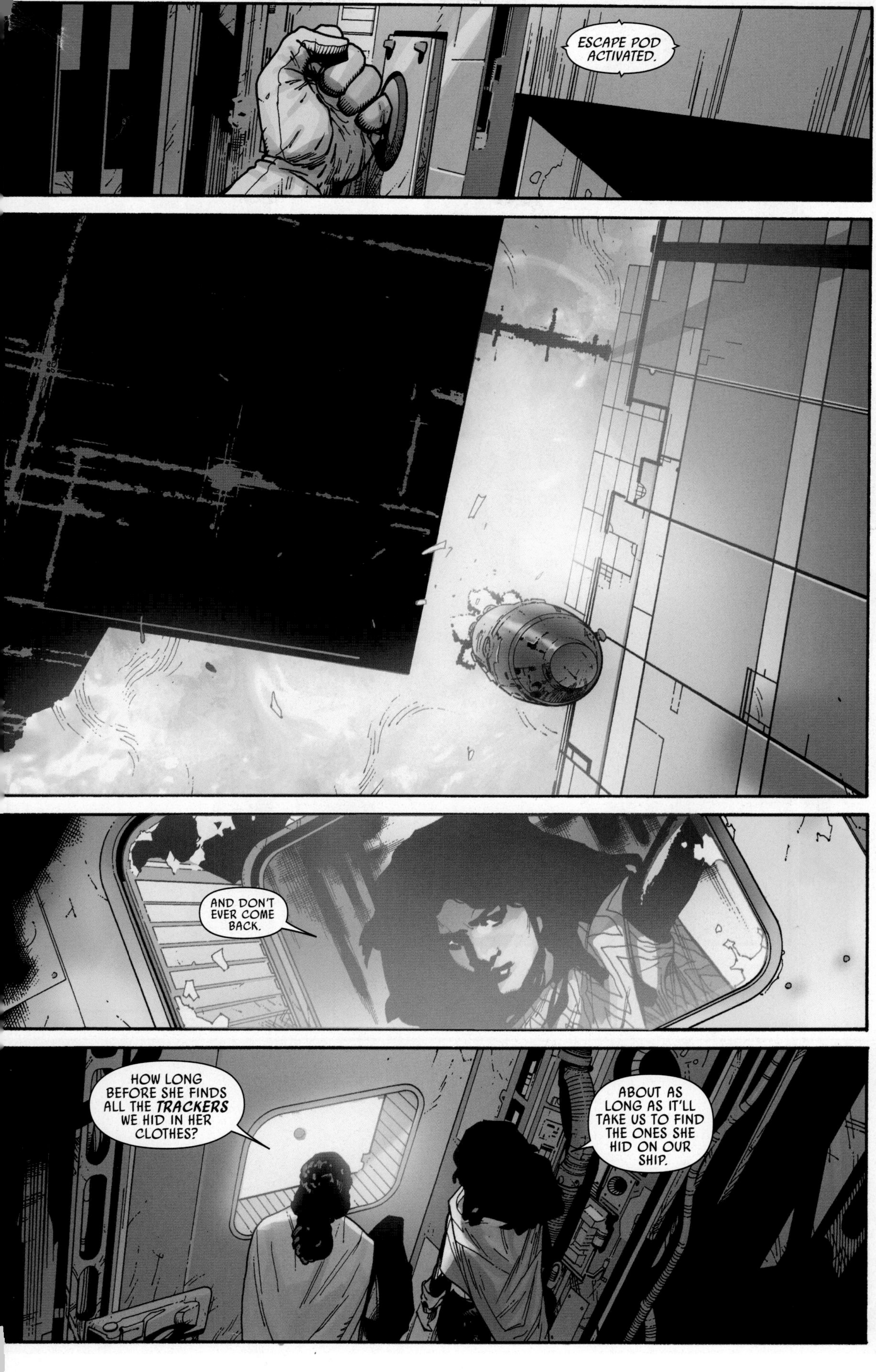
ESCAPE POD ACTIVATED.
AND DON'T EVER COME BACK.
HOW LONG BEFORE SHE FINDS ALL THE TRACKERS WE HID IN HER CLOTHES?
ABOUT AS LONG AS IT'LL TAKE US TO FIND THE ONES SHE HID ON OUR SHIP.

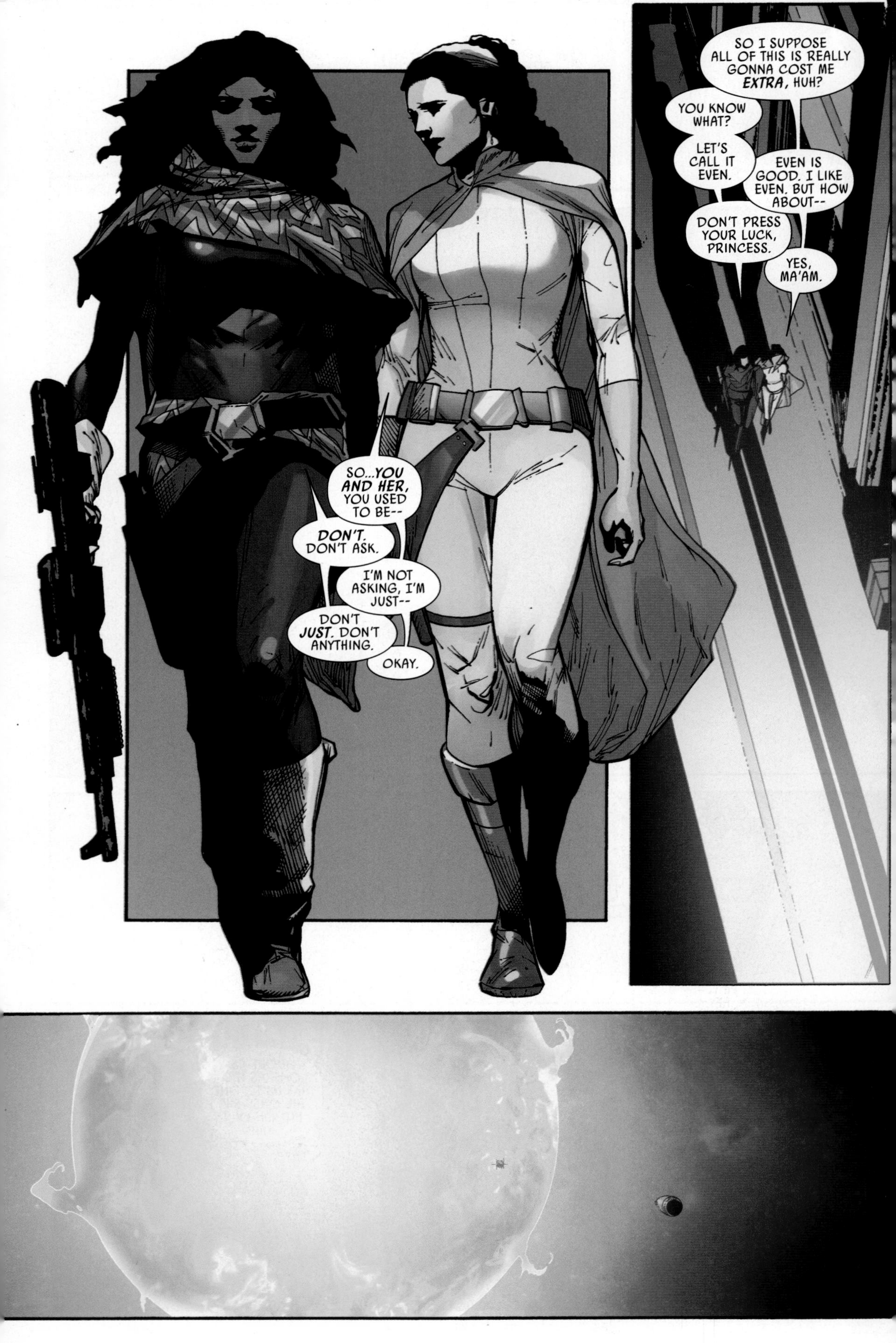
SO...YOU AND HER, YOU USED TO BE--
DON'T. DON'T ASK.
I'M NOT ASKING, I'M JUST--
DON'T JUST. DON'T ANYTHING.
OKAY.
SO I SUPPOSE ALL OF THIS IS REALLY GONNA COST ME EXTRA, HUH?
YOU KNOW WHAT?
LET'S CALL IT EVEN.
EVEN IS GOOD. I LIKE EVEN. BUT HOW ABOUT--
DON'T PRESS YOUR LUCK, PRINCESS.
YES, MA'AM.

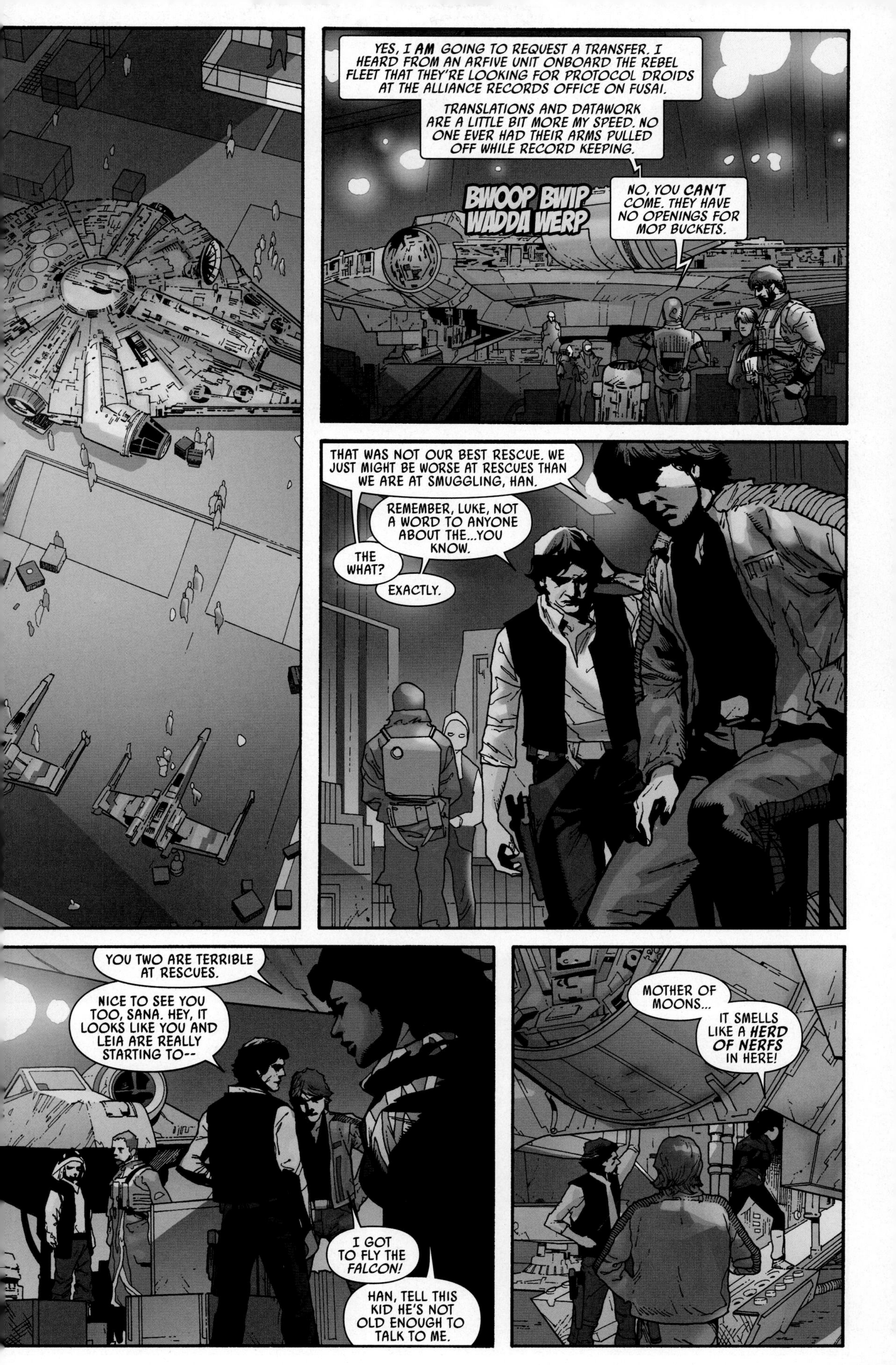

YES, I AM GOING TO REQUEST A TRANSFER. I HEARD FROM AN ARFIVE UNIT ONBOARD THE REBEL FLEET THAT THEY'RE LOOKING FOR PROTOCOL DROIDS AT THE ALLIANCE RECORDS OFFICE ON FUSAI.
TRANSLATIONS AND DATAWORK ARE A LITTLE BIT MORE MY SPEED. NO ONE EVER HAD THEIR ARMS PULLED OFF WHILE RECORD KEEPING.
BWOOP BWIP WADDA WERP
NO, YOU CAN'T COME. THEY HAVE NO OPENINGS FOR MOP BUCKETS.
THAT WAS NOT OUR BEST RESCUE. WE JUST MIGHT BE WORSE AT RESCUES THAN WE ARE AT SMUGGLING, HAN.
REMEMBER, LUKE, NOT A WORD TO ANYONE ABOUT THE...YOU KNOW.
THE WHAT?
EXACTLY.
YOU TWO ARE TERRIBLE AT RESCUES.
NICE TO SEE YOU TOO, SANA. HEY, IT LOOKS LIKE YOU AND LEIA ARE REALLY STARTING TO--
I GOT TO FLY THE *FALCON*!
HAN, TELL THIS KID HE'S NOT OLD ENOUGH TO TALK TO ME.
MOTHER OF MOONS...
IT SMELLS LIKE A ***HERD OF NERFS*** IN HERE!

I WANT YOU TO KNOW...I WON'T GIVE UP ON YOU.

I'LL GET YOU THE HELP YOU NEED, ENEB. WHETHER YOU WANT IT OR NOT.

HEH.

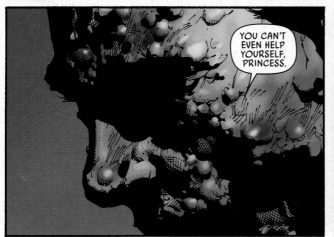

YOU CAN'T EVEN HELP YOURSELF, PRINCESS.

BUT SOMEDAY... YOU'LL WISH YOU'D LISTENED TO ME.

SOMEDAY.

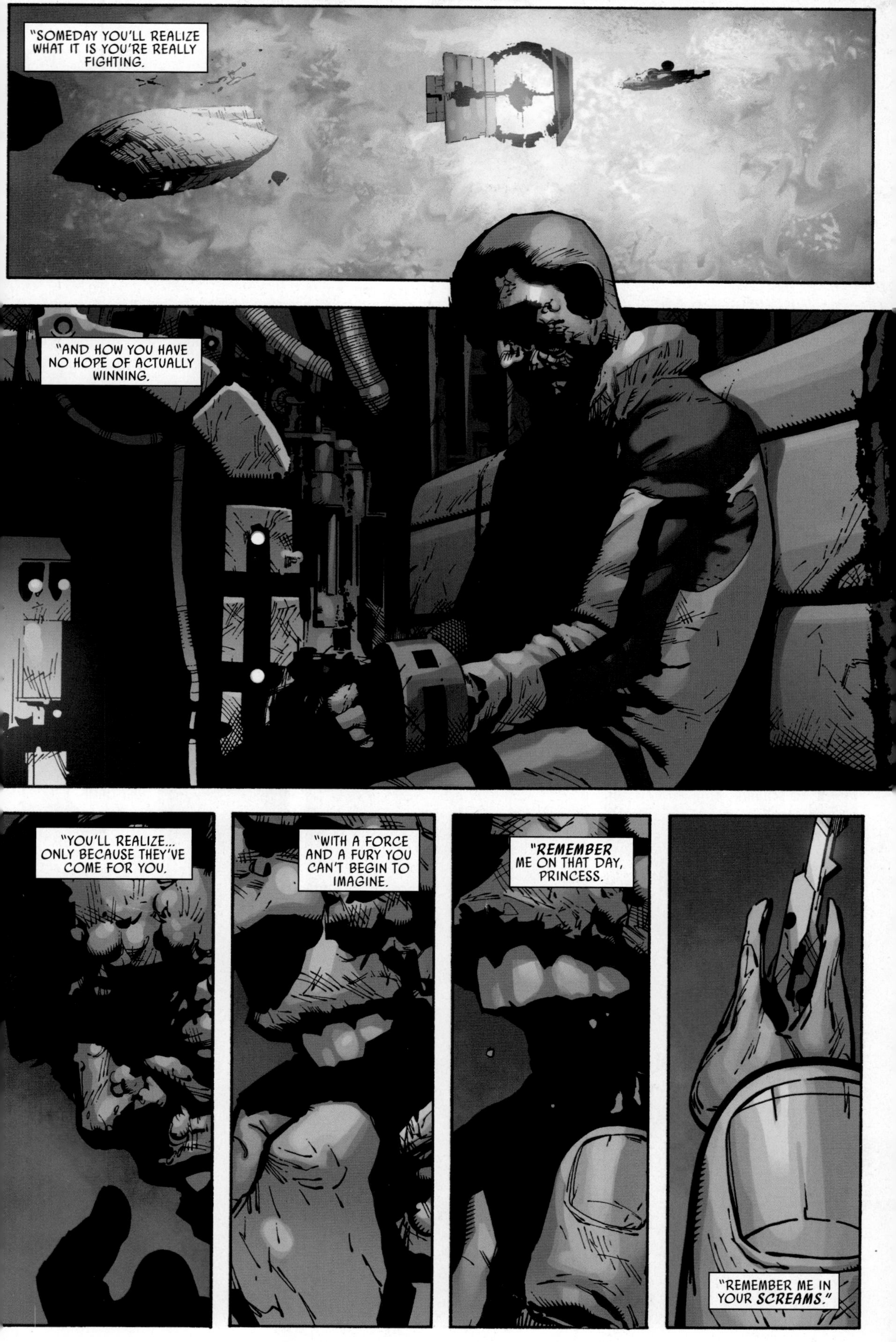
"SOMEDAY YOU'LL REALIZE WHAT IT IS YOU'RE REALLY FIGHTING.
"AND HOW YOU HAVE NO HOPE OF ACTUALLY WINNING.
"YOU'LL REALIZE... ONLY BECAUSE THEY'VE COME FOR YOU.
"WITH A FORCE AND A FURY YOU CAN'T BEGIN TO IMAGINE.
"REMEMBER ME ON THAT DAY, PRINCESS.
"REMEMBER ME IN YOUR SCREAMS."

DAYS LATER...

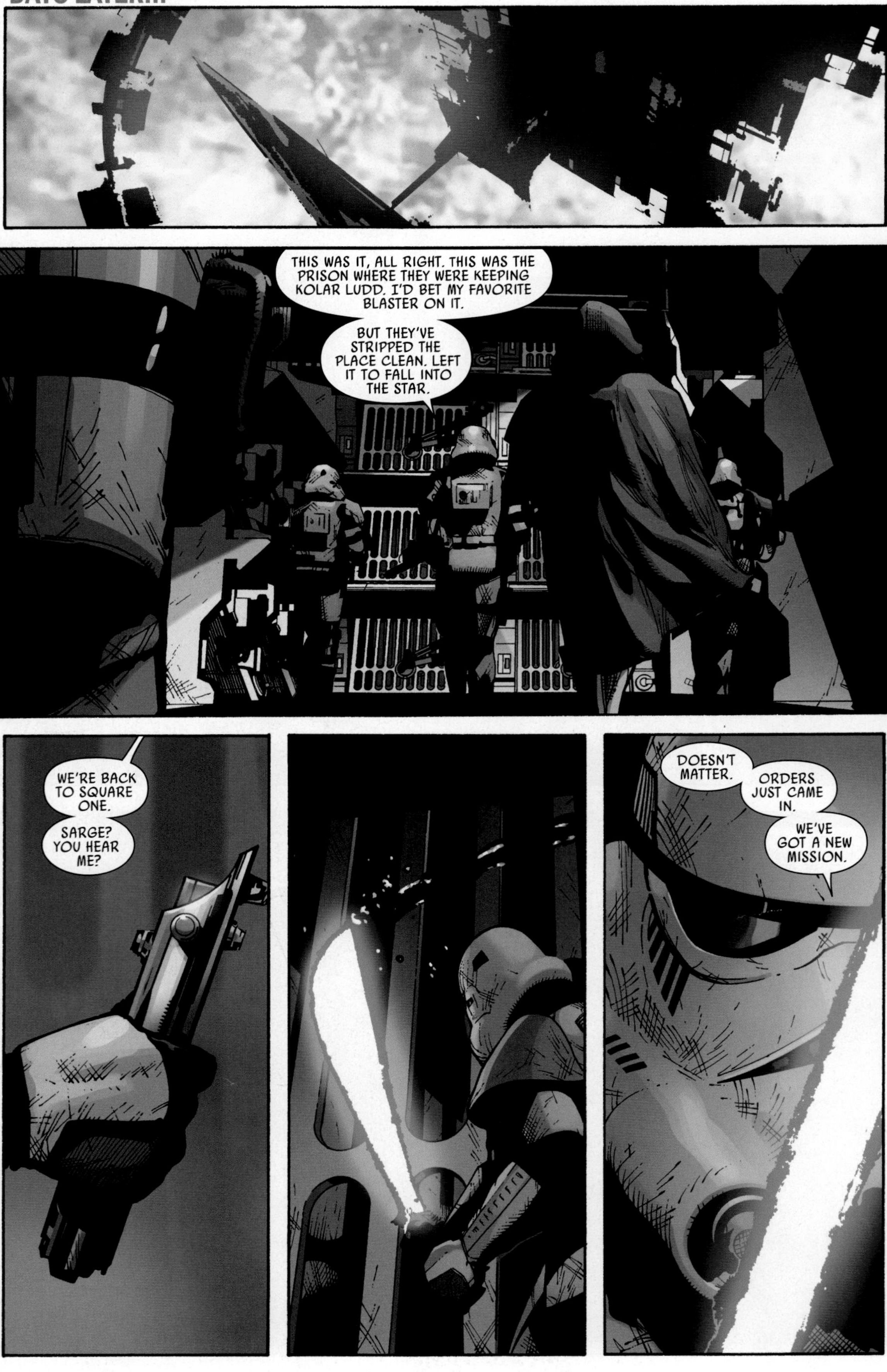

THIS WAS IT, ALL RIGHT. THIS WAS THE PRISON WHERE THEY WERE KEEPING KOLAR LUDD. I'D BET MY FAVORITE BLASTER ON IT.
BUT THEY'VE STRIPPED THE PLACE CLEAN. LEFT IT TO FALL INTO THE STAR.
WE'RE BACK TO SQUARE ONE.
SARGE? YOU HEAR ME?
DOESN'T MATTER.
ORDERS JUST CAME IN.
WE'VE GOT A NEW MISSION.

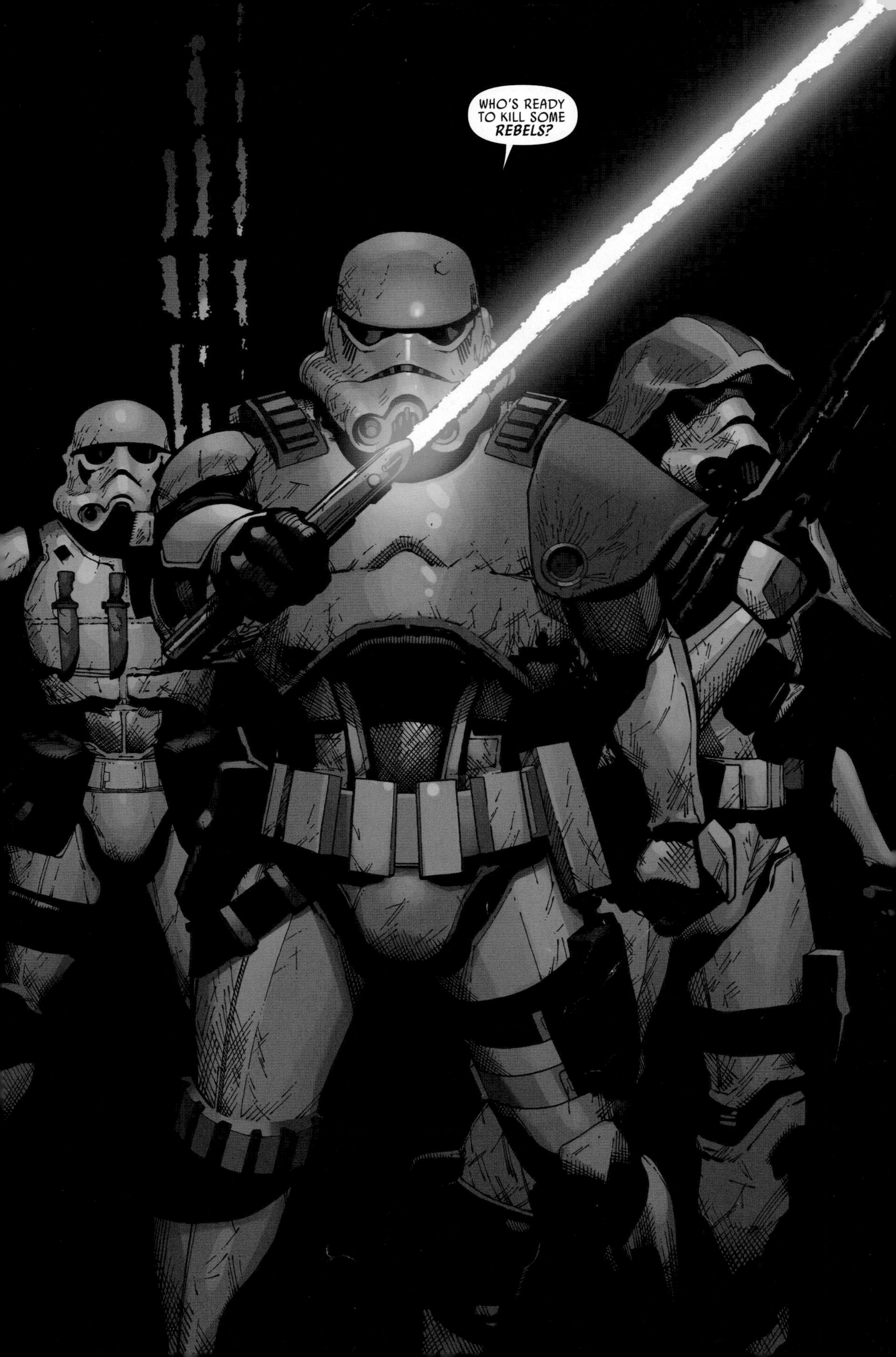
WHO'S READY TO KILL SOME *REBELS?*

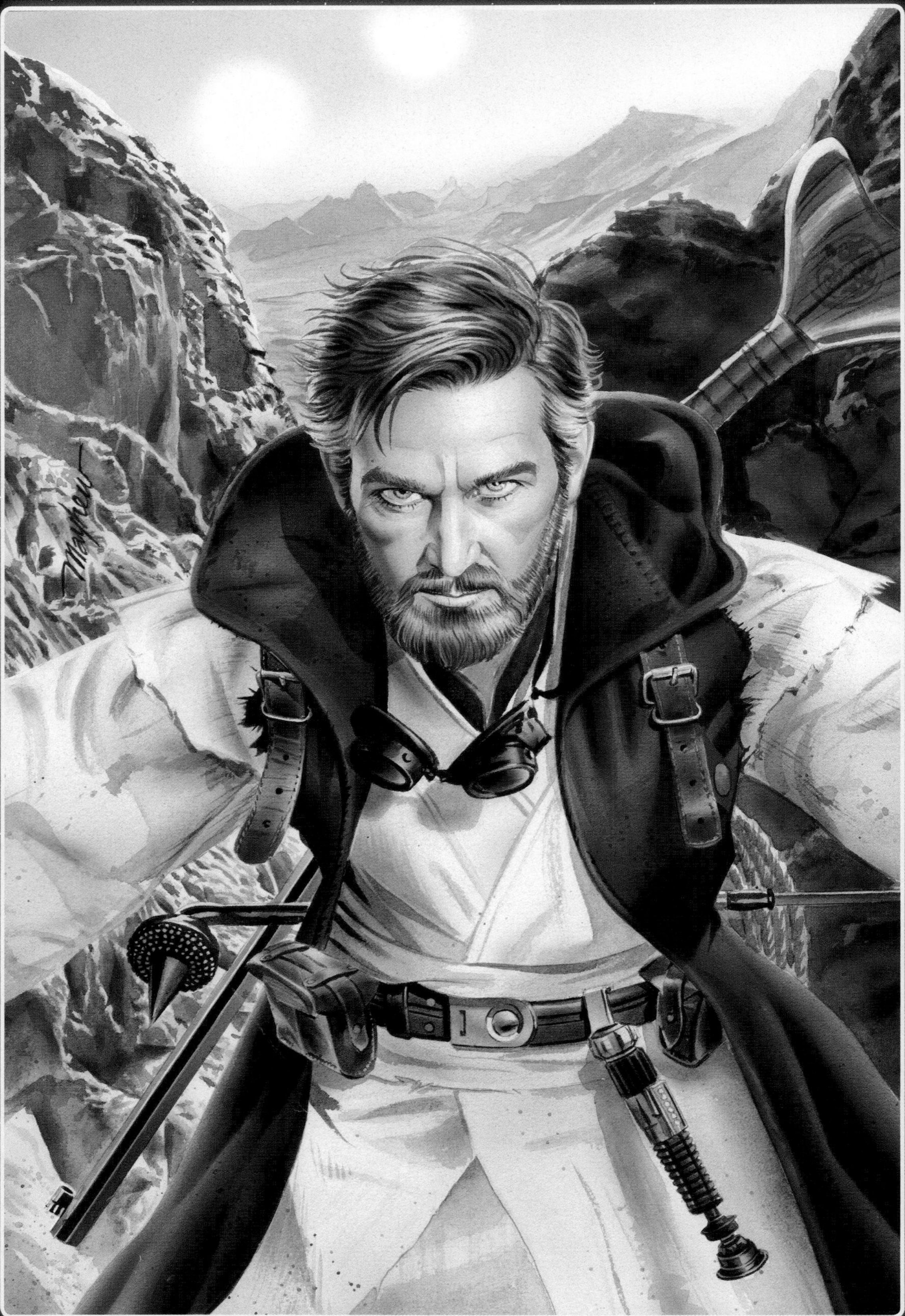

FROM THE JOURNALS OF

OLD BEN KENOBI

WHILE SEARCHING FOR ANSWERS IN HIS

QUEST TO BECOME A JEDI,

LUKE SKYWALKER HAS UNCOVERED A

JOURNAL WRITTEN BY JEDI MASTER

OBI-WAN KENOBI. THE JOURNAL DETAILS

KENOBI'S ADVENTURES DURING THE TIME

HE WAS IN HIDING ON TATOOINE--

INCLUDING WHEN OBI-WAN RESCUED

A YOUNG LUKE FROM JABBA THE HUTT'S

THUGS DURING THE GREAT DROUGHT.

WHAT FOLLOWS IS AN EXCERPT

FROM THAT JOURNAL.

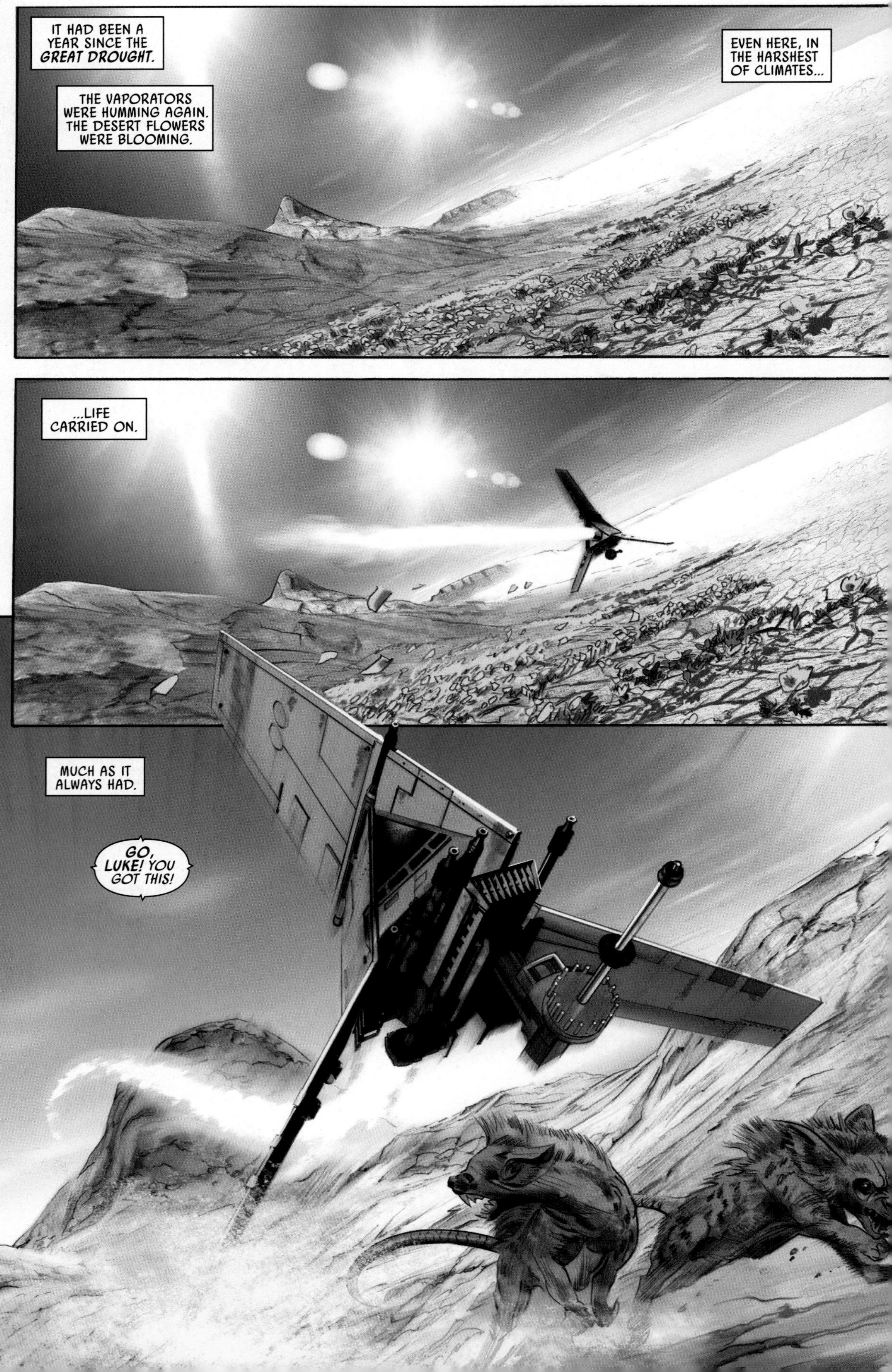
IT HAD BEEN A YEAR SINCE THE GREAT DROUGHT.
THE VAPORATORS WERE HUMMING AGAIN. THE DESERT FLOWERS WERE BLOOMING.
EVEN HERE, IN THE HARSHEST OF CLIMATES...
...LIFE CARRIED ON.
MUCH AS IT ALWAYS HAD.
GO, LUKE! YOU GOT THIS!

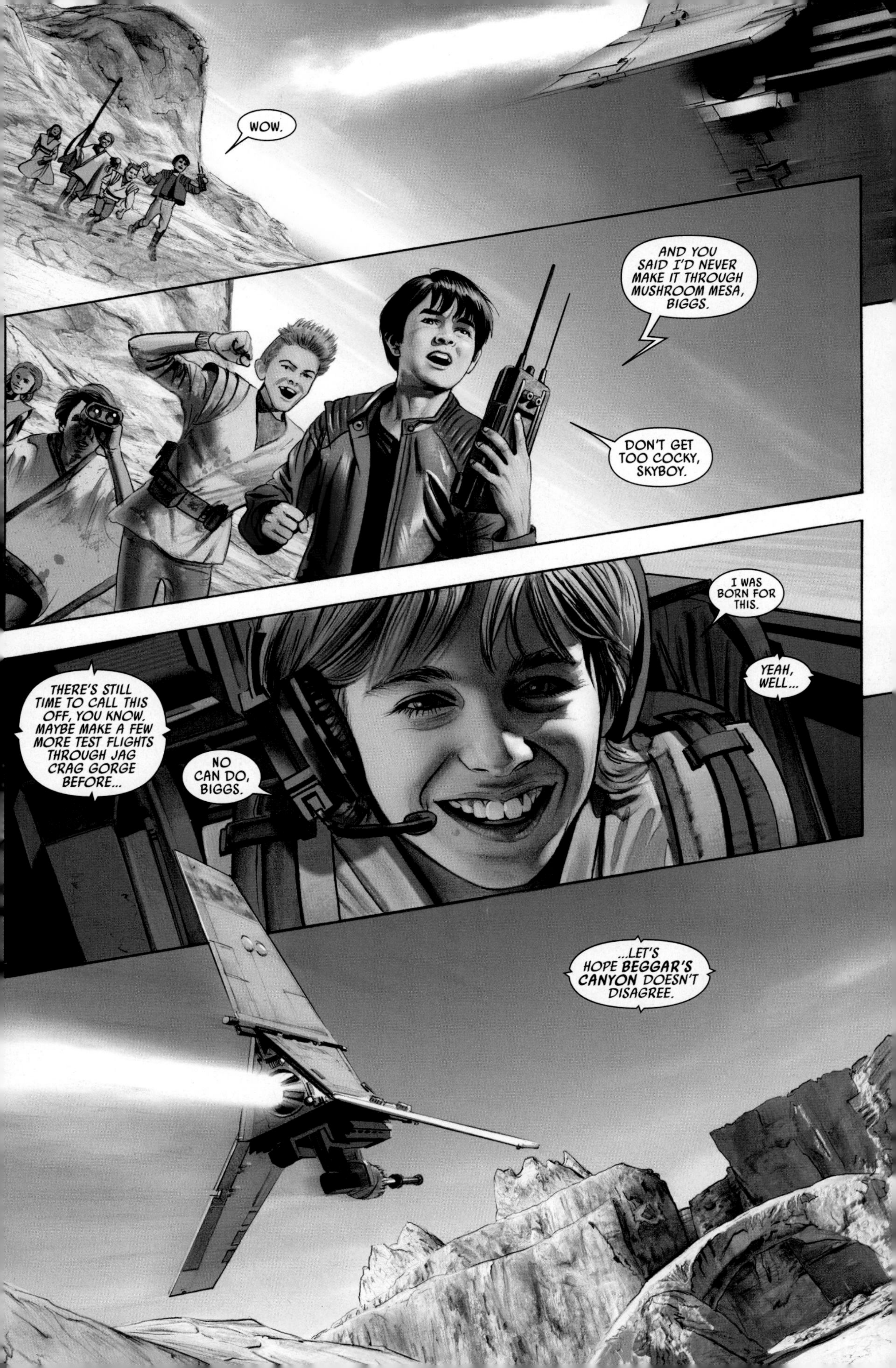
WOW.
AND YOU SAID I'D NEVER MAKE IT THROUGH MUSHROOM MESA, BIGGS.
DON'T GET TOO COCKY, SKYBOY.
I WAS BORN FOR THIS.
YEAH, WELL...
THERE'S STILL TIME TO CALL THIS OFF, YOU KNOW. MAYBE MAKE A FEW MORE TEST FLIGHTS THROUGH JAG CRAG GORGE BEFORE...
NO CAN DO, BIGGS.
...LET'S HOPE BEGGAR'S CANYON DOESN'T DISAGREE.

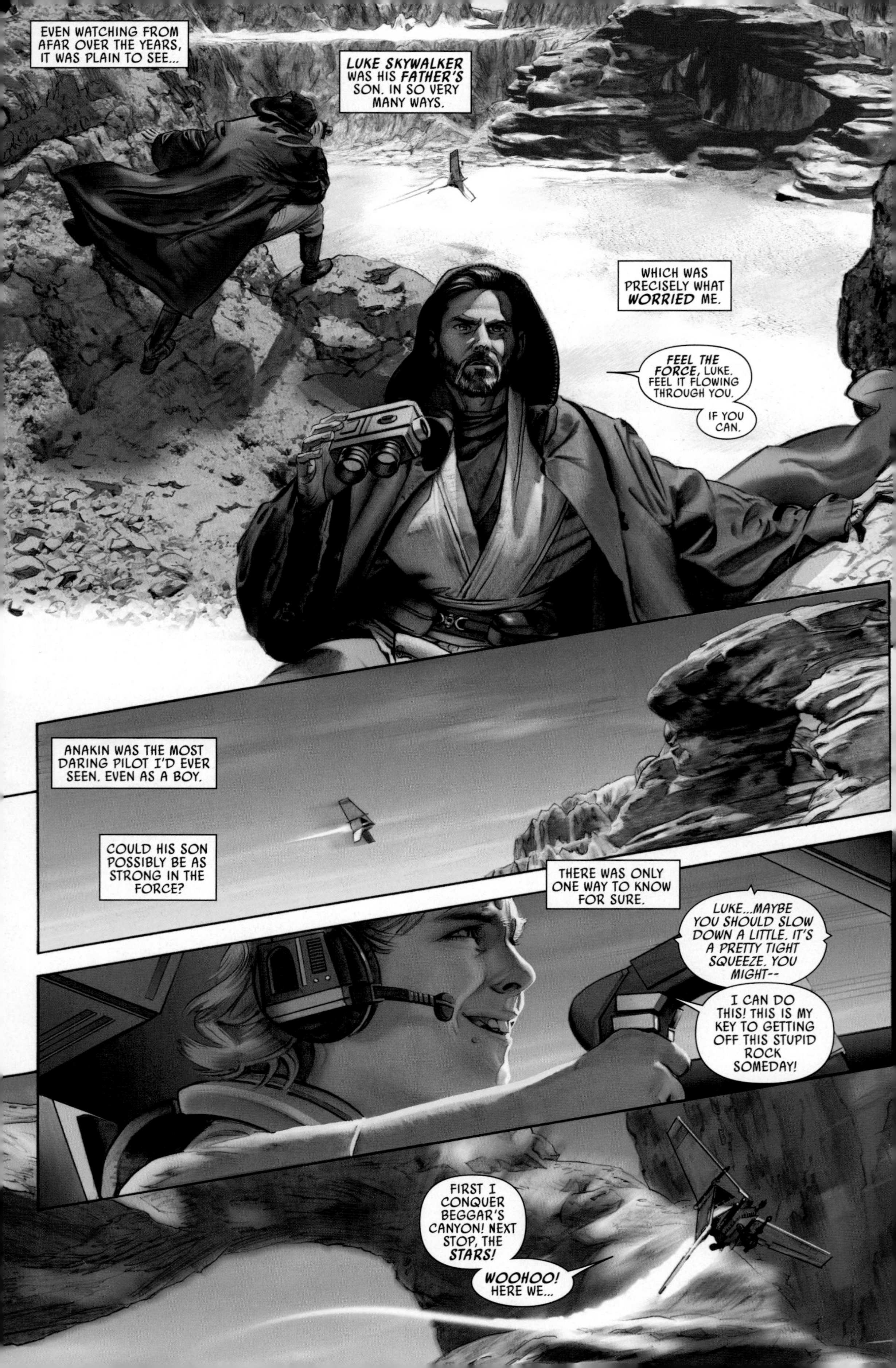
EVEN WATCHING FROM AFAR OVER THE YEARS, IT WAS PLAIN TO SEE...
LUKE SKYWALKER WAS HIS FATHER'S SON. IN SO VERY MANY WAYS.
WHICH WAS PRECISELY WHAT WORRIED ME.
FEEL THE FORCE, LUKE. FEEL IT FLOWING THROUGH YOU.
IF YOU CAN.
ANAKIN WAS THE MOST DARING PILOT I'D EVER SEEN. EVEN AS A BOY.
COULD HIS SON POSSIBLY BE AS STRONG IN THE FORCE?
THERE WAS ONLY ONE WAY TO KNOW FOR SURE.
LUKE...MAYBE YOU SHOULD SLOW DOWN A LITTLE. IT'S A PRETTY TIGHT SQUEEZE. YOU MIGHT--
I CAN DO THIS! THIS IS MY KEY TO GETTING OFF THIS STUPID ROCK SOMEDAY!
FIRST I CONQUER BEGGAR'S CANYON! NEXT STOP, THE STARS!
WOOHOO! HERE WE...

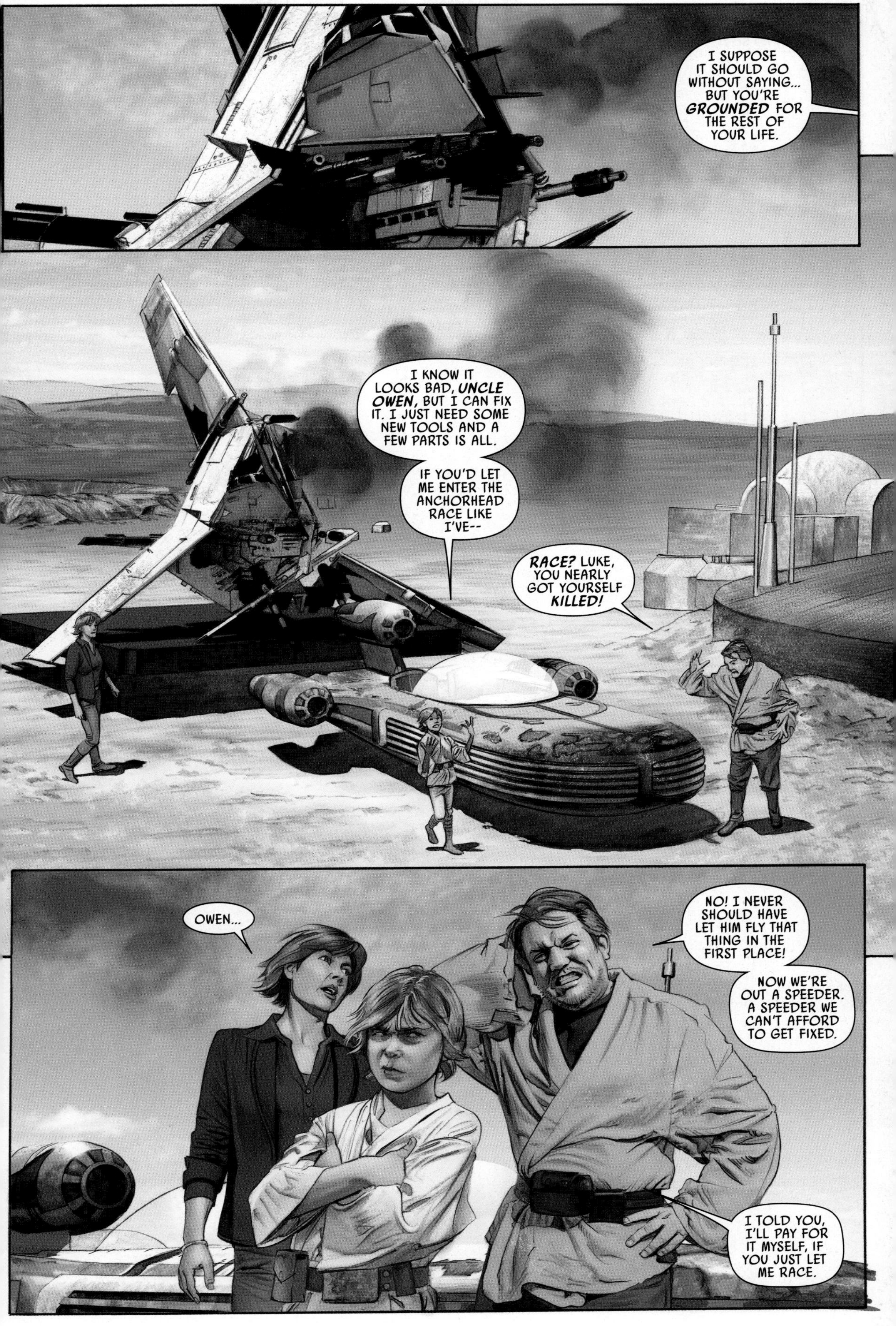
I SUPPOSE IT SHOULD GO WITHOUT SAYING... BUT YOU'RE **GROUNDED** FOR THE REST OF YOUR LIFE.
I KNOW IT LOOKS BAD, **UNCLE OWEN,** BUT I CAN FIX IT. I JUST NEED SOME NEW TOOLS AND A FEW PARTS IS ALL.
IF YOU'D LET ME ENTER THE ANCHORHEAD RACE LIKE I'VE--
RACE? LUKE, YOU NEARLY GOT YOURSELF **KILLED!**
OWEN...
NO! I NEVER SHOULD HAVE LET HIM FLY THAT THING IN THE FIRST PLACE!
NOW WE'RE OUT A SPEEDER. A SPEEDER WE CAN'T AFFORD TO GET FIXED.
I TOLD YOU, I'LL PAY FOR IT MYSELF, IF YOU JUST LET ME RACE.

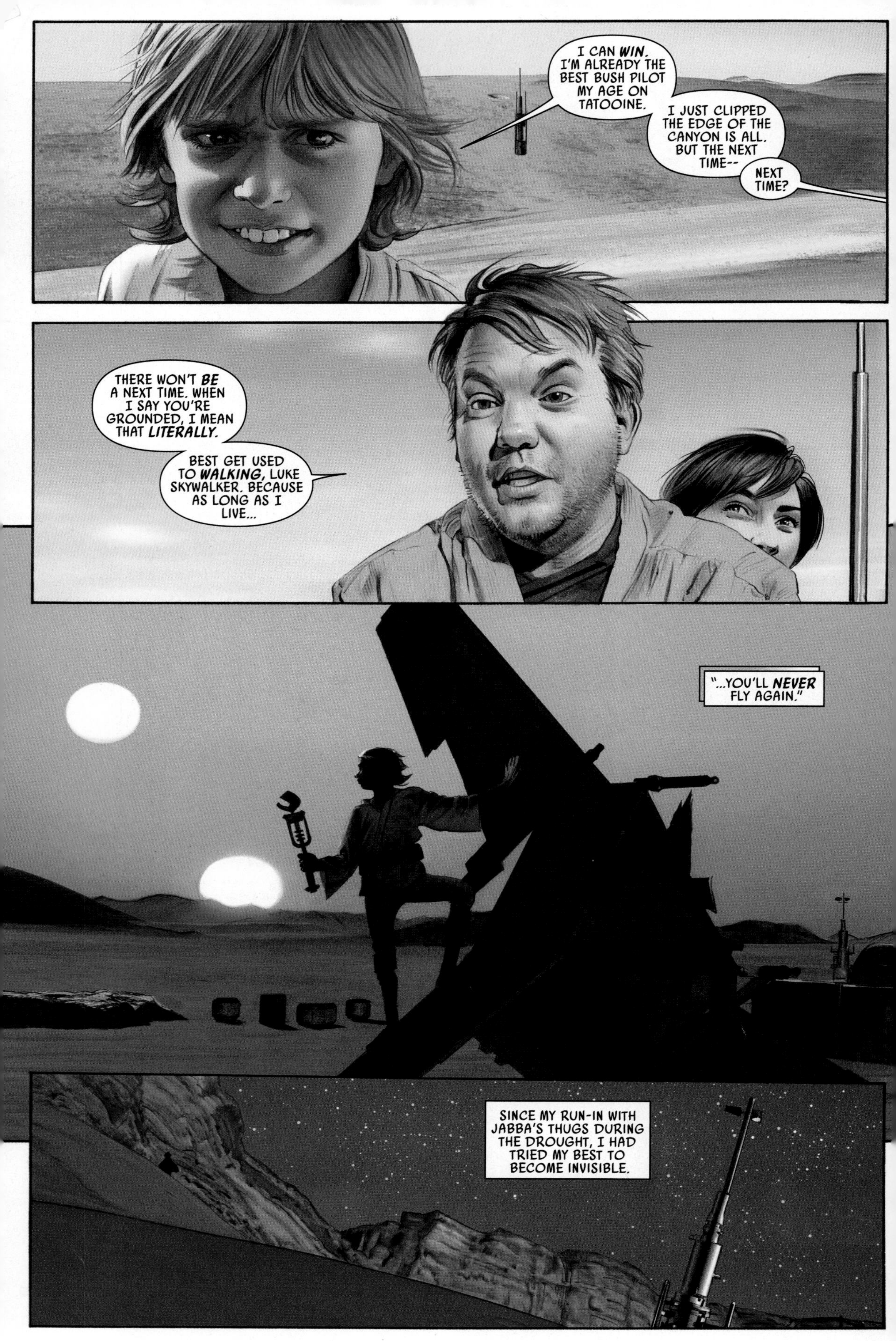
I CAN *WIN.* I'M ALREADY THE BEST BUSH PILOT MY AGE ON TATOOINE.
I JUST CLIPPED THE EDGE OF THE CANYON IS ALL. BUT THE NEXT TIME--
NEXT TIME?
THERE WON'T *BE* A NEXT TIME. WHEN I SAY YOU'RE GROUNDED, I MEAN THAT *LITERALLY.*
BEST GET USED TO *WALKING,* LUKE SKYWALKER. BECAUSE AS LONG AS I LIVE...
"...YOU'LL *NEVER* FLY AGAIN."
SINCE MY RUN-IN WITH JABBA'S THUGS DURING THE DROUGHT, I HAD TRIED MY BEST TO BECOME INVISIBLE.

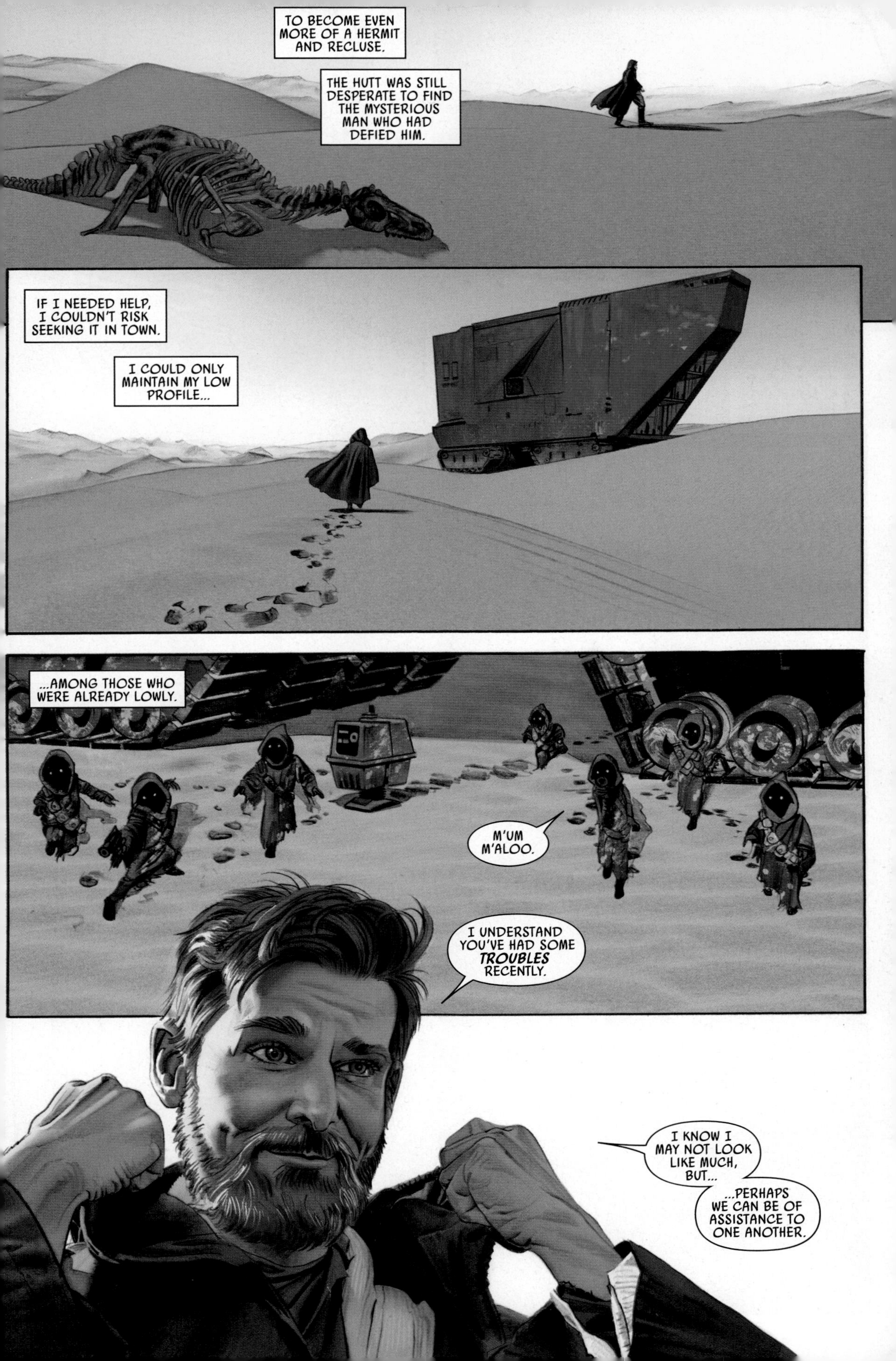
TO BECOME EVEN MORE OF A HERMIT AND RECLUSE.
THE HUTT WAS STILL DESPERATE TO FIND THE MYSTERIOUS MAN WHO HAD DEFIED HIM.
IF I NEEDED HELP, I COULDN'T RISK SEEKING IT IN TOWN.
I COULD ONLY MAINTAIN MY LOW PROFILE...
...AMONG THOSE WHO WERE ALREADY LOWLY.
M'UM M'ALOO.
I UNDERSTAND YOU'VE HAD SOME *TROUBLES* RECENTLY.
I KNOW I MAY NOT LOOK LIKE MUCH, BUT...
...PERHAPS WE CAN BE OF ASSISTANCE TO ONE ANOTHER.

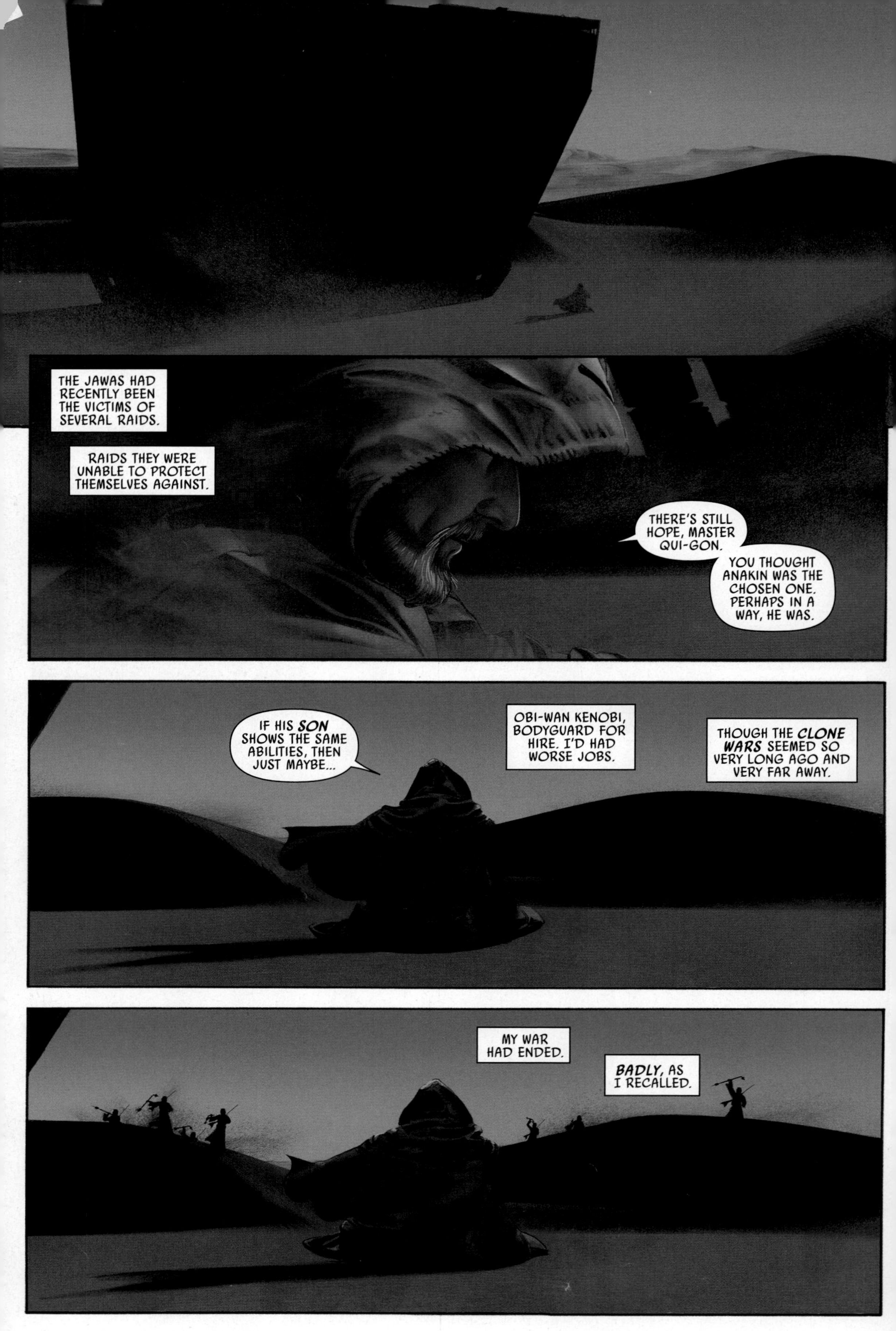
THE JAWAS HAD RECENTLY BEEN THE VICTIMS OF SEVERAL RAIDS.
RAIDS THEY WERE UNABLE TO PROTECT THEMSELVES AGAINST.
THERE'S STILL HOPE, MASTER QUI-GON.
YOU THOUGHT ANAKIN WAS THE CHOSEN ONE. PERHAPS IN A WAY, HE WAS.
IF HIS SON SHOWS THE SAME ABILITIES, THEN JUST MAYBE...
OBI-WAN KENOBI, BODYGUARD FOR HIRE. I'D HAD WORSE JOBS.
THOUGH THE CLONE WARS SEEMED SO VERY LONG AGO AND VERY FAR AWAY.
MY WAR HAD ENDED.
BADLY, AS I RECALLED.

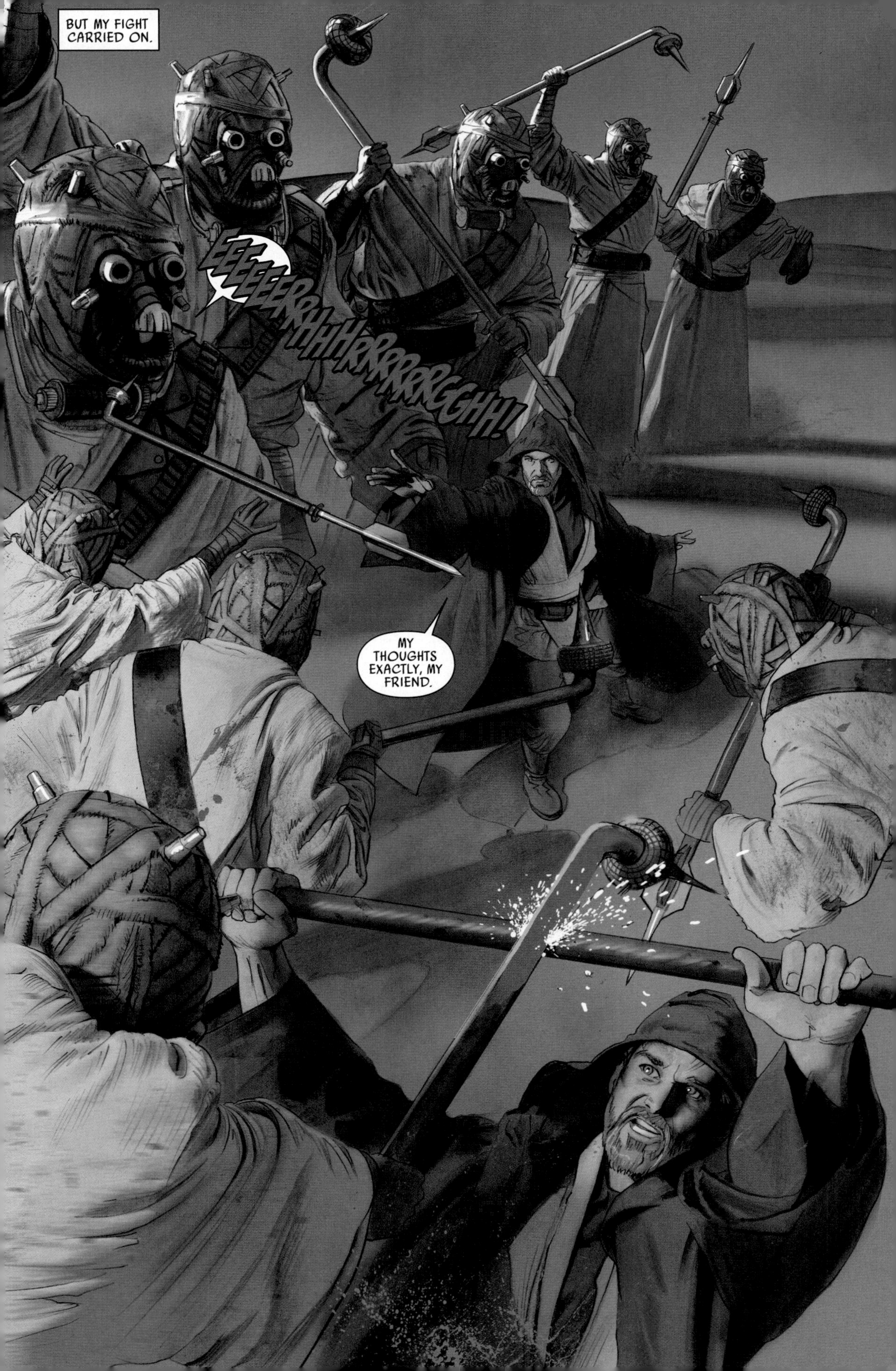
BUT MY FIGHT CARRIED ON.
EEEEEERRHHHRRRRRGGHH!
MY THOUGHTS EXACTLY, MY FRIEND.

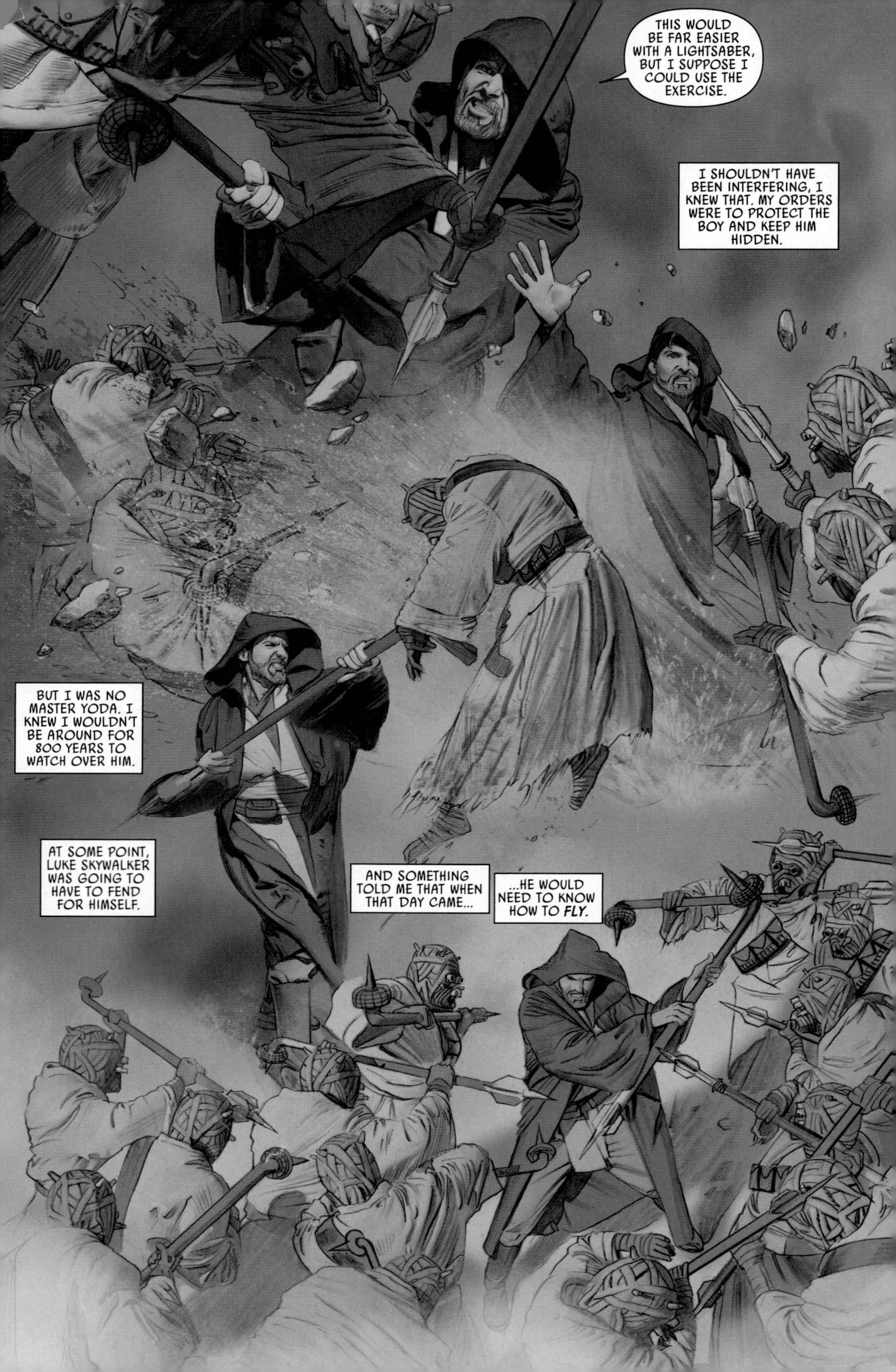

THIS WOULD BE FAR EASIER WITH A LIGHTSABER, BUT I SUPPOSE I COULD USE THE EXERCISE.
I SHOULDN'T HAVE BEEN INTERFERING, I KNEW THAT. MY ORDERS WERE TO PROTECT THE BOY AND KEEP HIM HIDDEN.
BUT I WAS NO MASTER YODA. I KNEW I WOULDN'T BE AROUND FOR 800 YEARS TO WATCH OVER HIM.
AT SOME POINT, LUKE SKYWALKER WAS GOING TO HAVE TO FEND FOR HIMSELF.
AND SOMETHING TOLD ME THAT WHEN THAT DAY CAME...
...HE WOULD NEED TO KNOW HOW TO *FLY*.

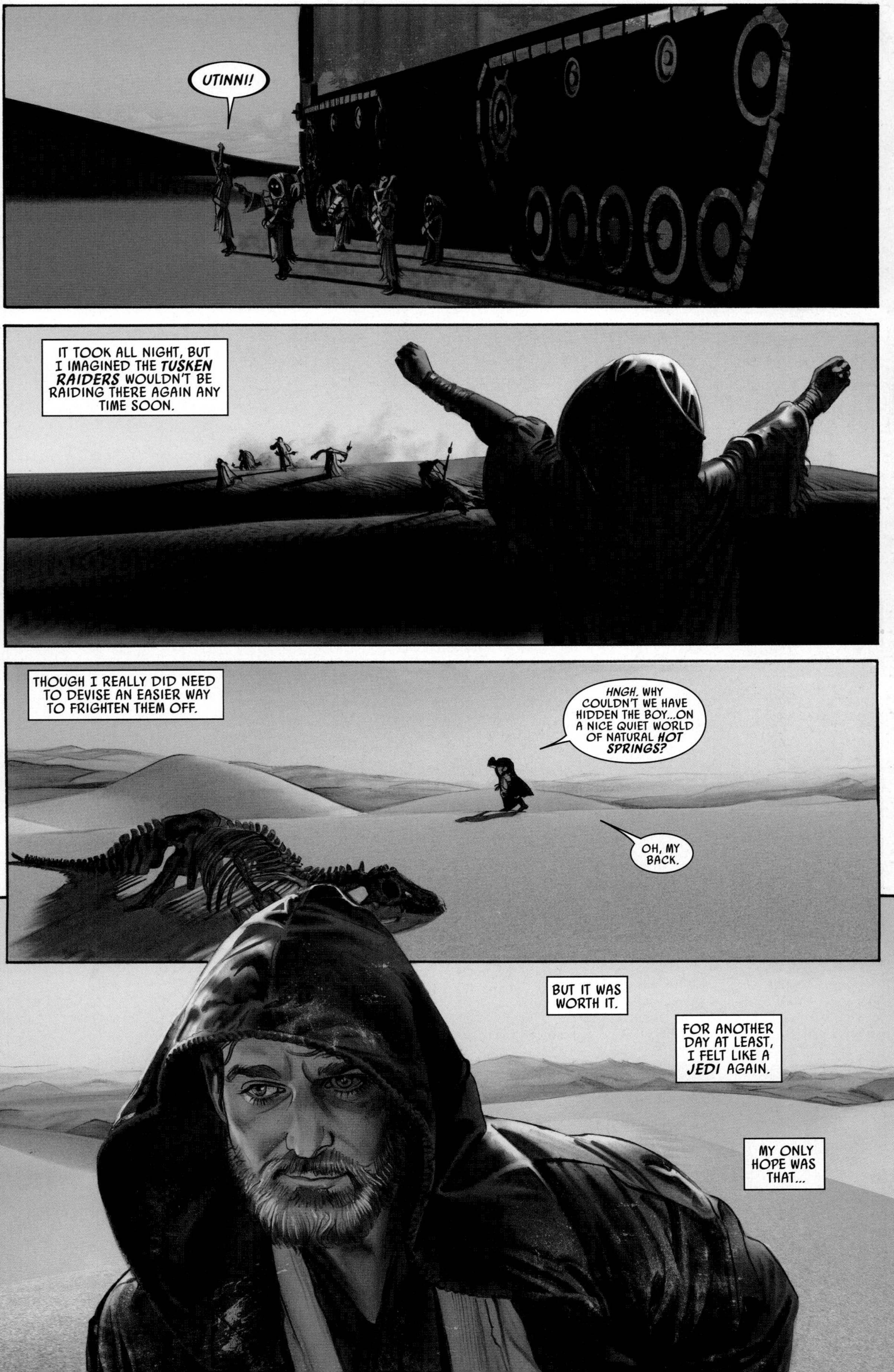
UTINNI!
IT TOOK ALL NIGHT, BUT I IMAGINED THE TUSKEN RAIDERS WOULDN'T BE RAIDING THERE AGAIN ANY TIME SOON.
THOUGH I REALLY DID NEED TO DEVISE AN EASIER WAY TO FRIGHTEN THEM OFF.
HNGH. WHY COULDN'T WE HAVE HIDDEN THE BOY...ON A NICE QUIET WORLD OF NATURAL HOT SPRINGS?
OH, MY BACK.
BUT IT WAS WORTH IT.
FOR ANOTHER DAY AT LEAST, I FELT LIKE A JEDI AGAIN.
MY ONLY HOPE WAS THAT...

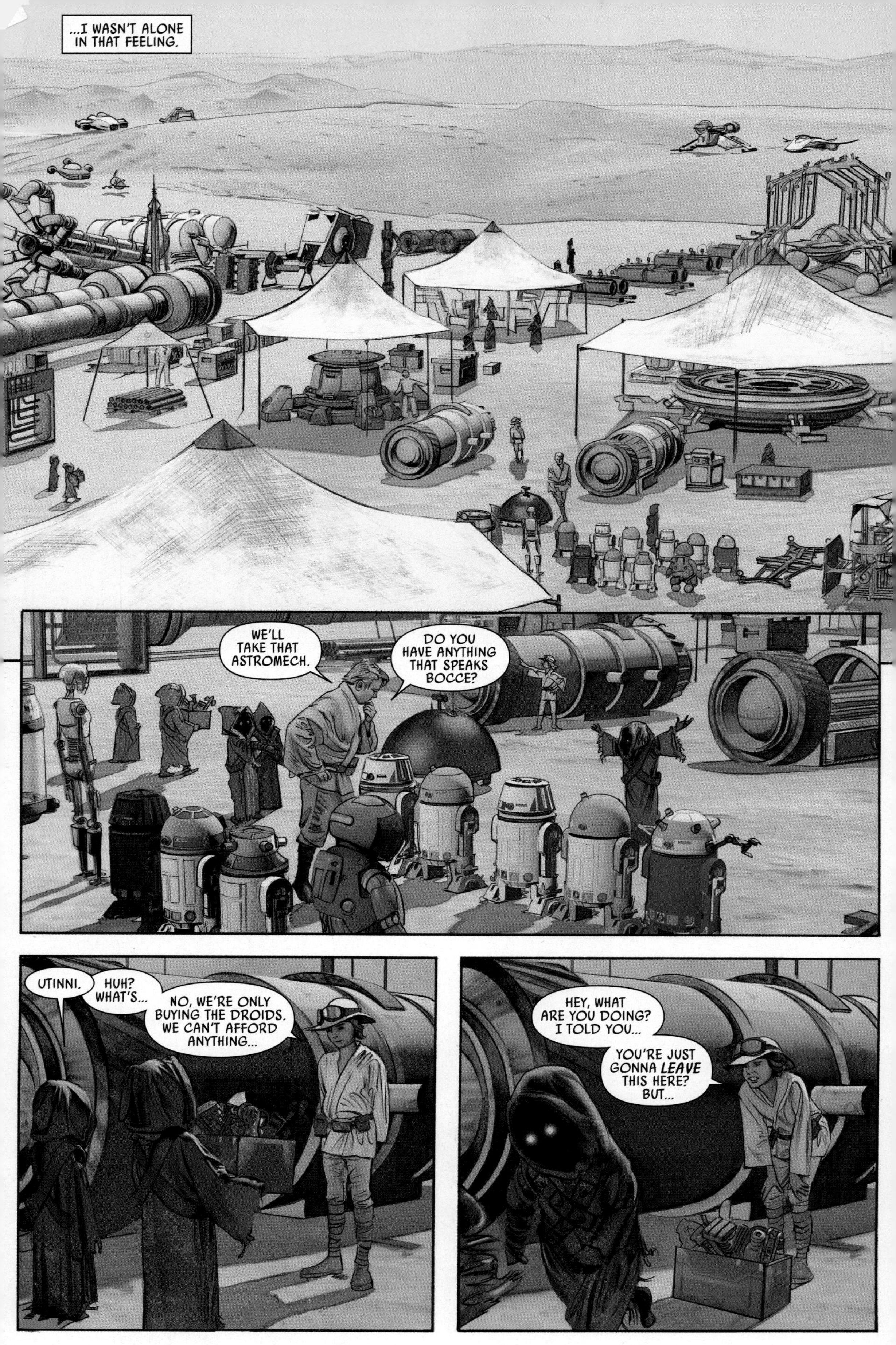
...I WASN'T ALONE IN THAT FEELING.
WE'LL TAKE THAT ASTROMECH.
DO YOU HAVE ANYTHING THAT SPEAKS BOCCE?
UTINNI.
HUH? WHAT'S...
NO, WE'RE ONLY BUYING THE DROIDS. WE CAN'T AFFORD ANYTHING...
HEY, WHAT ARE YOU DOING? I TOLD YOU...
YOU'RE JUST GONNA *LEAVE* THIS HERE? BUT...

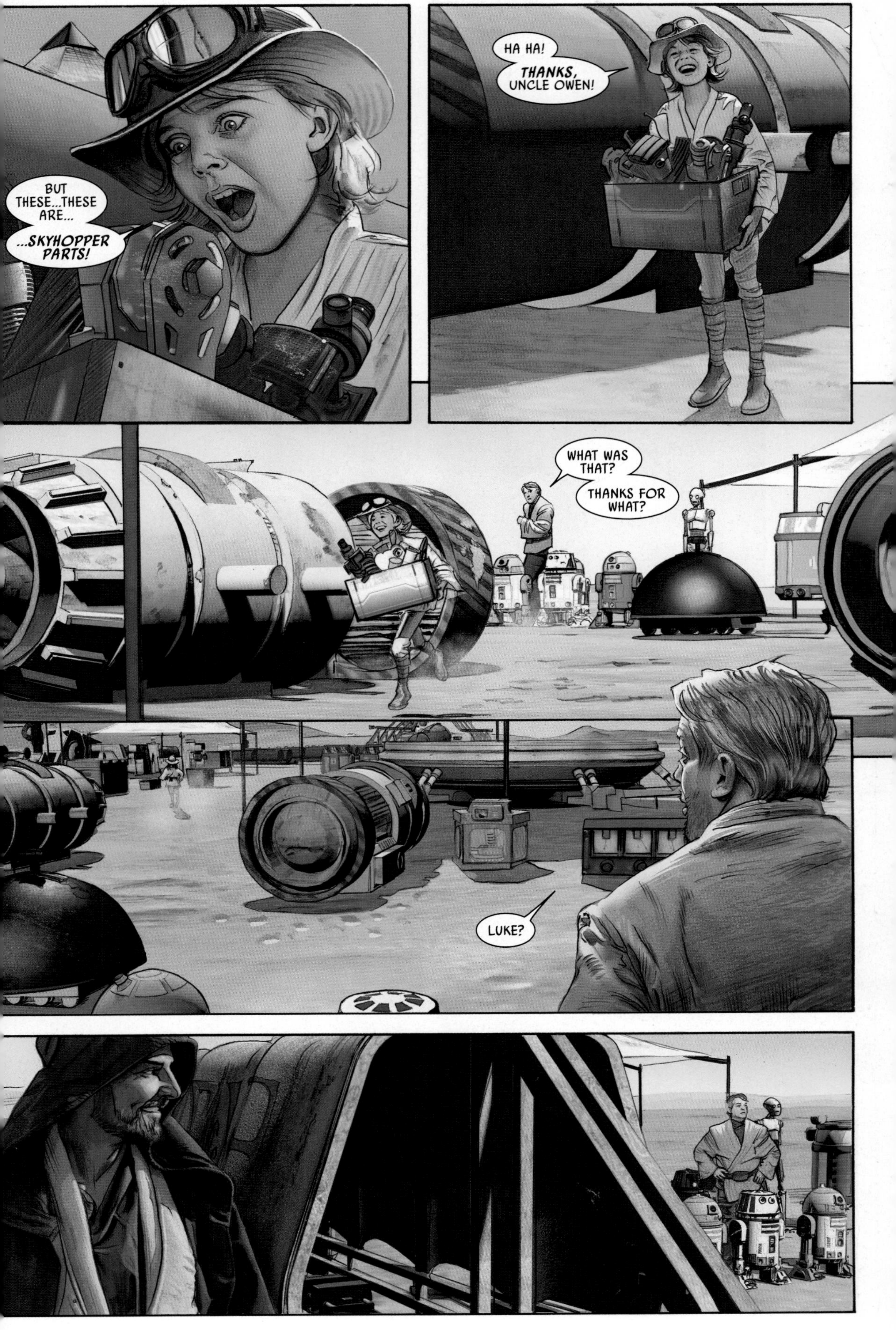
BUT THESE...THESE ARE...
...SKYHOPPER PARTS!
HA HA!
THANKS, UNCLE OWEN!
WHAT WAS THAT?
THANKS FOR WHAT?
LUKE?

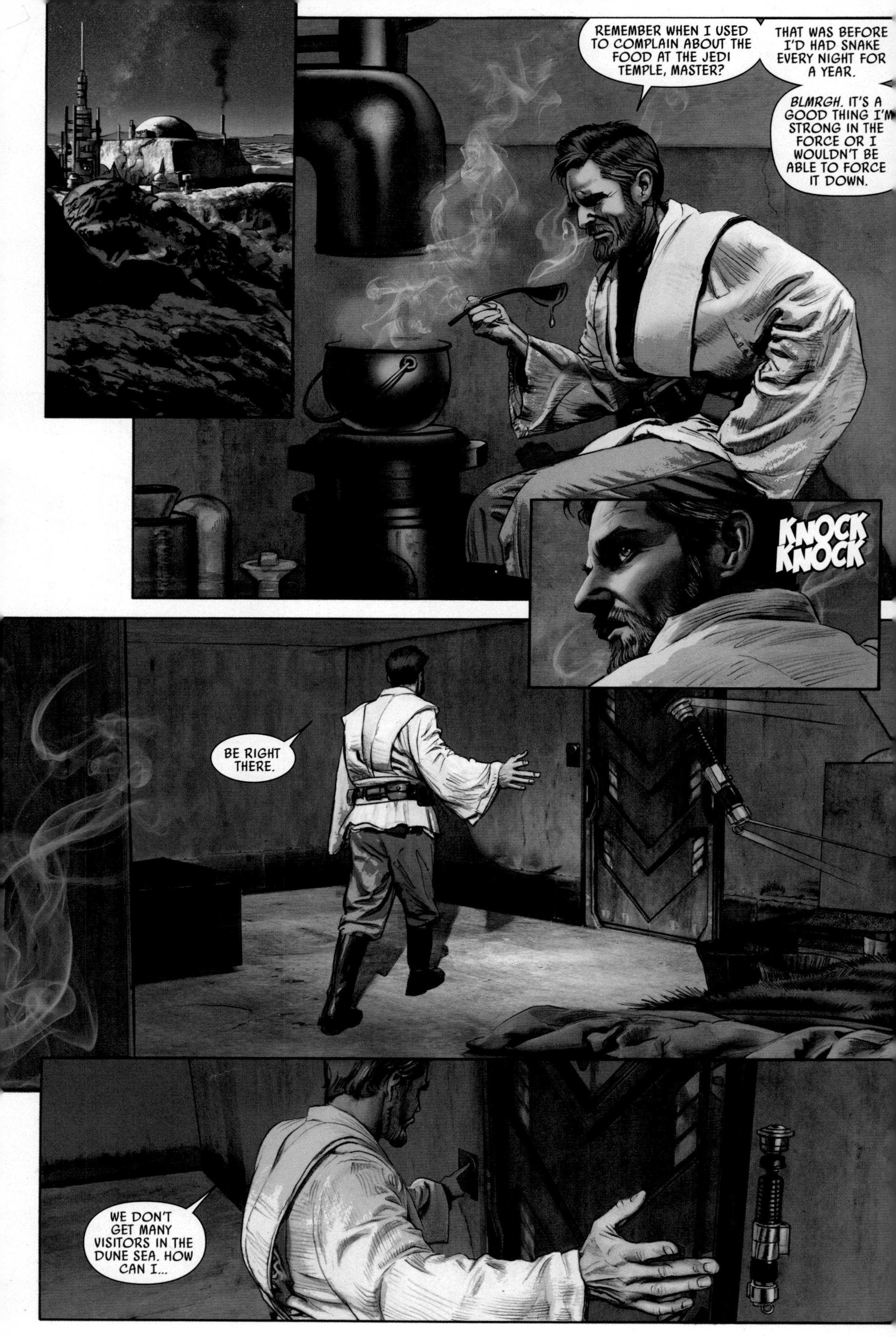
REMEMBER WHEN I USED TO COMPLAIN ABOUT THE FOOD AT THE JEDI TEMPLE, MASTER?
THAT WAS BEFORE I'D HAD SNAKE EVERY NIGHT FOR A YEAR.
BLMRGH. IT'S A GOOD THING I'M STRONG IN THE FORCE OR I WOULDN'T BE ABLE TO FORCE IT DOWN.
KNOCK KNOCK
BE RIGHT THERE.
WE DON'T GET MANY VISITORS IN THE DUNE SEA. HOW CAN I...

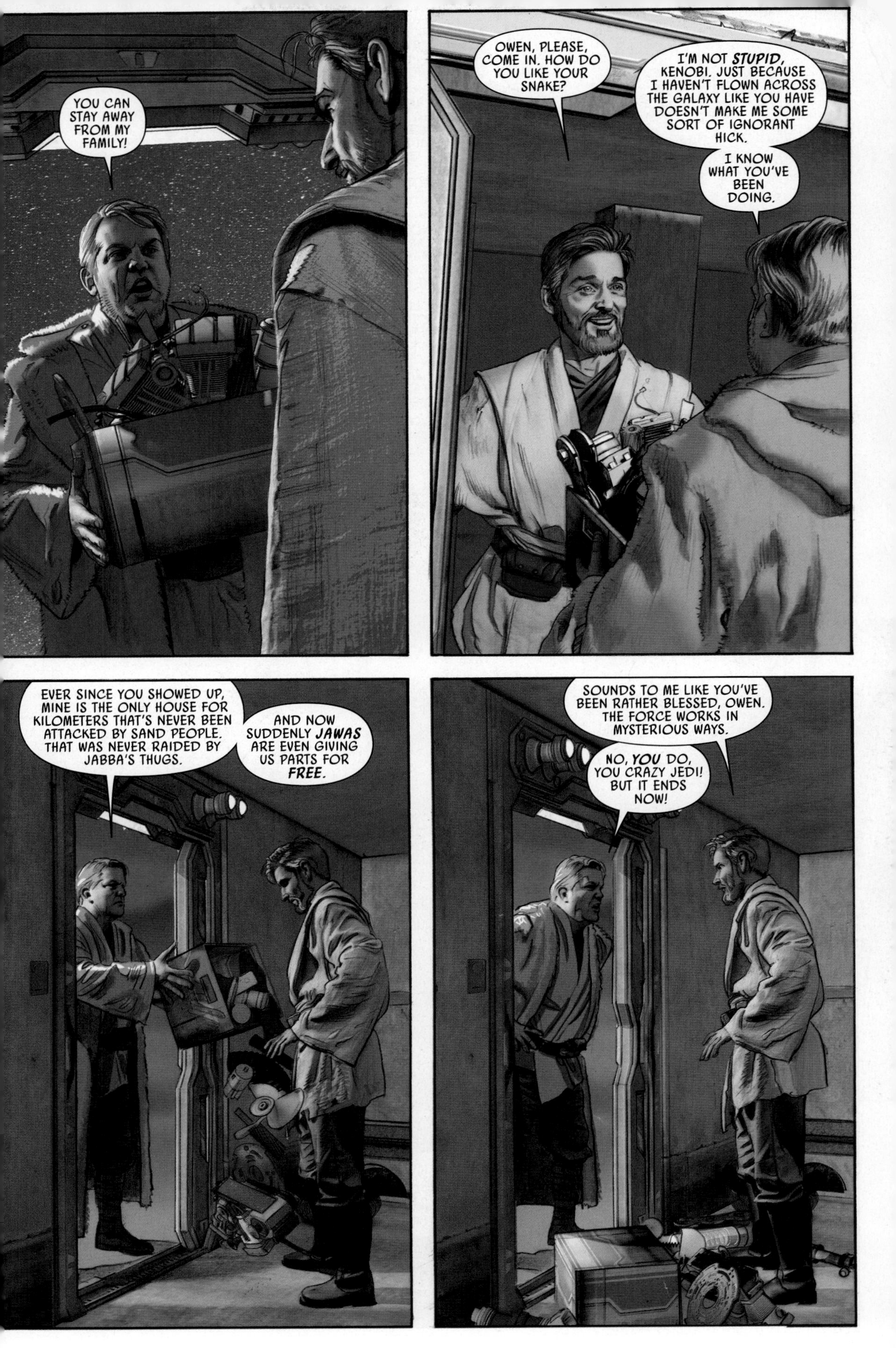
YOU CAN STAY AWAY FROM MY FAMILY!
OWEN, PLEASE, COME IN. HOW DO YOU LIKE YOUR SNAKE?
I'M NOT **STUPID**, KENOBI. JUST BECAUSE I HAVEN'T FLOWN ACROSS THE GALAXY LIKE YOU HAVE DOESN'T MAKE ME SOME SORT OF IGNORANT HICK.
I KNOW WHAT YOU'VE BEEN DOING.
EVER SINCE YOU SHOWED UP, MINE IS THE ONLY HOUSE FOR KILOMETERS THAT'S NEVER BEEN ATTACKED BY SAND PEOPLE. THAT WAS NEVER RAIDED BY JABBA'S THUGS.
AND NOW SUDDENLY **JAWAS** ARE EVEN GIVING US PARTS FOR **FREE**.
SOUNDS TO ME LIKE YOU'VE BEEN RATHER BLESSED, OWEN. THE FORCE WORKS IN MYSTERIOUS WAYS.
NO, **YOU** DO, YOU CRAZY JEDI! BUT IT ENDS NOW!

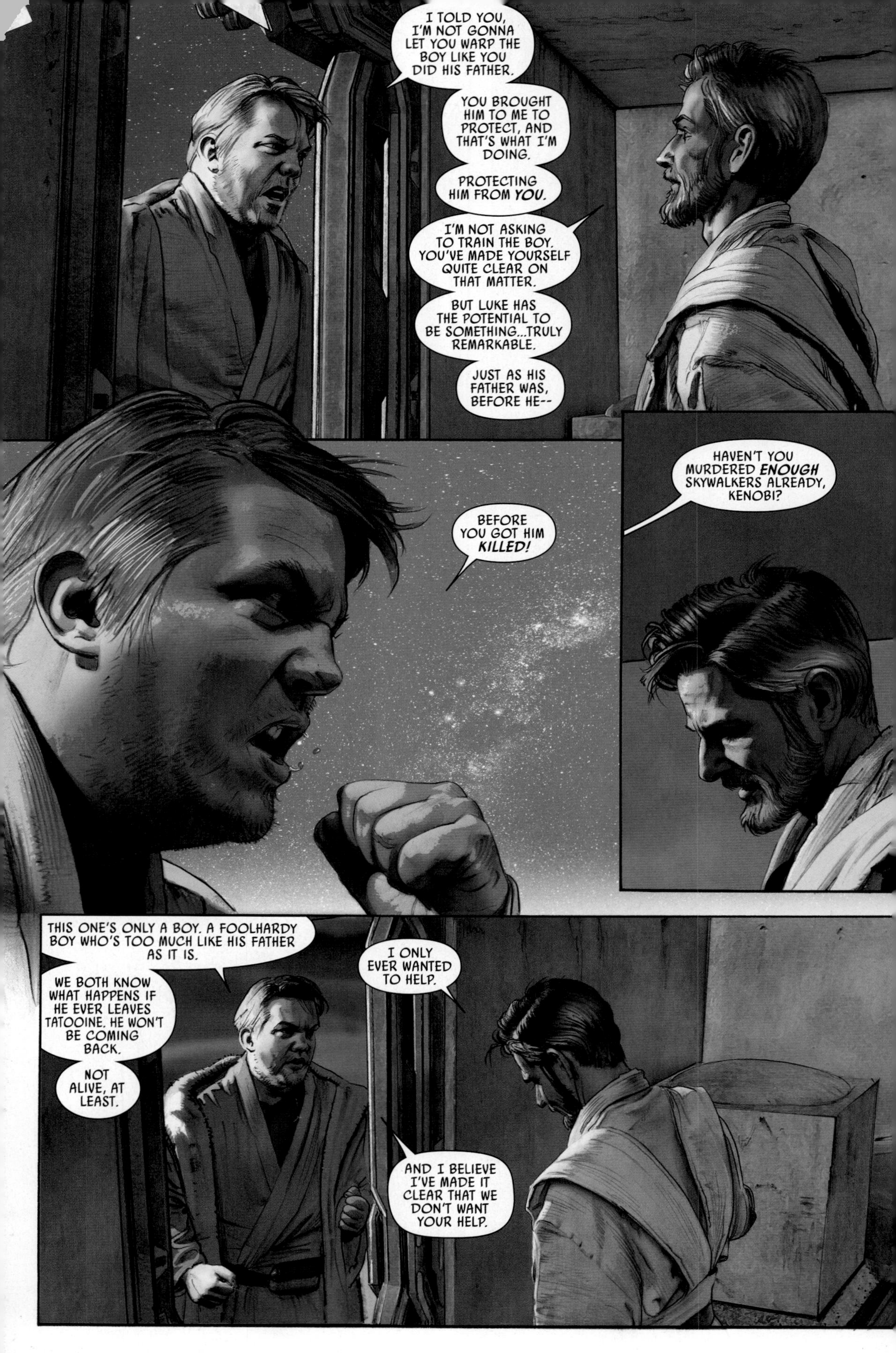

I TOLD YOU, I'M NOT GONNA LET YOU WARP THE BOY LIKE YOU DID HIS FATHER.
YOU BROUGHT HIM TO ME TO PROTECT, AND THAT'S WHAT I'M DOING.
PROTECTING HIM FROM *YOU.*
I'M NOT ASKING TO TRAIN THE BOY. YOU'VE MADE YOURSELF QUITE CLEAR ON THAT MATTER.
BUT LUKE HAS THE POTENTIAL TO BE SOMETHING...TRULY REMARKABLE.
JUST AS HIS FATHER WAS, BEFORE HE--
BEFORE YOU GOT HIM *KILLED!*
HAVEN'T YOU MURDERED *ENOUGH* SKYWALKERS ALREADY, KENOBI?
THIS ONE'S ONLY A BOY. A FOOLHARDY BOY WHO'S TOO MUCH LIKE HIS FATHER AS IT IS.
WE BOTH KNOW WHAT HAPPENS IF HE EVER LEAVES TATOOINE. HE WON'T BE COMING BACK.
NOT ALIVE, AT LEAST.
I ONLY EVER WANTED TO HELP.
AND I BELIEVE I'VE MADE IT CLEAR THAT WE DON'T WANT YOUR HELP.

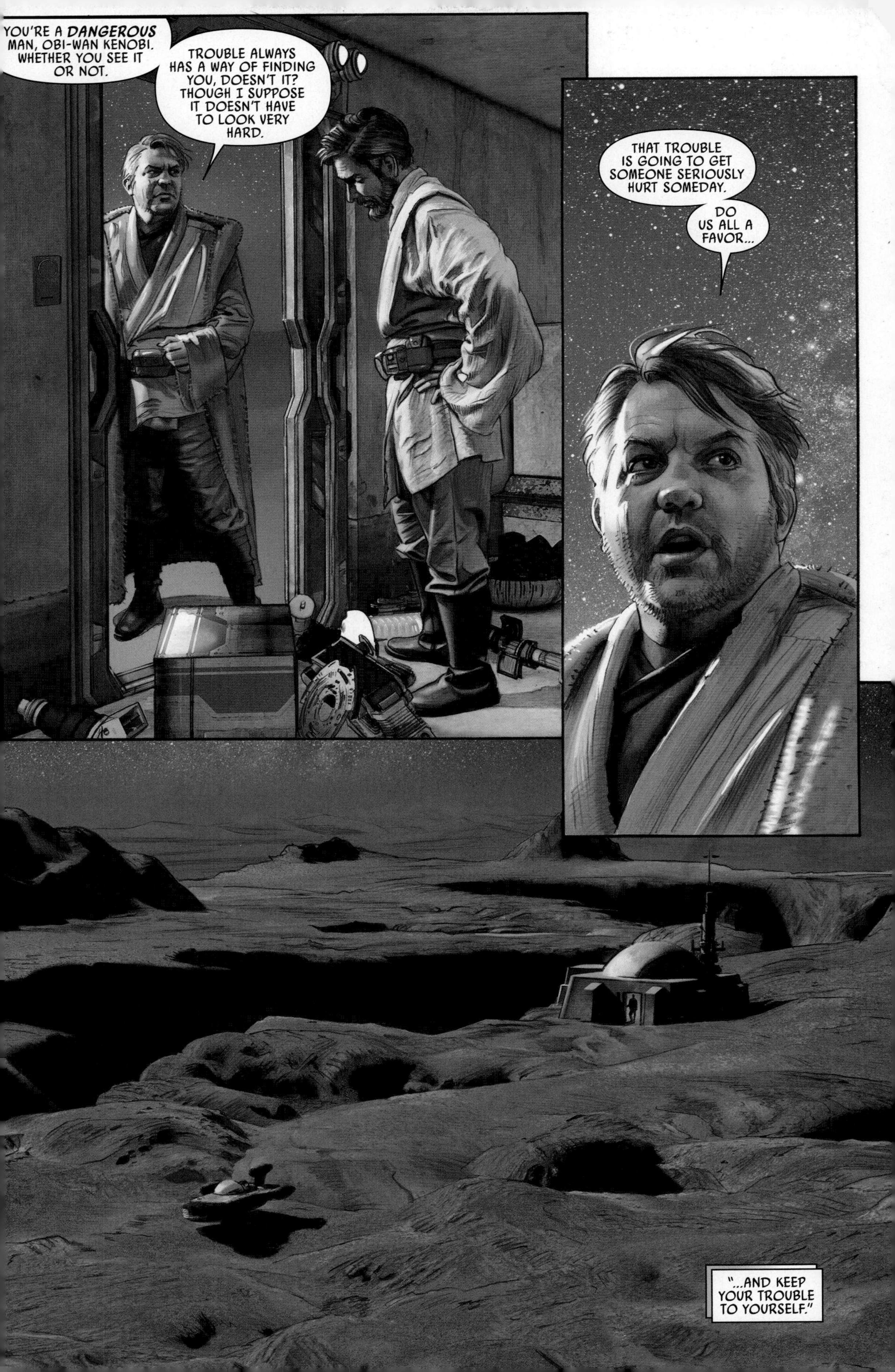
YOU'RE A DANGEROUS MAN, OBI-WAN KENOBI. WHETHER YOU SEE IT OR NOT.
TROUBLE ALWAYS HAS A WAY OF FINDING YOU, DOESN'T IT? THOUGH I SUPPOSE IT DOESN'T HAVE TO LOOK VERY HARD.
THAT TROUBLE IS GOING TO GET SOMEONE SERIOUSLY HURT SOMEDAY.
DO US ALL A FAVOR...
"...AND KEEP YOUR TROUBLE TO YOURSELF."

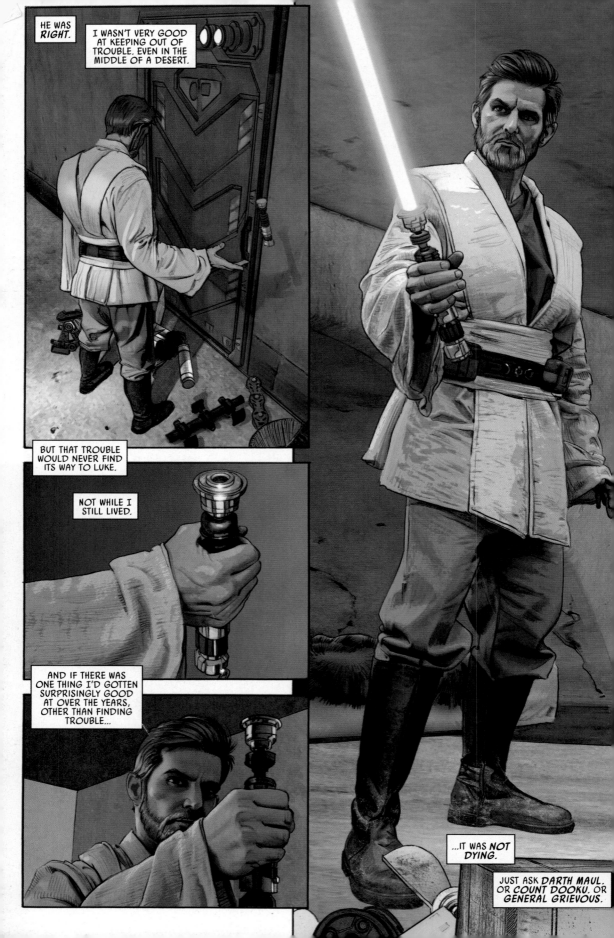

HE WAS *RIGHT*.

I WASN'T VERY GOOD AT KEEPING OUT OF TROUBLE. EVEN IN THE MIDDLE OF A DESERT.

BUT THAT TROUBLE WOULD NEVER FIND ITS WAY TO LUKE.

NOT WHILE I STILL LIVED.

AND IF THERE WAS ONE THING I'D GOTTEN SURPRISINGLY GOOD AT OVER THE YEARS, OTHER THAN FINDING TROUBLE...

...IT WAS *NOT DYING*.

JUST ASK *DARTH MAUL.* OR *COUNT DOOKU.* OR *GENERAL GRIEVOUS.*

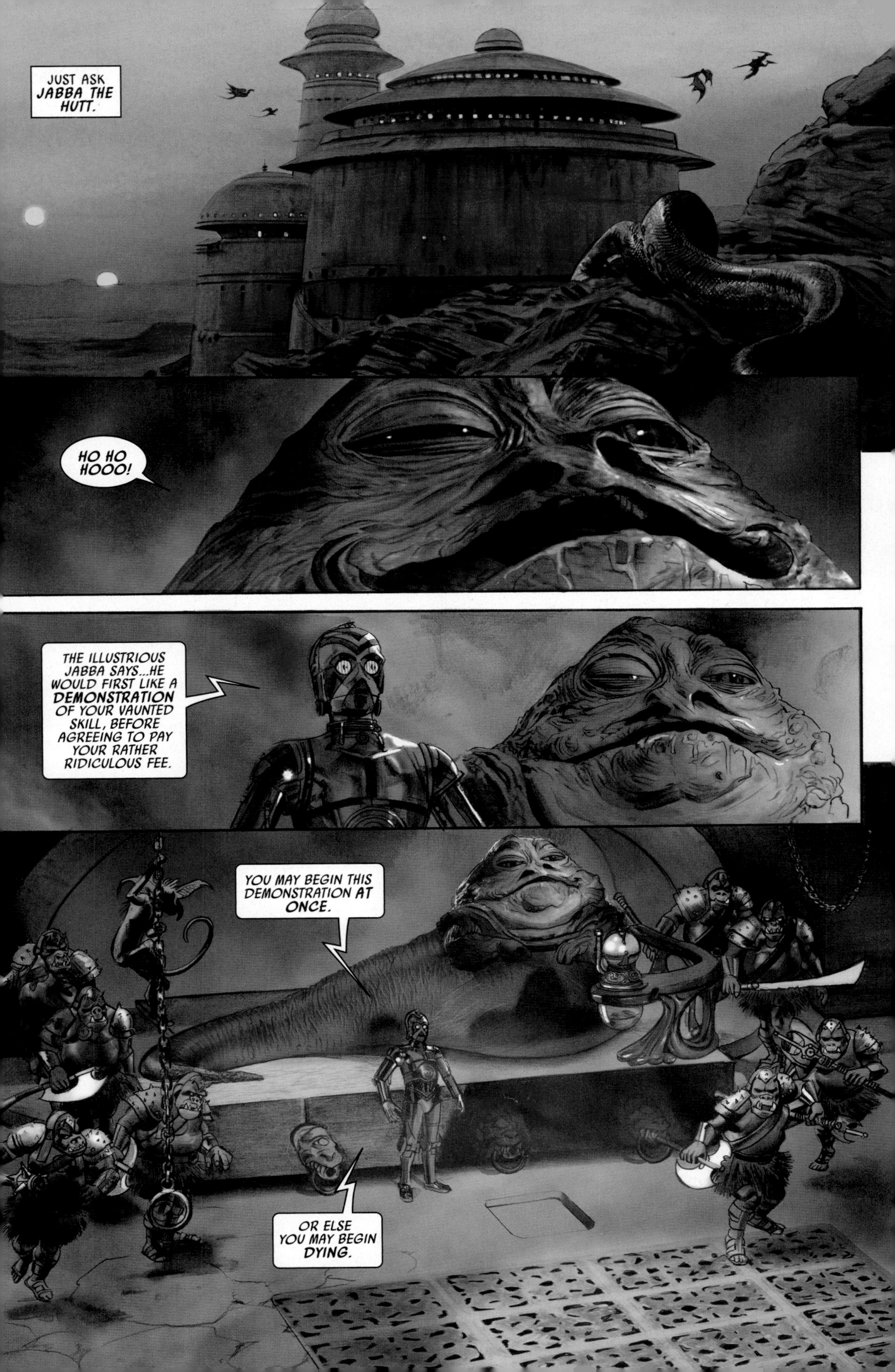
JUST ASK JABBA THE HUTT.
HO HO HOOO!
THE ILLUSTRIOUS JABBA SAYS...HE WOULD FIRST LIKE A DEMONSTRATION OF YOUR VAUNTED SKILL, BEFORE AGREEING TO PAY YOUR RATHER RIDICULOUS FEE.
YOU MAY BEGIN THIS DEMONSTRATION AT ONCE.
OR ELSE YOU MAY BEGIN DYING.

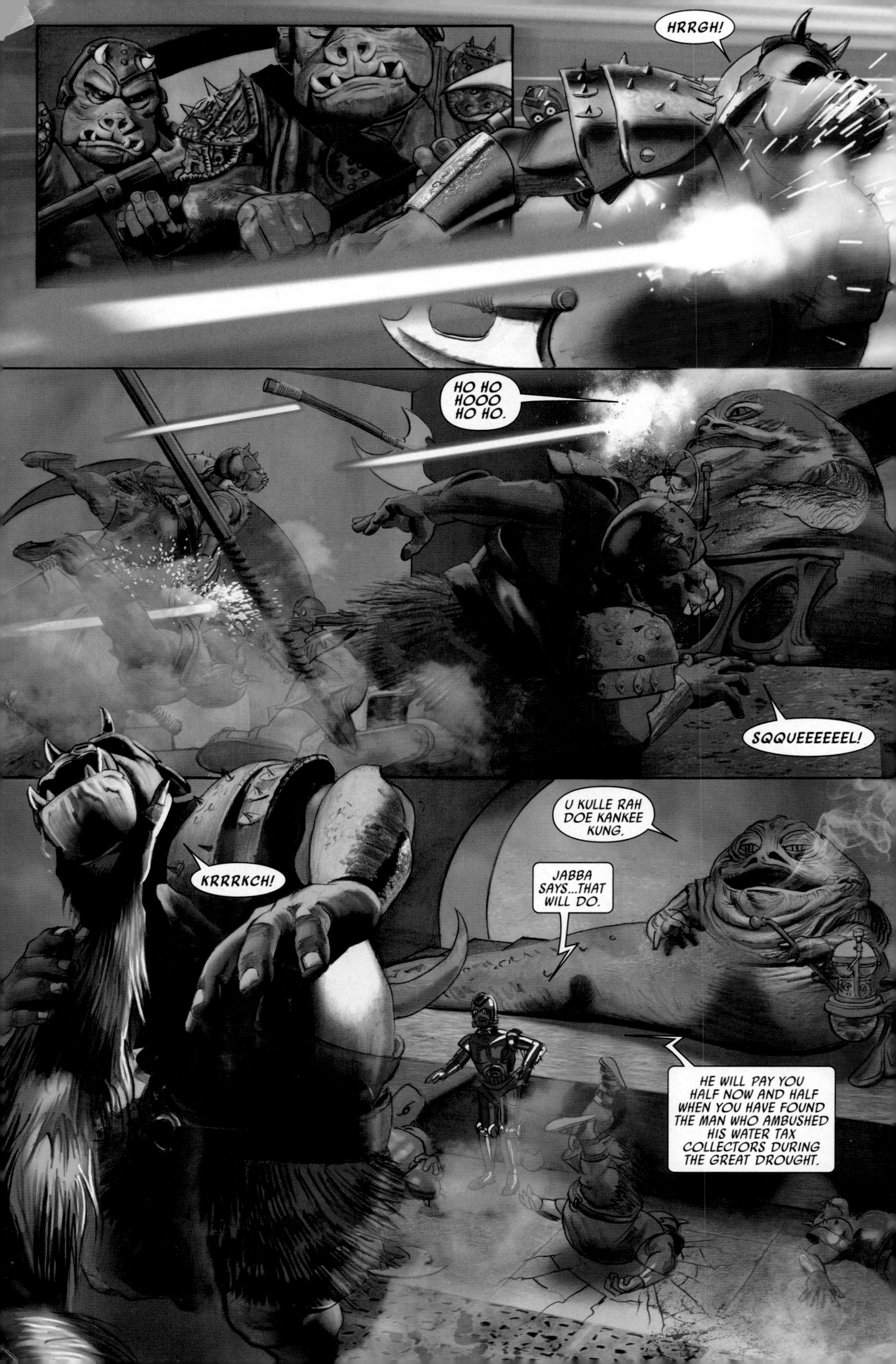
HRRGH!
HO HO HOOO HO HO.
SQQUEEEEEEL!
KRRRKCH!
U KULLE RAH DOE KANKEE KUNG.
JABBA SAYS...THAT WILL DO.
HE WILL PAY YOU HALF NOW AND HALF WHEN YOU HAVE FOUND THE MAN WHO AMBUSHED HIS WATER TAX COLLECTORS DURING THE GREAT DROUGHT.

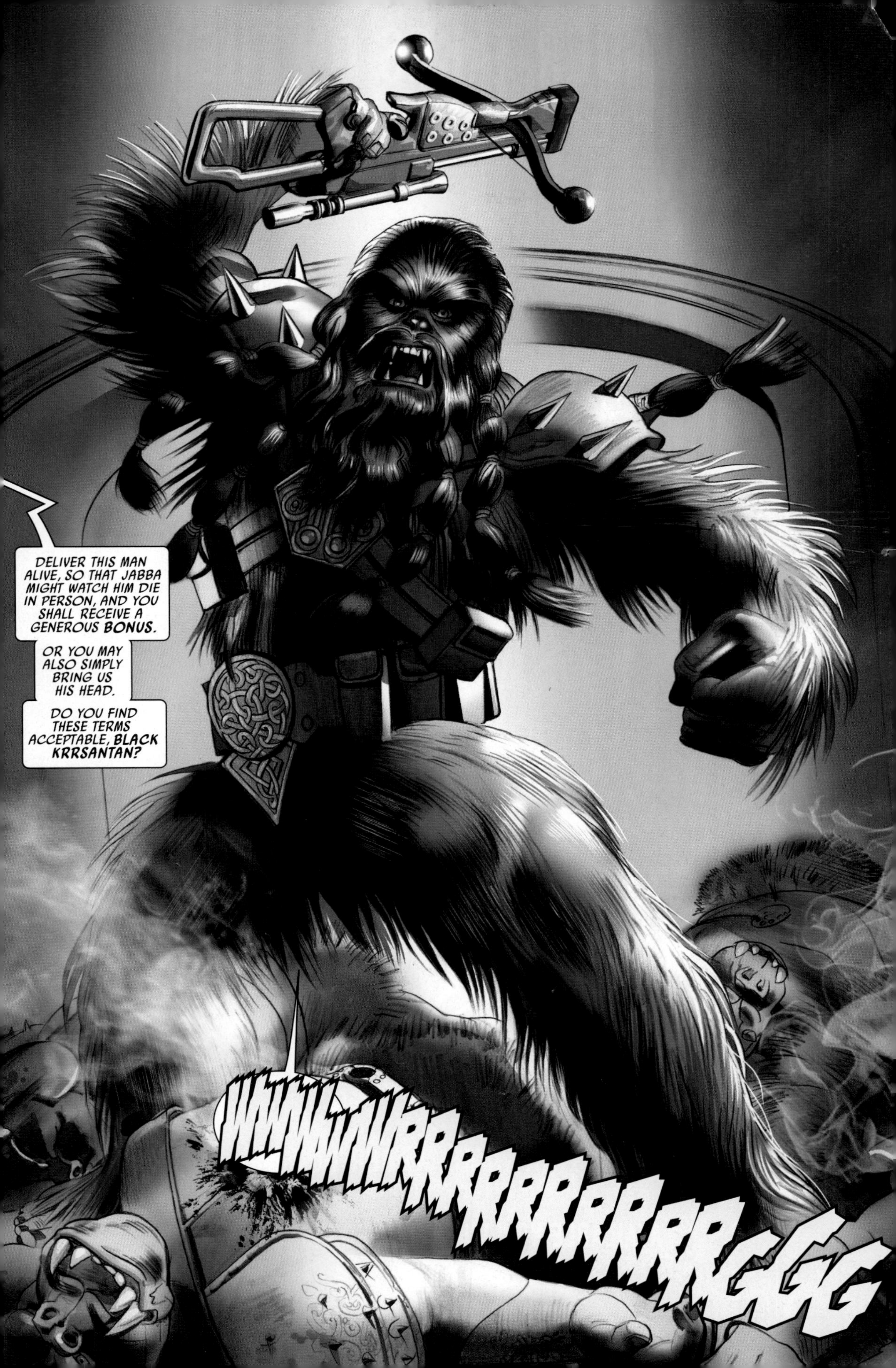
DELIVER THIS MAN ALIVE, SO THAT JABBA MIGHT WATCH HIM DIE IN PERSON, AND YOU SHALL RECEIVE A GENEROUS **BONUS.**
OR YOU MAY ALSO SIMPLY BRING US HIS HEAD.
DO YOU FIND THESE TERMS ACCEPTABLE, **BLACK KRRSANTAN?**
WWWWWWRRRRRRRRRRRRRRGGG

DARTH VADER TAKES ON THE REBELS IN THE EPIC CROSSOVER EVENT

STAR WARS: VADER DOWN

978-0-7851-9789-8

AVAILABLE NOW WHEREVER BOOKS ARE SOLD

WHAT IS A PRINCESS WITHOUT A WORLD?

STAR WARS: PRINCESS LEIA TPB

978-0-7851-9317-3

ON SALE NOW!

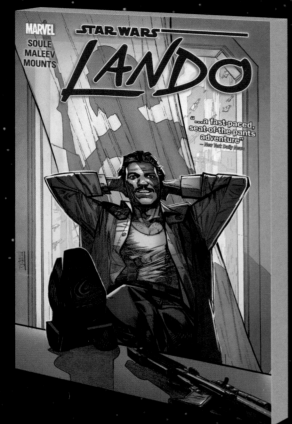

Y FAR, FAR AWAY!

F THE BIGGEST MOVIES IN HISTORY,
ERED INTERIORS!

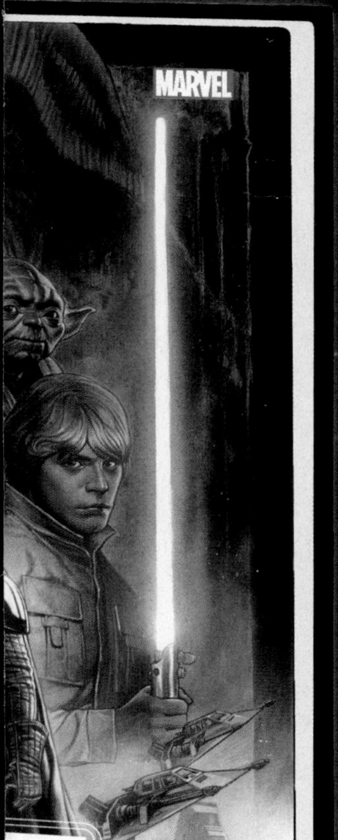
MARVEL
RE
ACK
WILLIAMS

PIRE STRIKES BACK HC

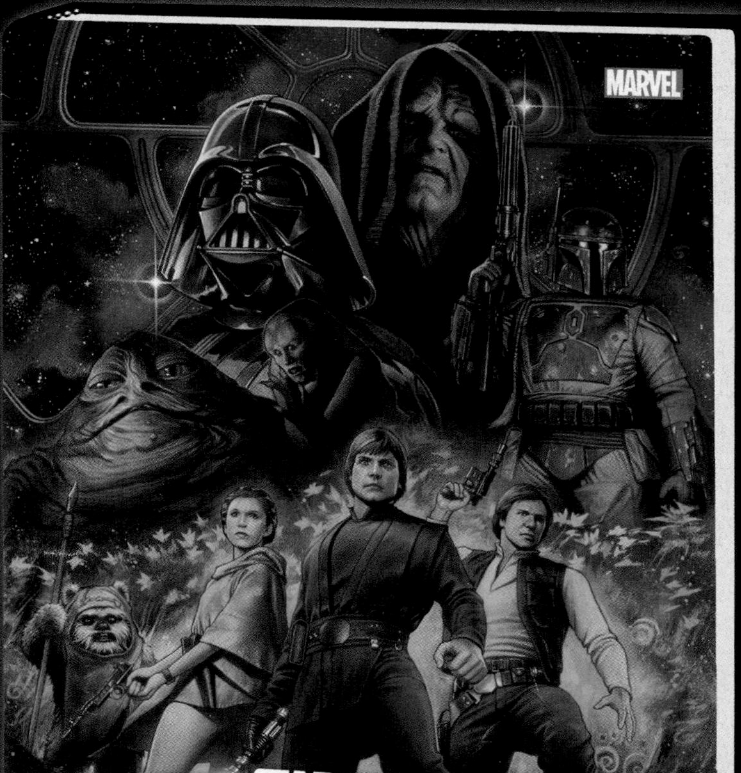
MARVEL
STAR WARS
RETURN OF THE
JEDI
EPISODE VI

STAR WARS: EPISODE VI – RETURN OF THE JEDI HC
978-0-7851-9369-2

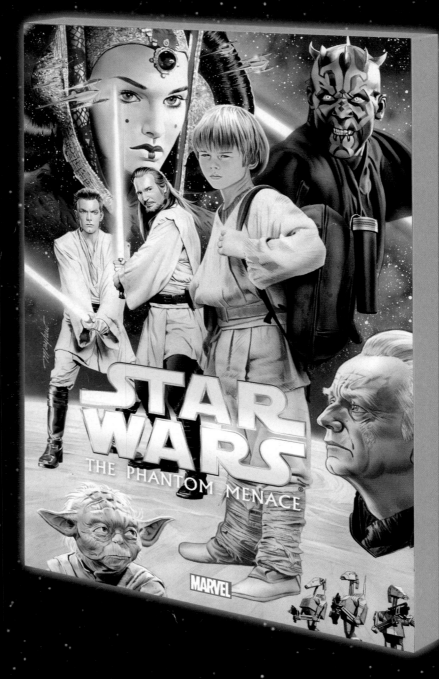